QUESTIONS OF THIRD CINEMA

QUESTIONS OF
THIRD CINEMA

Edited by Jim Pines and Paul Willemen

BFI PUBLISHING

First published in 1989 by the
British Film Institute
21 Stephen Street
London W1P 1PL

British Library Cataloguing in Publication Data

Questions of third cinema
   1. Developing countries cinema films, 1960–1981
   I. Pines, Jim   II. Willemen, Paul
   791.43'09172'4

   ISBN 0–85170–230–9

Cover design: Julia King

Typeset in 10 on 11½pt Sabon by
Fakenham Photosetting Limited, Fakenham, Norfolk
Printed by
St Edmundsbury Press, Bury St Edmunds, Suffolk

Contents

Preface

The principal characteristic of Third Cinema is really not so
much where it is made, or even who makes it, but, rather,
the ideology it espouses and the consciousness it displays.
The Third Cinema is that cinema of the Third World which
stands opposed to imperialism and class oppression in all
their ramifications and manifestations.
Teshome H. Gabriel, *Third Cinema in the Third World*,
p. 2.

Black Britain defines itself crucially as part of a diaspora. Its
unique cultures draw inspiration from those developed by
black populations elsewhere. In particular, the culture and
politics of black America and the Caribbean have become
raw materials for creative processes which redefine what it
means to be black, adapting it to distinctively British experiences and meanings. Black culture is actively made and
re-made.
Paul Gilroy, *There Ain't No Black in the Union Jack*, p. 154.

What relevance does the concept of Third Cinema have for film and
video practitioners working today? More specifically, how does it relate
to what Reece Auguiste has called 'the cinema of diasporic subjects
living and working in the metropolitan centres of London, Paris, New
York, etc.'? These were the sorts of question which partly inspired the
Third Cinema conference held in Edinburgh in 1986. We felt the time
was ripe for such a public critical debate, particularly in the light of
what had been happening in black independent film-making in Britain
since the early 1980s. Notwithstanding important economic and organisational questions – mainly to do with funding, distribution and
exhibition policy – which were the focus of several previous Black and
Third World film cultural events held in Britain, we wanted to shift the
debate to critical issues and flesh out the somewhat uneasy relationship
between (oppositional) critical practice/theory on the one hand, and
oppositional film and video practices on the other. For black (British)
practitioners in particular, this critical focus signalled the placement of
'theory' and questions of a (black) oppositional aesthetics high on the
cultural agenda.

Teshome Gabriel's seminal essay 'Towards a critical theory of Third World film' (included in this volume), and his book *Third Cinema in the Third World: The Aesthetics of Liberation*, provided another important source of inspiration. These texts offered a systematic approach to 'reading' Third World films and, by doing so, helped to realign the hitherto peripheral status of Third World 'Otherness', so as to make it – both critically and politically – the centre. The stress was now on 'difference' rather than 'otherness'. The crucial effect of this critical reformulation was the affirmation of the essential integrity of black and so-called Third World film cultures. Moreover, it helped to reinforce – at the conceptual level – what many of us felt was at the core of some of the developments which were taking place in Britain, where a number of black independent practitioners were challenging the old 'race relations' paradigms and experimenting with new forms of (black) representation. Hence the notion of a (black) diaspora which not only links these developments internationally, but also highlights the sheer complexity and richness of experience inscribed in 'diasporic subjects'. The idea of Third Cinema provided a useful (if somewhat tentative) way of framing a range of questions around the various forms of oppositional cultural production. In a very real sense, this represented an important first step towards 'theorising' black independent film culture.

Although Gabriel's reformulations effectively globalised the concept of Third Cinema and, in addition, recognised the importance of certain white European-American oppositional practices within this framework, there was nevertheless always the danger that we might fall into the trap of 'Third Worldism' or Third World essentialism. To some extent this trap had already been set by the particular history of 'Third Cinema' and by the nature of the debate itself, which the conference never fully resolved. Indeed, some of us (this writer included) were not prepared to completely abandon the tendency towards a kind of (cultural) nationalism, however 'awkward' or 'controversial' that ideological position might be.

Obviously, there was (is) a lot at stake, politically and culturally, and thus the need (expressed by some people) to repel any attempts 'to kidnap the concept of Third Cinema' was strongly present throughout the conference (and beyond). Third Cinema was a heated site of contestation which had to be secured, especially against the incursions of 'First World chauvinism'. As Clyde Taylor later put it, one of the 'most reliable characteristics' of this chauvinism is its 'denunciation of Third World postures of struggle for their particularism, i.e. ethnicity, nationalism, cultural nationalism, populism, etc., while concealing the use of such orientations for first world interests, disguised instead as internationalism, post-nationalism, cosmopolitanism – claiming postures of breadth and mobility that must necessarily rely on past or present

viii

imperialisms' ('Eurocentrics vs. New Thought at Edinburgh', *Framework* no. 34, pp. 140–1).

Another question constantly raised, in reference to Third Cinema, is the role of theory and its relationship to oppositional cultural practice. This is not a new or an original phenomenon, of course, as Homi Bhabha and others have indicated. But in relation to political film and video practice – and especially to 'Third World' film cultures – debates about the efficacy of theory have often taken on a particularly intense *moral* character. Notwithstanding the genuine fear that some practitioners seem to have whenever they hear that word – theory – there are at least three sets of problems that constantly need addressing. One centres on the nature of the theories themselves and the alleged elitism of which they are often accused; another has to do with the validity of theoretical work which draws on Western critical traditions; while another focuses on the need to avoid essentialist or prescriptive paradigms against which oppositional cultural practitioners are judged and evaluated (i.e. establishing an alternative hegemony operating under the guise of 'Third Cinema').

Fortunately, the dangerous (and still fairly common) assumption that 'theoretical work' is the domain of 'First World' intellectuals is easily disposable. But the notion that oppositional theoretical practice can somehow evolve in a Manichean vacuum – *our* theory vs. *their* theory – is more difficult to overcome, particularly where the articulation of self-identities is an integral part of the theoretical process. This leads directly to the question of whether there is a Third Cinema aesthetic, or, to put it slightly differently, whether it is possible (or even necessary) to erect an aesthetic paradigm which defines a broad range of oppositional cultural practices. Certainly Gabriel's notion of Third Cinema as 'guardian of popular memory' (Third Aesthetics), and Haile Gerima's interactive model emphasising the relationship between Audience/Community, Film-maker/Storyteller and Activist/Critic, point to a different kind of (non-Western) film culture which is not so much oppositional in the usual sense of the term, but simply more relevant politically and culturally to the milieu in which it is formed. In that respect, the use of the term 'Third Cinema aesthetics' is perhaps putting too fine a point on it since, as Clyde Taylor has argued, 'rather than search for a black or Third World film aesthetics we should interrogate the *Western* concepts of aesthetics as such, should recognise its determination through specific Western historical experiences and cultural exigencies' [ibid., p. 141].

The Edinburgh conference provided a lively forum for exploring a diverse range of issues relating to notions of Third Cinema, culture and politics, theoretical and oppositional practice, the role of national identities within cultural production, and so on. Although nothing concrete was resolved as such, much was debated, discovered, developed and given a new dynamic – and is aptly reflected in the essays collected in this volume. We therefore wish to thank all those who participated in the conference and allowed themselves to be exposed to intense but highly fruitful exchanges. We would also like to thank the Edinburgh International Film Festival, and especially its director Jim Hickey, not only for hosting the event but also for supporting the project from beginning to end.

The Third Cinema conference could not have happened without the financial support of the British Film Institute, and we duly thank them. We would also like to thank David Wilson and Geoffrey Nowell-Smith for supporting the publication of this volume, and for giving us constant but sympathetic nudges throughout the long editorial process. Teshome Gabriel helped us in many ways, proposing several excellent contributors whom we didn't know, and keeping on at us about the timeliness of this publication on Third Cinema. His support and enthusiasm are much appreciated. Finally, special thanks to June Givanni, who successfully undertook the formidable task of co-ordinating the Third Cinema conference, helping in no small measure to make it all become a reality.

Jim Pines

The Third Cinema Question: Notes and Reflections

Paul Willemen

In 1986, for its fortieth anniversary, the Edinburgh International Film Festival (EIFF) hosted a three-day conference organised by Jim Pines, June Givanni and myself, addressing the idea of a Third Cinema and its relevance to contemporary film culture.[*] Previous gatherings had been held in London and in Manchester to promote black film- and video-makers, but these events had concentrated on the presentation of that international sector's achievements and had addressed the most immediately pressing organisational and economic questions facing the practitioners involved.

In line with its traditional emphasis on the exploration of cultural issues, the EIFF set out to raise a different set of questions, described in the festival programme booklet in the following terms:

> With the major political and economic changes experienced in both the Euro-American sphere and in the so-called Third World since the late 70s, the issue of cultural specificity (the need to know which specific social-historical processes are at work in the generation of cultural products) and the question of how precisely social existence overdetermines cultural practices have taken on a new and crucial importance. The complexity of the shifting dynamics between intra- and inter-national differences and power relations has shown simple models of class domination at home and imperialism abroad to be totally inadequate.
>
> In addition, the blatantly ethnocentric aspects of 70s cultural theory have developed into crippling handicaps which under the pressure of current political and economic policies have caused Euro-American cultural theory to stagnate or, worse, to degenerate into either a naively sentimental leftism including its Third Worldist

---

[*] A version of this essay was published in *Framework* no. 34, 1987.

1

variant, or into 'post-modernism', with its contradictory thrust towards a pre-industrial nostalgia and towards bringing cultural-educational practice in line with the needs of a market economy and the entrepreneurial ideologies it requires.

Cultural activists outside the white Euro-American sphere, while taking note of 70s theory and its genuine achievements, have continued their own work throughout this period, formulating both in practice and in theory – in so far as these can be separated – a sophisticated approach to questions of domination/subordination, centre/periphery and, above all, resistance/hegemony. This work is of fundamental importance today, not only because of its ability to unblock the dead-ends of 70s cultural theories, but also and primarily because it opens out onto new practices of cinema: a cinema no longer captivated by the mirrors of dominance/independence or commerce/art, but grounded in an understanding of the dialectical relationship between social existence and cultural practice. The Edinburgh Conference will address the relevance and the implications of such a notion of Third Cinema.

The EIFF seemed the appropriate place for such an ambitious undertaking to initiate a fundamental critique of current European approaches to 'popular culture' by proposing that the notion of Third Cinema is far more relevant to contemporary cultural issues than any form of post-structural or any other kind of 'post-' theory. The implied polemical position in the way the conference was set up had a double thrust: by turning to Third Cinema as a potential way forward, the conference implied that left cultural theory in the UK and in the US has become a serious handicap in that it has become hypocritically opportunist (for example, the proliferation of attempts to validate the most debilitating forms of consumerism, with academics cynically extolling the virtues of the stunted products of cultural as well as political defeat) or has degenerated into a comatose repetition of 70s deconstructivist rituals. The turn to Third Cinema with all its Latin American connotations also repeated a gesture which had proved extremely productive in the early 70s: then a determined and systematic injection of 'foreign' cultural theories ranging from Althusser to Brecht, from Eco to the Soviet Formalists and from Lacan to Saussure had proved capable of reanimating the petrified body of English cultural criticism. Faced with a relapse into a state of suspended animation or worse, a reverting to 'left labourism' of the most parochially populist type (see, for example, the ideology of 'the community' in current cultural discourses), the conference was designed to draw attention to different, non-English approaches to cultural politics.

Mainly because the productivity and genuine achievements of British cultural criticism in the 70s must be seen as stemming from a salutary anti-Englishness and because the current degeneration of cultural theory correlates exactly with the abandonment of a critical rejection of English forms of cultural populism, the turn to Third Cinema can be seen as a rejection of parochialism as well as a critical engagement with the positive aspects of 70s theory. The political-cultural trends of the 80s have demonstrated the need for a drastic reappraisal of the terms in which radical practice had been conceived in the 70s: questions of gender and of cultural identity received new inflections, and traditional notions of class-determined identity were seen to be as inadequate as the forms of syndicalist struggle that corresponded to them. Some of the issues raised at the Edinburgh conference, such as the questions of Brechtian cinema and of cultural identity, received a new urgency but were now posed in a different context where not the radical white intelligentsia but the militant black cultural practitioners constituted the cutting edge of cultural politics and innovation. Their terms of reference were derived from a wide variety of sources and included 70s theories of subjectivity and Marxism in addition to the work of Fanon, C. L. R. James, black American writers and activists, Latin American and African film-makers, West Indian, Pakistani and Indian cultural traditions and intellectuals, etc. The cultural practices grounded in those – from an English point of view – 'other' currents, together with the impact of a whole series of physical acts of collective self-defence and resistance, offer the best chance yet to challenge and break down the ruling English Ideology, described so vividly in all its suffocating decrepitude in Tom Nairn's classic essay, 'The English Literary Intelligentsia' (*Bananas*, no. 3, 1976).

The notion of Third Cinema (and most emphatically not Third World Cinema) was selected as the central concept for a conference in Edinburgh in 1986, partly to re-pose the question of the relations between the cultural and the political, and partly to discuss whether there is indeed a kind of international cinematic tradition which exceeds the limits of both the national-industrial cinemas and those of Euro-American as well as English cultural theories.

The latter consideration is still very much a hypothesis relating to the emergence on an international scale of a kind of cinema to which the familiar realism vs modernism or post-modernism debates are simply irrelevant, at least in the forms to which Western critics have become accustomed. This trend is not unprecedented, but it appears to be gaining strength. One of its more readily noticeable characteristics seems to be the adoption of a historically analytic yet culturally specific mode of cinematic discourse, perhaps best exemplified by Amos Gitai's work, Cinema Action's *Rocinante*, Angelopoulos' *Travelling Players*, the films of Souleyman Cissé, Haile Gerima and Ousmane Sembene,

3

Kumar Shahani's *Maya Darpan* and *Tarang*, Theuring and Engström's *Escape Route to Marseilles*, the work of Safi Faye, the recent films of Yussif Chahine, Edward Yang's *Taipei Story*, Chen Kaige's *Yellow Earth*, the work of Allen Fong, the two black British films *Handsworth Songs* and *The Passion of Remembrance*, the Brazilian films of Joaquim Pedro de Andrade and Carlos Reichenbach, etc. The masters of this growing but still threatened current can be identified as Nelson Pereira dos Santos, Ousmane Sembene and Ritwik Ghatak, each summing up and reformulating the encounter of diverse cultural traditions into new, politically as well as cinematically illuminating types of filmic discourse, critical of, yet firmly anchored in, their respective social-historical situations. Each of them refused to oppose a simplistic notion of national identity or of cultural authenticity to the values of colonial or imperial predators. Instead, they started from a recognition of the many-layeredness of their own cultural-historical formations, with each layer being shaped by complex connections between intra- as well as inter-national forces and traditions. In this way, the three cited film-makers exemplify a way of inhabiting one's culture which is neither myopically nationalist nor evasively cosmopolitan. Their film work is not particularly exemplary in the sense of displaying stylistically inno-vative devices to be imitated by others who wish to avoid appearing outdated. On the contrary, it is their way of inhabiting their cultures, their grasp of the relations between the cultural and the social, which founded the search for a cinematic discourse able to convey their sense of a 'diagnostic understanding' (to borrow a happy phrase from Ray-mond Williams) of the situation in which they worked and to which their work was primarily addressed.

Third Cinema: Part I
The notion of a Third Cinema was first advanced as a rallying cry in the late 60s in Latin America and has recently been taken up again in the wake of Teshome Gabriel's book *Third Cinema in the Third World – The Aesthetics of Liberation* (1982). As an idea, its immediate inspi-ration was rooted in the Cuban Revolution (1959) and in Brazil's Cinema Nôvo, where Glauber Rocha provided an impetus with the publication of a passionate polemic entitled 'The Aesthetics of Hunger' (or 'The Aesthetics of Violence': *Revista Civilizacâo Brasileira* no. 3, July 1965). But as Michael Chanan reminded us in his introduction to *Twenty-five Years of the New Latin American Cinema* (British Film Institute and Channel 4, 1983), even at that stage the elaboration of an aesthetic felt to be appropriate to conditions in Latin America drew on the ideals of such far from revolutionary currents as Italian neo-realism and Grierson's notion of the social documentary, as well as on various kinds of Marxist aesthetics. What is becoming clearer now is that the

4

various manifestos and polemics arguing for a Third Cinema fused a number of European, Soviet and Latin American ideas about cultural practice into a new, more powerful (in the sense that it was able to conceptualise the connections between more areas of socio-cultural life than contemporary European aesthetic ideologies) programme for the political practice of cinema.

Two particular aspects of neo-realism and of the Griersonian approach may have recommended themselves to the many Latin American intellectuals who studied in Europe, which included such influential figures as Fernando Birri, Tomás Gutiérrez Alea and Julio García Espinosa, who all studied at the Centro Sperimentale in Rome. Firstly, both neo-realism and the British documentary were examples of an artisanal, relatively low-cost cinema working with a mixture of public and private funds, enabling directors to work in a different way and on a different economic scale from that required by Hollywood and its various national-industrial rivals. Secondly, contrary to the unifying and homogenising work of mainstream industrial cinemas, this artisanal cinema allowed, at least in principle and sometimes in practice, a more focused address of the 'national', revealing divisions and stratifications within a national formation, ranging from regional dialects to class and political antagonisms. What the Latin Americans appear to have picked up on was the potential for different cinematic practices offered by the European examples, rather than their actual trajectories and philosophies. Consequently, they did not follow the evolution of neo-realism into European art-house cinema, nor the relentless trek of the British documentary via Woodfall into the gooey humanism of TV plays and serials, while debased forms of the Griersonian documentary, lacking that genre's acute sense of aesthetic stylisation, survive in stunted forms in the backwaters of the British state-funded video sector.

The term Third Cinema was launched by the Argentinian film-makers Fernando Solanas and the Spanish-born Octavio Getino, who had made *La Hora de los Hornos* (1968) and published 'Hacia un Tercer Cine' ('Towards a Third Cinema', *Tricontinental* no. 13, October 1969). This was followed by the Cuban Julio García Espinosa's classic avant-gardist manifesto, 'For an Imperfect Cinema' (written in 1969 and published in *Cine Cubano* no. 66/67, 1970), which argued for an end to the division between art and life and therefore between professional, full-time intellectuals such as film-makers or critics and 'the people'. This utopian text, foreshadowing policies advocated during the Chinese Cultural Revolution, was followed by numerous writings both in Latin America and in post-68 Europe, in which notions of Third Cinema, Third World Cinema and Revolutionary Cinema tended to get lumped together to the point where they became synonymous. Simultaneously, in North Africa, a number of texts appeared

5

advocating approaches similar to the ones outlined in the Latin American texts: in 1967–8, in Cairo, a few critics and cineastes published the manifesto 'Jamaat as Cinima al jadida' ('Movement of the New Cinema'), and in Morocco the journal *Cinema 3*, founded by Nourdine Saïl, also published Third Cinema arguments. As Ferid Boughedir pointed out, other manifestos followed in the early 70s: 'Cinima al Badil' ('Alternative Cinema'), published in 1972 on behalf of a number of Arab cineastes in the Egyptian journal *At-Tariq*; the 'First Manifesto for a Palestinian Cinema' in 1972, issued at the Damascus Festival; and the 'Second Manifesto' issued later that year at the Carthage Festival, etc.

However, what seems to have happened with the public reception of these manifestos is that a number of crucial distinctions, often only marginally present in founding texts written under the pressures of urgent necessity, were overlooked. Firstly, the authors of the classic manifestos, collected by Chanan in *Twenty-five Years of the New Latin American Cinema*, forcefully state their opposition to a sloganised cinema of emotional manipulation. Any cinema that seeks to smother thought, including a cinema that relies on advertising techniques, is roundly condemned. Sanjines even accuses such strategies of going against revolutionary morality. In other words, a cinema that invites belief and adherence rather than promoting a critical understanding of social dynamics is regarded as worse than useless. All authors, from Birri to Espinosa and even the mystically inclined Glauber Rocha, stress the need for a cinema of lucidity. The widely expressed antagonism towards professional intellectuals is in fact an opposition to colonial and imperialist intellectuals, and this antagonism is never used to devalue the need for the most lucid possible critical intelligence to be deployed as an absolutely necessary part of making films. What is at stake here is the yoking together of the cognitive and the emotive aspects of the cinema. As Espinosa put it, this cinema is addressed 'in a separate or co-ordinated fashion at the intelligence, the emotions, the powers of intuition'. A major lesson to be learned from these manifestos is that they consistently warn against drifting into anti-intellectualism or, worse, shoddy intellectualism, emphasising the need to learn. What they do condemn is a particular kind of middle-class intellectual, not intellectual activity *per se*. The intellectuals condemned are only those whose 'expertise has usually been a service rendered, and sold, to the central authority of society', as Edward Said put it in *The Writer, the Text, and the Critic* (London, Faber & Faber, 1984, p. 2).

Secondly, the manifestos refuse to prescribe an aesthetics. The authors broadly agree about which aesthetic forms are not appropriate or are even damaging, but they also refuse to identify a particular formal strategy as the only way to achieve the activation of a revolutionary consciousness. Following Brecht, who vigorously protested against the attempt to elevate the use of 'distanciation devices' into an obligatory procedure, the Latin Americans insisted on the legitimacy of any procedure which was likely to achieve the desired results, i.e. an analytically informed understanding of the social formation and how to change it in a socialist direction. In Espinosa's words: 'Imperfect cinema can make use of the documentary or the fictional mode, or both. It can use whatever genre, or all genres … It can use cinema as a pluralistic art form or as a specialised form of expression.' Solanas and Getino talk about 'the infinite categories' of Third Cinema, and Sanjines noted that the forms of Revolutionary Cinema must change as the relations between 'author' and people change in particular circumstances. There are no general prescriptions other than negative ones in the sense that certain roads have been explored and found to be dead ends or traps. Glauber Rocha once recalled Nelson Pereira dos Santos quoting a line from a Portuguese poet: 'I don't know where I'm going, but I know you can't get there that way.'

One of the main differences between Third Cinema and the European notion of counter-cinema is this awareness of the historical variability of the necessary aesthetic strategies to be adopted. Whatever the explanation – and the weight of the modernist tradition in the arts may be a crucial factor here – and regardless of the political intentions involved, the notion of counter-cinema tends to conjure up a prescriptive aesthetics: to do the opposite of what dominant cinema does. Hence the descriptive definition of dominant cinema will dictate the prescriptive definition of counter-cinema. The proponents of Third Cinema were just as hostile to dominant cinemas but refused to let the industrially and ideologically dominant cinemas dictate the terms in which they were to be opposed.

To be fair, the two main UK counter-cinema theorists, Peter Wollen and Claire Johnston, never argued that the strategies and characteristics of counter-cinema should be canonised and frozen into a prescriptive aesthetics. They pointed to the importance of cinematic strategies designed to explore what dominant regimes of signification were unable to deal with. Theirs was a politics of deconstruction, not an aesthetics of deconstruction. The difference is worth noting. A politics of deconstruction insists on the need to oppose particular institutionally dominant regimes of making particular kinds of sense, excluding or marginalising others. An aesthetics of deconstruction proceeds from the traumatic discovery that language is not a homogeneous, self-sufficient system. Allon White put it most succinctly in an essay on 'Bakhtin, Sociolinguistics and Deconstruction' (in *The Theory of Reading*, ed. Frank Gloversmith, Sussex, 1984, pp. 138–9):

7

only for those who identify language as such with Saussurean *langue* does it appear paradoxical and impossible that dispersal, *différance*, lacks, absence, traces and all the modes of radical heterogeneity should be there at the heart of discourses which pretend to be complete. Much of the time, deconstruction is rediscovering in texts, with a kind of bemused fascination, all the indices of heteroglossia which Saussure excluded from consideration in his own model, by consigning them to the trashcan of *parole*. To discover that rationality (the logic of the signified) may be subverted by writing itself (the logic of the signifier) seems to put the 'whole Western episteme' into jeopardy, but is in fact a fairly trivial business.

The politics of deconstruction, then, insists on the need to say something different; an aesthetics of deconstruction dissolves into endlessly repeated difference-games, i.e. into the Varietal Thesis, as Meaghan Morris once put it.

Nevertheless, even a politics of deconstruction is circumscribed by its attention to the limits of dominant regimes of signification, whereas the Third Cinema polemicists avoided that trap – admittedly at the price of rather unhelpfully homogenising 'dominant cinema' itself, a mistake later corrected by Nelson Pereira dos Santos' *O Amuleto de Ogum* and *Na Estrada da Vida*, showing what can be done with a selective redeployment of the dominant cinema's generic elements while refusing to reduce the films to, or to imprison them in, that 'varietal' relationship. Dos Santos' films do not 'quote' elements of the dominant cinema in order to provide a nostalgic updating of a kind of cinema now associated with the past; he proposes instead a transformation of cinema which refuses to jettison all the components and aspects of that 'old' dominant cinema merely because they formed part of an unacceptable cinematic regime.

Thirdly, and most importantly, the Latin Americans based their notion of Third Cinema on an approach to the relations between signification and the social. They advocated a practice of cinema which, although conditioned by and tailored to the situations prevailing in Latin America, cannot be limited to that continent alone, nor for that matter to the Third World, however it is defined. The classic manifestos are fairly ambiguous on this point, making rather cursory references to Asian and African cinemas as well as to the work of Chris Marker or Joris Ivens. The clear, though not often explicitly stated, implication is that although Third Cinema is discussed in relation to Latin America, the authors of the manifestos see it as an attitude applicable anywhere. In *CinémAction* no. 1, Solanas took the opportunity to clarify the issue. It is worth quoting him at some length since he corrects many misconceptions that have accrued to the notion of Third Cinema:

First cinema expresses imperialist, capitalist, bourgeois ideas. Big monopoly capital finances big spectacle cinema as well as authorial and informational cinema. Any cinematographic expression ... likely to respond to the aspirations of big capital, I call first cinema. Our definition of second cinema is all that expresses the aspirations of the middle stratum, the petit bourgeoisie ...

Second cinema is often nihilistic, mystificatory. It runs in circles. It is cut off from reality. In the second cinema, just as in the first cinema, you can find documentaries, political and militant cinema. So-called author cinema often belongs in the second cinema, but both good and bad authors may be found in the first and in the third cinemas as well. For us, third cinema is the expression of a new culture and of social changes. Generally speaking, Third Cinema gives an account of reality and history. It is also linked with national culture ... It is the way the world is conceptualised and not the genre nor the explicitly political character of a film which makes it belong to Third Cinema ... Third Cinema is an open category, unfinished, incomplete. It is a research category. It is a democratic, national, popular cinema. Third Cinema is also an experimental cinema, but it is not practised in the solitude of one's home or in a laboratory because it conducts research into communication. What is required is to make that Third Cinema gain space, everywhere, in all its forms ... But it must be stressed that there are 36 different kinds of Third Cinema. (Reprinted in *L'Influence du troisième cinéma dans le monde*, ed. by *CinémAction*, 1979.)

Of course, these definitions beg a great many questions, the most immediate one being that of the viewers: is it possible to see a First Cinema film in a Third Cinema way? In Europe, most Third Cinema products have definitely been consumed in a Second Cinema way, bracketing the politics in favour of an appreciation of the authorial artistry. A pessimist might argue that the deeper a film is anchored in its social situation, the more likely it is that it will be 'secondarised' when viewed elsewhere or at a different time unless the viewers are prepared to interest themselves precisely in the particularities of the socio-cultural nexus addressed, which is still a very rare occurrence. Another point of interest is that the categories are not aligned with Marxist notions of class, presumably since all film-makers would then have to be seen as middle-class entrepreneurs, which is indeed what they are, even when making films clandestinely. Espinosa tackled that problem by arguing that no film-maker should be a full-time professional. Instead, Solanas aligns First, Second and Third Cinemas with three social strata: the bourgeoisie, the petit bourgeoisie and the people, the latter including industrial workers, small and landless peasants, the unemployed, the lumpenproletariat, students, etc. As a category, 'the people' seems to be used as a catch-all term designating all who are left after the bourgeoisie and most of the petit bourgeoisie have been deducted. This gives Third Cinema a basically negative definition. Moreover, if First Cinema was a capitalist-industrial-imperialist cinema and Second Cinema an individualist-petit bourgeois or unhappily capitalist one, Third Cinema is definitely presented as a socialist cinema. But the possibility of an anti-capitalist cinema drawing inspiration from pre-capitalist, feudal nostalgia is not taken into account. Neither did the authors of the manifestos always avoid attributing an essentially revolutionary consciousness to 'the people', the oppressed. As if the experience of oppression itself did not also have ideologically damaging effects, which is why a cinema of lucidity is such an essential prerequisite for a socialist cultural practice.

The manifestos also omit any mention of an aristocracy, as if that class simply didn't count in the cultural configuration. While this may be true to a large extent in Latin America, it is most certainly a handicap when considering Asian countries, not to mention European ones or the African social stratifications. Moreover, neither ethnic nor gender divisions are acknowledged in any of the manifestos, which confuses matters still further. These aspects of the Third Cinema texts do reinforce the impression that it was a notion developed by Latin Americans for Latin Americans and that the general applicability of the approach was added as an afterthought.

However, even though in this respect Third Cinema is not exactly defined with precision, two characteristics must be singled out as especially useful and of lasting value. One is the insistence on its flexibility, its status as research and experimentation, a cinema forever in need of adaptation to the shifting dynamics at work in social struggles. Because it is part of constantly changing social processes, that cinema cannot but change with them, making an all-encompassing definition impossible and even undesirable. The second useful aspect follows from this fundamental flexibility: the only stable thing about Third Cinema is its attempt to speak a socially pertinent discourse which both the mainstream and the authorial cinemas exclude from their regimes of signification. Third Cinema seeks to articulate a different set of aspirations out of the raw materials provided by the culture, its traditions, art forms etc., the complex interactions and condensations of which shape the 'national' cultural space inhabited by the filmmakers as well as their audiences.

Lineages

The Latin American manifestos must also be seen in the context of Marxist or Marxist-inspired cultural theories in general, where they mark a significant additional current with linkages passing both through Cuba and through Italy, as well as developing homegrown traditions of socialist and avant-gardist thought. The most direct connections in this respect, for a European reader, are with German cultural theory of the 1930s, with Brecht and also with Benjamin.

The relation with Brecht has been referred to earlier and may seem obvious, but the Benjamin connection is less well known. Susan Buck-Morss, one of the most perceptive and best informed commentators on Benjamin's work, drew attention to his statement about history writing which, *mutatis mutandis*, also applies to cinematic discourses and evokes the relationship which Solanas and Getino posited between film-making and the context within which film-makers work. In her essay 'The Flâneur, the Sandwichman and the Whore: The Politics of Loitering' (in *New German Critique*, no. 39, 1986), she quoted Benjamin: 'The events surrounding the historian and in which he takes part will underlie his presentation like a text written in invisible ink.' Similarly, underlining phrases from the *Passagenwerk*, she described a mode of inhabiting one's culture which comes close to the ideas put forward in the manifestos, except that Benjamin uses a characteristic metaphor to sum up the approach:

> In the face of 'the wind of history, [...] thinking means setting sails. *How* they are set is the important thing. What for others are digressions are for me the data that determine my course.' But this course is precarious. To cut the lines that have traditionally anchored Marxist discourse in production and sail off into the dreamy waters of consumption is to risk, politically, running aground.
>
> (*New German Critique*, op. cit., p. 107.)

Criticising the evocation of emotion without providing the knowledge that could change the situation, Benjamin's theory on dialectical images, although not mentioned in the manifestos, is present in their margins as they stress the relations with the viewer as being the productive site of cinematic signification. Paraphrasing Susan Buck-Morss, one could say that once 'the sails are set', it is not within the cinematic discourse but in the spaces between the referential world it conjures up and the real that the cognitive process is propelled.

Finally, in a direct parallelism with the aspirations of the Latin American cineastes, Benjamin wrote that he saw his work as one of educating 'the image-creating medium within us to see dimensionally, stereoscopically, into the depths of the historical shade'. Perhaps these echoes of Benjamin can be explained by the fact that 'It is in Benjamin's work of the 1930s that the hidden dialectic between avant-garde art and the utopian hope for an emancipatory mass culture can be grasped alive for the last time', according to Andreas Huyssen in the best book to date

11

on contemporary cultural dynamics, *After the Great Divide* (Indiana University Press, 1986, p. 16). He should have added: in the West, because the work resurfaced and continued in Latin America and in India in the 60s, although in modified forms.

In fact, the lineage goes back to the Soviet avant-gardes. Espinosa echoes Bogdanov's insistence that art practices must address the 'organisation of emotion and thought'. Rocha's violently emotional work echoes Tretyakov's reliance on shock to alter the psyche of the recipient of art. The Latin Americans' emphasis on lucidity echoes Brecht's confidence in the emancipatory power of reason, something he shared with many Soviet artists allied to Lunacharsky's Commissariat of the Enlightenment and their 'goal to forge a new unity of art and life by creating a new art and a new life' (ibid., p. 12) in one and the same movement. There are, then, clear continuities running from the Soviet artists via Tretyakov to Rocha, via Brecht to Solanas and via Benjamin to . . . E. Said?

However, it would be misleading to overlook the differences between the Brecht-Benjamin nexus and the Latin American manifestos. In the displacement of the political-cultural avant-garde from Europe to Latin America, some themes fell by the wayside while others were modified. Technological utopianism was the first casualty, as evidenced by Espinosa's notion of a technologically, as well as financially, poor cinema as being the most effective way forward for artists opposed to the Hollywood-dominated consciousness industries. The recourse to poor technology (e.g., black and white 16mm handheld camera techniques as opposed to studio technology, etc.) had become a necessity not only in Latin America but for all those who wished (and still wish) to contest the industrial cinema's domination. Secondly, compared to the Soviet and German socialist avant-gardes, the Latin Americans put an extraordinary, almost desperate stress on the need for lucidity in the struggle for a renewed attempt to integrate art and life. It is easy to see how changes that had come about since the 30s could give rise to a feeling of desperation in this respect. As Andreas Huyssen put it:

> The legitimate place of a cultural avant-garde which once carried with it the utopian hope for an emancipatory mass culture under socialism has been preempted by the rise of mass mediated culture and its supporting industries and institutions. It was the culture industry, not the avant-garde, which succeeded in transforming everyday life in the 20th century. And yet – the utopian hopes of the historical avant-garde are preserved, even though in distorted form, in this system of secondary exploitation euphemistically called mass culture. (ibid., p. 15)

The Latin American, Asian and African film-makers were, and to a

12

large extent still are, caught between the contradictions of technologised mass culture (its need to activate emancipatory wishes in order to redirect or defuse them by invoking an array of pleasures and organising them in such a way that the dominant pleasures become associated with conservative or individualist gratifications) and the need to develop a different kind of mass culture while being denied the financial, technological and institutional support to do so. Since the culture industry has become extremely adept at orchestrating emotionality while deliberately atrophying the desire for understanding and intellectuality, it makes sense for the Latin American avant-gardes to emphasise lucidity and the cognitive aspects of cultural work, thus reversing the hierarchy between the cognitive and the emotive, while of course maintaining the need to involve both.

The third main difference is due to two absences in Latin America. The absence of a powerful fascist culture with its aestheticisation of politics, as exemplified in Nazi Germany. In Latin America, political power has been wielded in more nakedly repressive ways, perhaps because the populist ideologies required by national-fascist regimes could never be successfully passed off as a domestic aspiration: imperialist forces were too obviously in play for that strategy to work. The second absence is the experience of Stalinism's rigorous subordination of cultural workers to the requirements of the elite of the Party bureaucracy. Whatever could be said of Cuba's cultural policies, the effervescence of Cuba's cinema in the 60s was such a welcome contrast to the cinemas of other 'existing socialisms' that the shortcomings of prevailing Marxist theories of culture were not a major issue for Latin American cultural practitioners. The Allende period in Chile only reinforced this optimism for a while. Consequently the Latin Americans were better able to reconnect with the emancipatory drive of 20s and 30s cultural theory than their European counterparts, who had been traumatised by the experience of World War Two and by the degeneration of the once revered Soviet regime. For them, the dangers inherent in the avant-garde rhetoric about the fusion of art and life were all too apparent. It took the Latin Americans' reformulations under different circumstances, and in the context of a wave of successful independence struggles, to put the question back on the political-cultural agenda. Their emphasis on lucidity also functioned positively in that respect as a warning against subordinating the critical-cognitive dimensions of cultural work to the emotive-utopian harnessing of popular aspirations to a (necessarily) centrally dictated strategy of a political party (if that party is at all serious about gaining power).

Finally, the Latin Americans also pioneered, alongside their filmmaking work, a 'Third Cinema' critical practice which proceeded from the same impulses towards 'historical lucidity', something which the

Europeans never achieved as far as cinema was/is concerned. Not only did the cineastes write manifestos, they also engaged in a critical reconstruction of their cinematic histories. In conjunction with them, historian-critics such as Paulo Emilio Salles Gomes and Jean-Claude Bernadet in Brazil consistently worked towards a type of criticism that sought to understand individual texts and contemporary trends in film-making in relation to the historical processes, institutions and struggles from which these texts and currents received their formative impulses. It took longer for those critical practices to travel to Europe than it took the films. Only recently, and indirectly, has the critical equivalent of Third Cinema gained ground in the West and, not surprisingly, it is mainly (but not exclusively: see for instance Meaghan Morris on *Crocodile Dundee* in *Art & Text*, no. 25) practised by critics and theorists who themselves try to reconnect with as well as extend aspects of 30s German cultural theories: for example, the work of Fredric Jameson, Eric Rentschler, Miriam Hansen, writers associated with the US-based journal *New German Critique*, the writings of Alexander Kluge. In Britain, the work on British and Irish cinema published by the Ireland-based John Hill and the work of Peter Wollen come to mind, along with Claire Johnston's essay on *Maeve*, as all too rare examples. Perhaps fittingly, this return to critical theory went together with a rediscovery of the massive importance of a Soviet theoretician's long neglected work: that of Mikhail Bakhtin.

Third Cinema: Part II

Recently, Teshome Gabriel reformulated some of the Third Cinema theses, pointing out that 'Third Cinema includes an infinity of subjects and styles as varied as the lives of the people it portrays . . . [its] principal characteristic is really not so much where it is made, or even who makes it, but, rather, the ideology it espouses and the consciousness it displays.' Although still confining it *de facto* to so-called Third World countries, nearly always overlooking Asia (which may be due to the difficulty of obtaining prints for study rather than to oversight), Gabriel's unambiguous affirmation that Third Cinema can be practised anywhere opens the way towards a different conceptualisation of Third Cinema and its contemporary relevance. Instead of Epstein's notion of 'photogenie' or difference theory (the 'varietal thesis'), which are theories of consumption, Third Cinema refers to production, and its corresponding theory of consumption would then be Bakhtin's theory of reading, including its emphases on inner speech and the profoundly social aspects of discourse.

However, perhaps because of his committed internationalism, Gabriel risks contradicting himself by not facing head on the question of the national. If Third Cinema is as varied as the lives of the people it

14

portrays (I would prefer to say: as varied as the social processes it inhabits), it must follow that it espouses nationally specific forms, since the lives of people are governed and circumscribed by histories and institutions made 'nationally specific' by the very existence of the boundaries framing the terrain where a particular government's writ runs, by the legal and educational systems in place there, etc.

Nevertheless, Gabriel also wrote *Towards a Critical Theory of Third World Films* (reprinted in this collection) in which Third Cinema and genuine Third World cinema expressive of Third World needs are equated. Whether or not China, India or South Korea can meaningfully be regarded as Third World areas, Gabriel's essay raises another serious problem: is it theoretically possible to find a unifying aesthetic for non-Euro-American cinemas? If the answer is 'yes' as his otherwise stimulating analyses tend to suggest, then Third Cinema is undoubtedly not nearly as varied as the lives of the people it portrays. But, going one step further, the way Gabriel seeks to substantiate the argument for a unifying aesthetic leads to two conflicting results. Firstly, and in spite of the stated contrary intention, Third Cinema is once more defined in terms of its difference from Euro-American cinema, thus implicitly using Hollywood and its national-industrial rivals as the yardstick against which to measure the other's otherness. Secondly, Gabriel demonstrates also that the various non-Euro-American cinematic regimes organise time and space in their own specific ways. That is to say, using a Bakhtinian term, non-Euro-American cinema is characterised by a different chronotope. In his study of Bakhtin's work, Tzvetan Todorov defined the chronotope as 'the set of distinctive features of time and space within each literary genre' (*Mikhail Bakhtin: The Dialogical Principle*, Manchester University Press, 1984, p. 83). Bakhtin himself was a little less restrictive. He talked about an image of 'historical time condensed in space' (*Speech Genres & Other Late Essays*, University of Texas Press, 1986, p. 49) and of

> the ability to *see time*, to *read time*, in the spatial whole of the world and, on the other hand, to perceive the filling of space not as an immobile background, a given that is completed once and for all, but as an emerging whole, an event – this is the ability to read in everything *signs that show time in its course*, beginning with nature and ending with human customs and ideas (all the way to abstract concepts) ... The work of the seeing eye joins here with the most complex thought processes.
>
> (ibid., p. 24)

Consequently, chronotopes are time-space articulations characteristic of particular, historically determined conceptions of the relations between the human, the social and the natural world, i.e. ways of conceptualising social existence. Gabriel's argument that a different chronotope determines the narrative images and rhythms of non-Euro-American cinemas is convincing. However, his analysis stops short of specifying how, for instance, the chronotope of Ghatak's films, with their intricate interweaving of historical, biographical, natural and emotional temporal rhythms, not to mention musical and speech rhythms, in spaces disrupted by edges and boundaries themselves condensing historical and symbolic meanings, differs from Joaquim Pedro de Andrade's telescoping of historical, allegorical and fantasy times in *O Homem do Pau Brasil,* or the representation of historical time in terms of the relation between linear-evential time and cyclical-ritual time in a space divided according to varieties of sacred-profane oppositions, as in Sembene's *Ceddo.* Secondly, the chronotopes of neither the first nor the second cinemas are as homogeneous as Gabriel's argument (and the use of the term Euro-American in these notes) would suggest. Chantal Akerman and Bette Gordon's films each in their own way deploy space-time worlds at variance with dominant Euro-American cinemas. Similarly, some of Mario Bava's horror films operate within the confines of fantasy time and logic (in which the narrative is propelled by the working through of a single, highly condensed but basically static fantasy structure), whereas Roger Corman's work is marked by the imbrication of sacred-ritual and profane-linear time structures, although both tend to use space in very similar ways. Then there is the question of the differences between the chronotopes of 'commercial' Indian cinemas and those of Japanese, Hollywood or Latin American ones. In addition, there appear to be marked differences between black British and black American films in spite of their shared opposition to Hollywood. These differences relate more to the varying relations between these films and their respective 'host' cinemas, a relationship that also informs the differences between British and American independent-political cinemas in general. For example, the black British cinema can be seen as organising time-space relations differently from both dominant and experimental-independent British cinemas, and this complex differentiation from its immediate industrial-social-cultural context is a more pertinent (over)determining process than, for example, any reference to black African cinemas. Moreover, within the black British cinema there are further important distinctions to be made between films drawing on Asian and on Caribbean cultural discourses and histories.

Gabriel's homogenisation of the Third Cinema chronotope into a single aesthetic 'family' is thus premature, although the analysis of the differentiation between Euro-American cinema and its 'other' constitutes the necessary first step in this politically indispensable and urgent

16

task of expelling the Euro-American conceptions of cinema from the centre of film history and critical theory. The difficulties of such a project are not to be underestimated, as is demonstrated by the consistent shorthand usage of the term Euro-American in this discussion: readers of these notes are bound to have some idea of what is meant by that term, while a distinction between Islamic and Buddhist cinemas is likely to be received with puzzlement, although it is in all probability a pertinent distinction to make.

The national

One important factor which programmes Gabriel's premature re-homogenisation of Third Cinema, after his insistence on its infinite variability, is his principled but costly avoidance of the national question. The effectiveness with which the national socio-cultural formations determine particular signifying practices is not addressed. Admittedly, the national question itself has a different weight in various parts of the globe, but the forced as well as the elective internationalism of cinema – especially of a cinema with inadequately developed industrial infrastructures – tends to bracket national-cultural issues too quickly. And yet if any cinema is determinedly 'national', even 'regional', in its address and aspirations, it is Third Cinema.

Since Hollywood established its dominance in the world market, from 1919 onwards, the call for a cinema rooted in national cultures has been repeated in a variety of ways, perhaps most vocally by national bourgeoisies cynically invoking the 'national culture' in order to get the state to help them monopolise the domestic market. Initially, these calls took the form of arguments for an authorial cinema, within a national industry if possible, outside of its institutions if necessary. The split between a national-dominant cinema competing with Hollywood and a national authorial cinema – which also existed within Hollywood, as Solanas acknowledged – has been mirrored in the split between a politically oriented militant cinema opposing mainstream entertainment cinema and a personal-experimental cinema opposing the literariness of author-cinema, even if these categories tended to overlap at times. These mirror-divisions have developed since the mid-20s, each giving rise to its own institutions but none being able to challenge the industrial-political domination of Hollywood. At best, some countries (especially in Asia) have managed to prevent Hollywood from destroying their local film industry, but even these countries failed to make a significant international impact. The post-World War Two era up to 1975 (the Vietnamese victory over the US) has been characterised by intense struggles over 'national' film cultures, and has seen the rise of authorial cinemas while the dominant industrial cinemas' ideological and economic functions within national as well as in international

17

capitalist structures began to shift towards television. In countries without advanced film production sectors, the question of the national was also and immediately a political question, i.e. the question of national liberation and the right to speak in one's own cultural idioms. But although these questions are fairly recent ones as far as cinema is concerned, they had been rehearsed for over a century in relation to literature, the fine arts, theatre, music, etc.

In fact, the West invented nationalism, initially in the form of imperialism as nation-states extended their domination over others, creating at one and the same time the hegemonic sense of the 'national culture' and the 'problem' of national identity for the colonised territories. The issue of national-cultural identity arises only in response to a challenge posed by the other, so that any discourse of national-cultural identity is always and from the outset oppositional, although not necessarily conducive to progressive positions. This holds true for the colonising nation as well as for the colonised one(s) it calls into being. The responses to this reciprocal but antagonistic formation of identities fall into three types.

The first option is to identify with the dominant and dominating culture, which is easy for the metropolitan intelligentsia such as the infamous Thomas Macaulay, who disguised armed and economic force under the cloak of cultural superiority. This option is less comfortable for the colonised intelligentsia who may aspire to the hegemonic culture but can never really belong to it. However, the rewards for such an aspiration are sufficiently attractive for many of them to pursue it with vigour: there is the promise of advancement under colonial rule and of becoming the 'national' leadership to which a retreating coloniser will wish to bequeath power.

The second option is to develop the antagonistic sense of national identity by seeking to reconnect with traditions that got lost or were displaced or distorted by colonial rule or by the impact of Western industrial-military power. In spite of the undoubted mobilising power of such national-populist ideologies, this option presents considerable difficulties and dangers. The main ones derive from the need to reinvent traditions, to conjure up an image of pre-colonial innocence and authenticity, since the national-cultural identity must by definition be founded on what has been suppressed or distorted. The result is mostly a nostalgia for a pre-colonial society which in fact never existed, full of idyllic villages and communities peopled by 'authentic' (read folkloric) innocents in touch with the 'real' values perverted by imperialism or, in the most naive versions, perverted by technology.

Alternatively, particular aspects of some culture are selected and elevated into essentialised symbols of the national identity: the local answer to imperialism's stereotypes. Mirroring imperialism's practices, such efforts mostly wind up presenting previously existing relations of domination and subordination as the 'natural' state of things.

And then, of course, there are the political monstrosities that occur when such idealised and essentialised notions of national identity achieve some kind of power: for example, the wholesale massacres of 'others', the 'others' required to define the 'national identity' and to function as scapegoats for the fact that the 'original idyllic existence' still seems as far away as ever.

African and Asian as well as Latin American intelligentsia have negotiated these problems for a very long time and have come up with a variety of solutions, among which are Third Worldist types of internationalism (the displacement from national identity to continental identity), the controlled mixture of feudalism and advanced capitalism practised in Japan, the displacement of the national to the racial (negritude, for example), etc. In the second half of the 20th century, however, together with the widespread struggles for national liberation and independence, a different approach has gained strength. Although often still riddled with residues of backward-looking idealisations of what the 'original' culture must have been like before the impact of Western rapaciousness, this third option refused both national chauvinism and identification with the aggressor in favour of a more complex view of social formations and their dynamics, including the fraught relationship with the West. As the Moroccan Zaghloul Morsy put it: 'Whether we try to refute it, liberate ourselves from it or assent to it . . . the West is here with us as a prime fact, and ignorance or imperfect knowledge of it has a nullifying effect on all serious reflection and genuinely artistic expression' (*Main Trends in Aesthetics and the Sciences of Art*, ed. M. Dufrenne, New York, 1979, p. 40).

It is one of the contentions of these notes that the opposite holds true as well: Asian, African and Latin American cultures are with us as a fact and ignorance of them has an equally nullifying effect on all serious reflection . . . in the West. While the bourgeois nationalist intellectuals of the liberated countries talked about effecting a synthesis of East and West or of North and South in order to forge a new hegemony, militant intellectuals rejected that illusion and opted for a rhetoric of becoming: the national culture would emerge from a struggle waged by the existing people and not by the idealised figment of a ruralist fantasy. It is in this process of struggle that the intellectuals would find a role. In that context, liberation did not refer to the freeing of some previously existing but temporarily suppressed state of culture. On the contrary, political and economic liberation would be a necessary precondition for the emergence of a popular culture, a point most cogently made by Solanas when he stressed the experimental nature of Third Cinema. In each case, the specific circumstances of the country involved – its pre-

19

colonial as well as colonial history, etc. – would determine the particular shape and dynamics of the culture once it has been freed to evolve according to its own needs and aspirations. Consequently, the question of the national became not irrelevant but secondary: the primary task was to address the existing situation in all its often contradictory and confusing intricacy with the maximum lucidity. The expression of cultural and national identity as well as personal identity would be an inevitable by-product in the sense that a discourse about and addressing particular social processes would necessarily bear the imprint of those processes in the same way that any discourse bears the imprint of those it addresses, along with the traces of the (over)determining forces that shape it. Cultural identity no longer precedes the discourse as something to be recovered; it is by trying to put an understanding of the multifarious social-historical processes at work in a given situation into discourse that the national-cultural-popular identity begins to find a voice. Tradition(s) can no longer be seen as sacred cows: some are to be criticised, others to be mobilised or inflected – an attitude exemplified by Sembene's and Cissé's work. Nationalist solidarity thus gives way to the need for critical lucidity which becomes the intellectual's special task. His/her contribution becomes the provision of a critical understanding likely to assist the struggles at hand. As Louis Althusser put it in a letter to Régis Debray: '[Intellectuals] are entrusted by the people in arms with the guardianship and extension of scientific knowledge. They must fulfil this mission with the utmost care, following in the footsteps of Marx, who was convinced that nothing was more important for the struggles of the workers' movements and those waging those struggles than the most profound and accurate knowledge' (in Debray, *A Critique of Arms*, Penguin, 1977, p. 267).

Edward Said formulated it in this way: 'The history of thought, to say nothing of political movements, is extravagantly illustrative of how the dictum "solidarity before criticism" means the end of criticism.' And he went on to say: 'Even in the very midst of a battle in which one is unmistakably on one side against another, there should be criticism, because there must be critical consciousness if there are to be issues, problems, values, even lives to be fought for' (*The World, the Text, and the Critic*, London, Faber & Faber, 1984, p. 28). So although the national may indeed not be the most important issue, to skip the question of the national and slide directly towards an international aesthetic also eliminates the defining characteristics of Third Cinema itself: the aim of rendering a particular social situation intelligible to those engaged in a struggle to change it in a socialist direction.

That the question of the national cannot be divorced from the question of Third Cinema is also evident from an example which most Third Cinema theorists tend to overlook in spite of the striking similarities presented by it: the cultural practice advocated at Santiniketan in India in the 20s and 30s. The Tagore-founded institution in Bengal developed an aesthetic on the interface between nature and culture, unifying the Janus-faced relationship of the artist to both under the terms of the 'environment' and the 'living tradition'. It saw culture as layered into regional specificities while insisting on a critical internationalism. In Geeta Kapur's words:

As an artist, Rabindranath's commitment to the living tradition came first and foremost through his creative choices, through his working the great range of artistic forms [...] as for example his use as a poet of Upanishadic verse, Baul songs and folk lullabies. At the same time he enjoined his colleagues to resist spiritual and aesthetic (as for that matter political) codification of forms on any rigid national or ethnic grounds, to open themselves out to the world art movements, thus enlivening their own practice and making it internationally viable and contemporary.
(In *K. G. Subramanyan*, Lalit Kala Akademi, New Delhi, 1987, p. 17)

She added: 'This after all would be the best test of a living tradition.' At Santiniketan, a concerted attempt was made to organise the liberating effects of such an orientation towards the complexities of a contemporary 'environment' and of vernacular vocabulary and skills into a coherent aesthetic approach which was deeply embedded in the Indian national independence movement. The political and the cultural were fused into a radical curriculum in which students at Santiniketan

were introduced to craftsmen at work; they were encouraged to rework traditional materials and techniques and the objects produced were exhibited and sold in local fairs [an equivalent of the exhibition practices associated with Third Cinema and its screenings at informal popular gatherings as well as in student milieux and in radical institutions] with the hope of recycling the taste and skills of craftsmen-artists into the urban middle-class milieu with the young artist forming a double link. A new Indian sensibility was to be hypothesised, created, designed ... [Popular art] inclined them to visual narratives (derived from the great myths as well as from tribal fables), to hybrid figural iconography and swift stylistic abbreviations.

(ibid, p. 18)

Summing up the pedagogic approach of Nandalal Bose, 'the most courageous artist of the nationalist period', Geeta Kapur emphasises

21

that this constituted a practice of 'images derived from popular sources serving political-populist purposes with a radical effect on both' (ibid., p. 19). The dialogic relation with the popular, the stress on the vernacular, the double reference to both the regional and the international, the hybridisation practices, the recourse to the most inexpensive means of artistic production, the project of creating a new national culture, all these features recur in the writings of the Third Cinema polemicists. In addition, the Cuban as well as the Indian varieties of this current were deeply embedded in anti-imperialist struggles for national-cultural as well as political and economic autonomy.

This should not, of course, obscure the differences between Santiniketan and the Latin Americans, the most obvious of which are the latter's overtly Marxist approach and the fact that the political practice of a capital-intensive, inherently 'modern' mass-media technology such as cinema required a drastic reconceptualisation of the nature of the dialogue with the popular. Moreover, Santiniketan is not the only antecedent of Third Cinema in this respect: the Brazilian theatrical and literary avant-gardes of the 20s, especially those associated with Oswald de Andrade, the Pau Brasil and the Anthropofagia manifestos, come to mind, as do the Mexican muralists in the 30s, etc., all of which address similar sets of tensions and contradictions. In that regard, the references to Italian neo-realism and to Grierson in the manifestos cannot be taken at face value. They function as a symptom. The European reference is then a symptom of the productive cultural hybridisation inherent in the position from which the Latin American cineastes speak, rather than functioning as a designation of origins. Finally, the absence in that context of references to Jean Rouch also speaks volumes. Rouch is a reference for African film-makers as opposed to Latin American ones, except for the rather jokey allusions in the Brazilian comedy *Ladroes de Cinema* (1977). His absence from the classic Third Cinema manifestos thus operates as a marker of the marginalisation of African cinemas by the Latin Americans at the time. The argument that it might have been overlooked because of Rouch's ethnographic rather than explicitly political discourse would not be very convincing, since Griersonian social democracy and its admiration for strongly centralised (but benevolent) state authority does figure in the texts in spite of its dubious politics. Moreover, Rouch can be seen as a most intriguing father figure for Third Cinema, more so than Ivens or Marker, since it is with *Moi un noir* (1957) that he invented an African Third Cinema style of film-making – and that precisely because of the dialogic relation set up between Rouch and his main protagonist, 'Robinson' (i.e. Oumarou Ganda), which structures the filmic process, its stylistic aspects along with its fiction (see for example the points made by Jim Hillier in *Cahiers du Cinéma*, vol. 2, London, Routledge &

Kegan Paul/British Film Institute, 1986, pp. 223–5). It is significant that Rouch's film and the emergence of a Third Cinema in Africa date back to the very year in which Ghana became the first African nation-state to gain independence from its colonising power.

Bakhtin

For the theoretical elaboration of the interplay between utterances and their socio-historical setting(s), the most useful inspiration available to date is the work of Mikhail Bakhtin. In particular, his concepts of dialogue, otherness and the chronotope provide productive ways in which Teshome Gabriel's pioneering work might be built upon, allowing us to rethink the whole issue of cultural politics in the process. Although Bakhtin does not directly address the question of the national, he is very much concerned with the issue of socio-historical specificity. His discussion of discursive genres outlines the way he poses the problem:

> The work is oriented, first, towards its [...] recipients, and towards certain conditions of performance and perception. Second, the work is oriented towards life, from the inside, so to speak, by its thematic content. [...] Every genre has its methods, its ways of seeing and understanding reality, and these methods are its exclusive characteristic. The artist must learn to see reality through the eyes of the genre. [...] The field of representation changes from genre to genre [...] it delineates itself differently as space and time. This field is always specific.
>
> (Quoted in T. Todorov, op. cit., pp. 82–3)

Bakhtin then goes on to make another link by defining genre as a fragment of collective memory:

> Cultural and literary traditions [...] are preserved and continue to live, not in the subjective memory of the individual nor in some collective 'psyche', but in the objective forms of culture itself. [...] In this sense, they are intersubjective and interindividual, and therefore social. [...] The individual memory of creative individuals almost does not come into play.
>
> (Quoted in T. Todorov, op. cit., p. 85)

Bakhtin's translators, biographers and commentators, K. Clark and M. Holquist, emphasise the proximity of such an approach to cultural tradition to Bakhtin's concept of the chronotope:

> In each place and period a different set of time/space categories

obtained, and what it meant to be human was in a large measure determined by these categories. The Greeks saw time as cyclical, for example, while the Hebrews assigned greatest value to the future.
(*Mikhail Bakhtin*, Harvard University Press, 1984, p. 278)

The component parts of discourses/utterances are themselves 'socialised':

Within the arena of [...] every utterance an intense conflict between one's own and another's word is being fought out. Each word is a little arena for the clash of and criss-crossing of differently oriented social accents. A word in the mouth of a particular individual is a product of the living interaction of social forces.
(Quoted in Clark and Holquist, op. cit., p. 220)

The reason for this is that

No utterance can be attributed to the speaker exclusively; it is the *product of the interaction of the interlocutors*, and, broadly speaking, the product of the whole complex *social situation* in which it has occurred.
(Quoted in T. Todorov, op. cit., p. 30, original emphases)

Bakhtin goes so far as to characterise individual utterances as corridors in which echo a multiplicity of voices, a corridor shaped by the interaction, whether direct or indirect, delayed or anticipated, between interlocutors, so that what is actively unspoken or what is simply, silently assumed, exerts as effective a determining force upon the discourse as the speaker's project. In addition to the interlocutors and to the social situation — itself alive with remembered, half-remembered, anticipated and temporarily dormant discourses — there is the echo of the generic whole that resounds in every word that functions within it. However, Bakhtin's plurivocal cultural spaces do not present some egalitarian jostle of intersecting voices of the type that deconstructive notions of intertextuality evoke. On the contrary:

Just as [social diversity] is constrained by the rules imposed by the single state, the diversity of discourses is fought against by the aspiration, correlative to all power, to institute a common language. [...] The common language is never given but in fact always ordained, and at every moment of the life of the language it is opposed to genuine heterology.
(Todorov, op. cit., p. 57)

Cultural specificity is thus never a closed, static terrain; it is never a systemic whole like a code:

> Culture cannot be enclosed within itself as something ready made. The unity of a particular culture is an open unity [in which] lie immense semantic possibilities that have remained undisclosed, unrecognised, and unutilised.
> (*Speech Genres & Other Late Essays*, pp. 5–6)

The clear implication here is that just as there is a hierarchy imposed upon the diversity of discourses, the institutionalised exercise of power bears upon which semantic possibilities shall remain unrecognised or unutilised. In the case of cinema, this means that social power has its word to say in what kind of discourses are made as well as in how people read them. The silence of the oppressed may be an active form of resistance, a refusal. It may also be the result of a socially induced incapacity to activate certain registers of meaning, the exercise of social power having succeeded in blocking access to a number of semantic possibilities. It is important to stress this particular effect of power, since it is often overlooked by people who study the way consumers use products of the cultural industries: questions of pleasure are often emphasised at the expense of an examination of the stunting and restrictive effects of dominant discursive regimes which constantly repeat the ruling out of certain types of making sense.

Having sketched the parameters of a possible typology of the dynamics shaping cultural formations, Bakhtin makes some particularly challenging points with far-reaching implications, especially for the community-oriented populist tendencies currently dominant among left cultural practitioners in the UK as well as in the US. In a short journalistic piece he warned:

> In our enthusiasm for specification we have ignored questions of the interconnection and interdependence of various areas of culture; we have frequently forgotten that the boundaries of these areas are not absolute, that in various epochs they have been drawn in various ways; and we have not taken into account that the most intense and productive life of culture takes place on the boundaries of its individual areas and not in places where these areas have become enclosed in their own specificity.
> (*Speech Genres*, p. 2)

This warning helps to explain the sterility of classic modernist positions but also, and more importantly, of attempts to enclose cultural practices within class or ethnic or gender specificities. This point is

25

developed into a fully fledged critique of practices that advocate identification between the intellectual-artist and 'the people' or any other social grouping. In the following quotation, Bakhtin refers to attempts to understand 'foreign cultures', but his remarks apply with equal force and pertinence to social strata other than one's own, regardless of whether these strata are defined in terms of class, ethnicity or gender. Bakhtin wrote:

> There exists a very strong, but one-sided and thus untrustworthy idea that in order better to understand a foreign culture, one must enter into it, forgetting one's own, and view the world through the eyes of this foreign culture. [...] Of course, the possibility of seeing the world through its eyes is a necessary part of the process of understanding it; but if this were the only aspect [...] it would merely be duplication and would not entail anything enriching. *Creative understanding* does not renounce itself, its own place and time, its own culture; and it forgets nothing. In order to understand, it is immensely important for the person who understands to be *located outside* the object of his or her creative understanding – in time, in space, in culture. In the realm of culture, outsideness is a most powerful factor in understanding. [...] We raise new questions for a foreign culture, ones that it did not raise for itself; we seek answers to our own questions in it; and the foreign culture responds to us by revealing to us its new aspects and new semantic depths. Without *one's own* questions one cannot creatively understand anything other or foreign. Such a dialogic encounter of two cultures does not result in merging or mixing. Each retains its own unity and *open* totality, but they are mutually enriched.
>
> (*Speech Genres*, pp. 6–7)

One must be 'other' oneself if anything is to be learned about the meanings of limits, or borderlines; of the areas where 'the most intense and productive life of culture takes place'.

Trinh T. Minh-ha, in an equally provocative introduction to a special issue of *Discourse* (no. 8, 1986–7), echoes Bakhtin's concern with the productivity of otherness:

> Otherness has its own laws and interdictions. [...] And difference in this context undermines opposition as well as separatism. Neither a claim for special treatment, nor a return to an authentic core (the 'unspoiled' Real Other), it acknowledges in each of its moves the coming together and drifting apart both within and between identity/ies. What is at stake is not only the hegemony of Western cultures, but also their identities as unified cultures: in other words,

the realisation that there is a Third World in every First World, and vice-versa. (p. 3)

Remembering Bakhtin's point about the unequal power relations between discourses, these considerations lead us far from the post-modern or the multiculturalist free play of differences, the republican carnival of voices, towards a politics of otherness as the precondition for any cultural politics. If outsideness is the prerequisite for creative understanding, it also follows that outsideness is a position as threatening as it is productive. Threatening for the 'insider' whose limits become visible in ways not accessible to him/her; productive precisely in so far as structuring limits, horizons, boundaries, become visible and available for understanding.

If we return to the Latin American manifestos through the prism of Bakhtin's theories, their insistence on a lucid presentation of social forces and of reality, coupled with the pursuit of socialist aspirations, can be seen in a somewhat different light. Viewed from this perspective, Third Cinema is a cinema neither of nor for 'the people', nor is it simply a matter of expressing opposition to imperialism or to bourgeois rule. It is a cinema made by intellectuals who, for political and artistic reasons at one and the same time, assume their responsibilities as socialist intellectuals and seek to achieve through their work the production of social intelligibility. Moreover, remembering Edward Said's point about the need for criticism, their pursuit of the creative understanding of particular social realities takes the form of a critical dialogue – hence the need for both lucidity and close contact with popular discourses and aspirations – with a people itself engaged in bringing about social change. Theirs is not an audience in the Hollywood or in the televisual sense, where popularity is equated with consumer satisfaction and where pleasure is measured in terms of units of the local currency entered on the balance sheet. Theirs, like Brecht's, is a fighting notion of popularity, as is clear from Solanas' insistence on Third Cinema being an experimental cinema engaged in a constant process of research. And like Brecht, the Latin Americans reserve the right to resort to any formal device they deem necessary to achieve their goals, as is clear from their refusal to straitjacket themselves into a codified Third Cinema aesthetic.

Speaking in the forms of cinema, i.e. making films, or in other genres of audiovisual discourse, thus necessarily means entering into a dialogue, not only with the historical uses of these genres – since these discourses inevitably reverberate in, for example, Third Cinema's sound-image articulations – but also with the power relations enshrined in those historical uses of dominant narrative regimes, along with the entire cultural networks within which the experiences of making and viewing are located. Third Cinema is most emphatically not simply concerned with 'letting the oppressed speak with their own voices': that would be a one-sided and therefore an untrustworthy position. Those voices will only speak the experience of oppression, including the debilitating aspects of that condition. Third Cinema does not seek to induce guilt in or to solicit sympathy from its interlocutors. Instead, it addresses the issue of social power from a critical-but-committed position, articulating the joining of 'the intelligence, the emotions, the powers of intuition', as Espinosa put it, so as to help achieve socialist ideals.

Because of the realisation of the social nature of discourse, the Third Cinema project summons to the place of the viewer social-historical knowledges, rather than art-historical, narrowly aesthetic ones. These latter knowledges would be relevant only in so far as they form part of the particular nexus of socio-historical processes addressed.

As for Third Cinema and otherness or outsideness, it is no accident but a logical consequence that a sense of non-belonging, non-identity with the culture one inhabits, whether it be nationally defined, ethnically or in any other way, is a precondition for 'the most intense and productive aspects of cultural life'. Although that may be too strong a formulation since it obviously is possible to be 'other' in some respects and to be 'in and of' the culture at the same time, the fact remains that it is in this disjuncture, in this in-between position, that the production of social intelligibility thrives, at least as far as socialist cultural practices are concerned. The price paid for such a position is invariably the hostility of representatives of the hegemonic culture, whether these are active apologists for the ruling ideologies or merely guilty intellectuals who hope to wash away the taint of their middle-class position by abdicating all intellectual responsibilities. But that hostility is actively to be welcomed as an indication that we are on the right track.

What is at stake, from my point of view, in the re-actualisation of the Third Cinema debates in the UK in the 80s, is the conviction that outsideness/otherness is the only vantage point from which a viable cultural politics may be conducted in the UK. The negotiation of the problems involved in otherness as a positional necessity is the precondition for a critical-cultural practice in Britain, as witnessed by the work of black film-makers who now constitute the most intellectually and cinematically innovative edge of British cultural politics, along with a few 'others' such as Cinema Action (the makers of the most intelligent film about Englishness in the 80s, *Rocinante*), Mark Karlin (whose programmes on Nicaragua constitute an example of Third Cinema's adaptability to televisual modes of discourse) and some film-makers such as Pat Murphy who move between Ireland and the UK. While the work of these film-makers seems to have little in common from a formal, aesthetic point of view, they nevertheless share a systematic demarcation from the genres to which they ostensibly belong: *Burning an Illusion* is as different from the prevailing social-realist dramas as *Territories* is from modernist-experimental video- and film-making; *Rocinante* is as different from road movie romances as *Anne Devlin* is from biographical films with strong, political heroines, etc. In each case, the difference is not generated by a surfeit of formal innovation or by the pursuit of a marketable variation on a theme, but because the prevailing generic codifications are too restrictive for the articulation of their social-analytical purposes.

Together with these film-making activities, theoretical-critical work also needs to address its Englishness, its parochial limits, its ethnocentricity and insularity. This requires a particular emphasis to be given to 'otherness', to the dialogue with unfamiliar cultural practices and traditions, while refusing to homogenise every non-Euro-American culture into a globalised 'other'. The challenge to English aspirations towards universality is not to pose a counter-universality but actively to seek to learn about as well as promote other ways of making sense. When we learn how the work of Ritwik Ghatak, Kumar Shahani or Carlos Reichenbach is 'specific' to the cultural formations that produced them, perhaps we will learn to see better how our homegrown theories and films bear the imprint of an incapacitatingly restrictive Englishness (Americans may substitute their own -ness where appropriate). Therefore, the notion of Third Cinema is relevant to the UK for its exemplification of an approach to the relations between the social and the cultural as well as for its very 'otherness' in the sense of something it is necessary both to learn from and about: to learn from Third Cinema film-makers and intellectuals while endeavouring to make more breathing space within the UK for the emergence of otherness as a challenge to the English Ideology.

Consequently, my primary aim in drawing attention to the issues which the notion of Third Cinema allows me to raise is an attempt to help change the (film) culture which I inhabit by evoking a historical narrative, of sorts, which is intended to conjure up an anticipated, desirable but necessarily utopian image of what a socialist critical-cultural practice might/should be.

Towards a critical theory of
Third World films

Teshome H. Gabriel

Wherever there is a film-maker prepared to stand up against commercialism, exploitation, pornography and the tyranny of technique, there is to be found the living spirit of *New Cinema*. Wherever there is a film-maker, of any age or background, ready to place his cinema and his profession at the service of the great causes of his time, there will be the living spirit of *New Cinema*. This is the correct definition which sets *New Cinema* apart from the commercial industry because the commitment of industrial cinema is to untruth and exploitation.

The Aesthetics of Hunger
Glauber Rocha [Brazil]

Insert the work as an original fact in the process of liberation, place it first at the service of life itself, ahead of art; *dissolve aesthetics in the life of society*: only in this way, as [Frantz] Fanon said, can decolonisation become possible and culture, cinema, and beauty – at least, what is of greatest importance to us – become *our culture, our films, and our sense of beauty.*

Towards a Third Cinema
Fernando Solanas and Octavio Gettino [Argentina]

Frantz Fanon, in his attempts to identify the revolutionary impulse in the peasant of the Third World, accepted that culture is an act of insemination upon history, whose product is liberation from oppression.[1] In my search for a methodological device for a critical inquiry into Third World films, I have drawn upon the historical works of this ardent proponent of liberation, whose analysis of the steps of the genealogy of Third World culture can also be used as a critical framework for the study of Third World films. This essay is, therefore, divided into two parts and focuses on those essential qualities Third World films possess rather than those they may seem to lack. The first part lays the formulation for Third World film culture and filmic institutions based on a critical and theoretical matrix applicable to Third World needs. The second part is an attempt to give material substance to the analytic constructs discussed previously.

From pre-colonial times to the present, the struggle for freedom from oppression has been waged by the Third World masses, who in their maintenance of a deep cultural identity have made history come alive. Just as they have moved aggressively towards independence, so has the evolution of Third World film culture followed a path from 'domination' to 'liberation'. This genealogy of Third World film culture moves from the First Phase in which foreign images are impressed in an alienating fashion on the audience, to the Second and Third Phases in which recognition of 'consciousness of oneself' serves as the essential antecedent for national and, more significantly, international consciousness. There are, therefore, three phases in this methodological device.

Phases of Third World films

Phase I – The unqualified assimilation
The industry: Identification with the Western Hollywood film industry. The link is made as obvious as possible and even the names of the companies proclaim their origin. For instance, the Nigerian film company, Calpenny, whose name stands for California, Pennsylvania and New York, tries to hide behind an acronym, while the companies in India, Egypt and Hongkong are not worried being typed the 'Third World's Hollywood', 'Hollywood-on-the-Nile', and 'Hollywood of the Orient' respectively.
The theme: Hollywood thematic concerns of 'entertainment' predominate. Most of the feature films of the Third World in this phase sensationalise adventure for its own sake and concern themselves with escapist themes of romance, musicals, comedies etc. The sole purpose of such industries is to turn out entertainment products which will generate profits. The scope and persistence of this kind of industry in the Third World lies in its ability to provide reinvestable funds and this quadruples their staying power. Therefore, in cases where a counter-cinematic movement has occurred the existing national industry has been able to ingest it. A good example is in the incorporation of the 'cinema nôvo' movement in the Brazilian Embrafilme.

31

Style: The emphasis on formal properties of cinema, technical brilliance and visual wizardry, overrides subject matter. The aim here is simply to create a 'spectacle'. Aping Hollywood stylistically, more often than not, runs counter to Third World needs for a serious social art.

Phase II – The remembrance phase

The industry: Indigenisation and control of talents, production, exhibition and distribution. Many Third World film production companies are in this stage. The movement for a social institution of cinema in the Third World such as 'cinema moudjahid' in Algeria, 'new wave' in India and '*engagé* or committed cinema' in Senegal and Mozambique exemplifies this phase.

The theme: Return of the exile to the Third World's source of strength, i.e. culture and history. The predominance of filmic themes such as the clash between rural and urban life, traditional versus modern value systems, folklore and mythology, identifies this level. Sembene Ousmane's early film *Mandabi* about a humble traditional man outstripped by modern ways characterises this stage. *Barravento* ('The Turning Wind'), a poetic Brazilian film about a member of a fishermen's village who returns from exile in the city, is a folkloric study of mysticism. The film from Burkina Faso (Upper Volta), *Wend Kûuni* ('God's Gift'), attempts to preserve the spirit of folklore in a brilliant recreation of an old tale of a woman who is declared a witch because of her conflicts with custom when she refused to marry after the disappearance of her husband. While the most positive aspect of this phase is its break with the concepts and propositions of Phase I, the primary danger here is the uncritical acceptance or undue romanticisation of ways of the past.

It needs to be stressed that there is a danger of falling into the trap of exalting traditional virtues and racialising culture without at the same time condemning faults. To accept totally the values of Third World traditional cultures without simultaneously stamping out the regressive elements can only lead to 'a blind alley', as Fanon puts it, and falsification of the true nature of culture as an act or agent of liberation. Therefore, unless this phase, which predominates in Third World film practices today, is seen as a process, a moving towards the next stage, it could develop into opportunistic endeavours and create cultural confusion. This has been brilliantly pointed out by Luis Ospina of Colombia in his self-reflexive film *Picking on the People*, in which he criticises the exploitative nature of some Third World film-makers who peddle Third World poverty and misery at festival sites in Europe and North America and do not approach their craft as a tool of social transformation. An excellent case in point is the internationally acclaimed film *Pixote* by Hector Babenco. According to a *Los Angeles Times* correspondent in Rio de Janeiro, Da Silva, the young boy who played the title role of the film, was paid a mere $320. The correspondent writes: 'In a real-life drama a juvenile judge in Diadema, a suburb of Sao Paulo, last week released Da Silva, now 16, to the custody of his mother after his arrest on charges of housebreaking and theft.' According to Da Silva's mother, who sells lottery tickets for her living, 'after a trip to Rio when he got no work, he told me, "Mother, they have forgotten me, I am finished."' In the meantime Mr Babenco, the now famous film director, was about to shoot his next feature, *The Kiss of the Spider Woman*, in collaboration with producers in Hollywood.[2]

The style: Some attempts to indigenise film style are manifest. Although the dominant stylistic conventions of the first phase still predominate here, there appears to be a growing tendency to create a film style appropriate to the changed thematic concerns. In this respect, the growing insistence on spatial representation rather than temporal manipulation typifies the films in this phase. The sense of a spatial orientation in cinema in the Third World arises out of the experience of an 'endless' world of the large Third World mass. This nostalgia for the vastness of nature projects itself into the film form, resulting in long takes and long or wide shots. This is often done to constitute part of an overall symbolisation of a Third World thematic orientation, i.e. the landscape depicted ceases to be mere land or soil and acquires a phenomenal quality which integrates humans with the general drama of existence itself.

Phase III – The combative phase

The industry: Film-making as a public service institution. The industry in this phase is not only owned by the nation and/or the government, it is also managed, operated and run for and by the people. It can also be called a cinema of mass participation, one enacted by members of communities speaking indigenous language, one that espouses Julio García Espinosa's polemic of 'An Imperfect Cinema',[3] that in a developing world, technical and artistic perfection in the production of a film cannot be the aims in themselves. Quite a number of social institutions of cinema in the Third World, some underground like Argentina's 'Cine Liberacion' and some supported by their governments – for instance, 'Chile Films' of Allende's Popular Unity Socialist government – exemplify this phase. Two industrial institutions that also exemplify this level are the Algerian L'Office National pour le Commerce et l'Industrie Cinématographique (ONCIC) and Cuba's Institute of Film Art and Industry (ICAIC).

The theme: Lives and struggles of Third World peoples. This phase signals the maturity of the film-maker and is distinguishable from either Phase I or Phase II by its insistence on viewing film in its ideological ramifications. A very good example is Miguel Littin's *The Promised*

33

Land, a quasi-historical mythic account of power and rebellion, which can be seen as referring to events in modern-day Chile. Likewise, his latest film *Alsino and the Condor* combines realism and fantasy within the context of war-torn Nicaragua. The imagery in *One Way or Another* by the late Sara Gómez Yara, of an iron ball smashing down the old slums of Havana, not only depicts the issue of women/race in present-day Cuba but also symbolises the need for a new awareness to replace the old oppressive spirit of *machismo* which still persists in socialist Cuba. The film *Soleil O*, by the Mauritanian film-maker Med Hondo, aided by the process of Fanonian theses, comes to the recognition of forgotten heritage in the display of the amalgam of ideological determinants of European 'humanism', racism and colonialism. The failure of colonialism to convert Africans into 'white-thinking blacks' depicted in the film reappears in a much wider symbolic form in his later film, *West Indies*, where the entire pantheon of domination and liberation unfolds in a ship symbolic of the slave-ship of yesteryear.

The style: Film as an ideological tool. Here, film is equated or recognised as an ideological instrument. This particular phase also constitutes a framework of agreement between the public (or the indigenous institution of cinema) and the film-maker. A Phase III film-maker is one who is perceptive of and knowledgeable about the pulse of the Third World masses. Such a film-maker is truly in search of a Third World cinema – a cinema that has respect for the Third World peoples. One element of the style in this phase is an ideological point-of-view instead of that of a character as in dominant Western conventions. *Di Cavalcanti* by Glauber Rocha, for instance, is a take-off from 'Quarup', a joyous death ritual celebrated by Amazon tribes.[4] The celebration frees the dead from the hypocritical tragic view modern man has of death. By turning the documentary of the death of the internationally renowned Brazilian painter Di Cavalcanti into a chaotic/celebratory montage of sound and images, Rocha deftly and directly criticised the dominant documentary convention, creating in the process not only an alternative film language but also a challenging discourse on the question of existence itself. Another element of style is the use of flashback – although the reference is to past events, it is not stagnant but dynamic and developmental. In *The Promised Land*, for instance, the flashback device dips into the past to comment on the future, so that within it a flash-forward is inscribed. Similarly, when a flash-forward is used in Sembene's *Ceddo* (1977), it is also to convey a past and future tense simultaneously to comment on two historical periods.

Since the past is necessary for the understanding of the present, and serves as a strategy for the future, this stylistic orientation seems to be ideologically suited to this particular phase.

It should, however, be noted that the three phases discussed above are not organic developments. They are enclosed in a dynamic which is dialectical in nature; for example, some Third World film-makers have taken a contradictory path. *Lucía*, a Cuban film by Humberto Solás, about the relations between the sexes, belongs to Phase III, yet Solás' latest film, *Cecilia*, which concerns an ambitious mulatto woman who tries to assimilate into a repressive Spanish aristocracy, is a regression in style (glowing in spectacle) and theme (the tragic mulatto) towards Phase I. Moving in the opposite direction, Glauber Rocha's early Brazilian films like *Deus e O Diabo na Terra do Sol* (literally 'God and the Devil in the Land of the Sun', but advertised in the United States as 'Black God, White Devil'!) and *Terra em Transe* ('The Earth Trembles') reflect a Phase II characteristic, while his last two films, *A Idade da Terra* ('The Age of Earth') and *Di Cavalcanti*, both in their formal properties and subject matter manifest a Phase III characteristic in their disavowal of the conventions of dominant cinema. According to Glauber Rocha, *A Idade da Terra* (which develops the theme of *Terra em Transe*) and *Di Cavalcanti* disintegrate traditional 'narrative sequences' and rupture not only the fictional and documentary cinema style of his early works, but also 'the world cinematic language' under 'the dictatorship of Coppola and Godard'.[5]

The dynamic enclosure of the three phases posits the existence of grey areas between Phases I and II, and II and III. This area helps to identify a large number of important Third World films. For instance, the Indian film *Manthan* ('The Churning'), the Senegalese film *Xala* ('Spell of Impotence'), the Bolivian film *Chuquiago* (Indian name for La Paz), the Ecuadorean film *My Aunt Nora*, the Brazilian film *They Don't Wear Black Tie* and the Tunisian film *Shadow of the Earth* occupy the grey area between Phase II and III. The importance of the grey areas cannot be over-emphasised, for not only do they concretely demonstrate the *process of becoming* but they also attest to the multi-faceted nature of Third World cinema and the need for the development of new critical canons.

Components of critical theory

From the above it can be seen that the development of Third World film culture provides a critical theory particular to Third World needs. I would like to propose at this stage an analytic construct consisting of three components that would provide an integrative matrix within which to approach and interpret the Three Phases drawn out from the Third World's cultural history. The components of critical theory can be schematised as follows:

Component 1: *Text*
   The intersection of codes and sub-codes; the chief thematic and formal characteristics of existing films and the rules of that filmic grammar. And the transformational procedures whereby new 'texts' emerge from old.
Component 2: *Reception*
   The audience: the active interrogation of images versus the passive consumption of films. The issue of alienated and non-alienated identity and the ideal/inscribed or actual/empirical spectatorship illustrates this component of critical theory.
Component 3: *Production*
   The social determination where the wider context of determinants informs social history, market considerations, economy of production, state governance and regulation composes this stage of the critical constructs. Here, the larger historical perspective, the position of the institution of indigenous cinema in progressive social taste, is contexted. The overriding critical issue at this juncture is, for instance, the unavoidable ultimate choice between the classical studio system and the development of a system of production based on the lightweight 16mm or video technology. The pivotal concern and the single most significant question at this stage, therefore, is: 'Precisely what kind of institution is cinema in the Third World?'

Confluence of phases and critical theory

Each phase of the Third World film culture can be described in terms of all the three components of critical theory, because each phase is necessarily engaged in all the critical operations. For instance, Phase I is characterised by a type of film that simply mirrors, in its concepts and propositions, the *status quo*, i.e. the text and the rules of the grammar are identical to conventional practices. The consequence of this type of 'mimicking' in the area of 'reception' is that an alienated identity ensues from it precisely because the spectator is unable to find or recognise himself/herself in the images. The mechanisms of the systems of 'production' also acknowledge the *status quo* – the reliance is on the studio systems of controlled production and experimentation.

   If we apply the components of critical theory to Phase II only, a slight shift in the text and the rules of the grammar is noticeable. Although the themes are predominantly indigenised, the film language remains trapped, woven and blotted with classical formal elements, and remains stained with conventional film style. In terms of 'reception' the viewer, aided by the process of memory and an amalgam of folklore and mythology, is able to locate a somewhat diluted traditional identity. The third level of critical theory also composes and marks the process of indigenisation of the institution of cinema where a position of self-determination is sought.

Finally, the three components of critical theory find their dynamic wholeness in Phase III – the Combative Phase. Here, the text and sub-texts go through a radical shift and transformation – the chief formal and thematic concerns begin to alter the rules of the grammar. Another film language and a system of new codes begin to manifest themselves. With regard to 'reception' we discover that the viewer or subject is no longer alienated because recognition is vested not only in genuine cultural grounds but also in an ideological cognition founded on the acknowledgment of the decolonisation of culture and total liberation.

The intricate relationships of the three *phases* of the evolution of Third World film culture and the three analytic constructs for filmic institutions help to establish the stage for a confluence of a unique aesthetic exchange founded on other than traditional categories of film conventions (see fig. 1).

Summary of the development of film culture and filmic institutions

Phases

A. Assimilation phase
B. Remembrance phase
C. Combative phase

DISTINCTIVE

Critical theory

A. Text
B. Reception
C. Production

INTERSECTING

Confluences of phases and critical theory

INTEGRATIVE

Figure 1

Here, A and B find themselves in a larger historical perspective C. It is a wider context of indigenisation and self-determination which conditions levels A and B to give up their position of dominance to C, a stage which composes and marks the union of Third World film culture and the social institutions of cinema.

This new Third World cinematic experience, inchoate as it is, is in the process of creating a concurrent development of a new and throbbing social institution capable of generating a dynamic and far-reaching influence on the future socio-economic and educational course of the Third World.

I contend that the confluence obtained from the interlocking of the *phases* and the critical *constructs* reveals underlying assumptions concerning perceptual patterns and film viewing situations. For instance, with respect to fiction film showing in Third World theatres, rejection on cultural grounds forces incomplete transmission of meaning. That is, the intended or inscribed meaning of the film is deflected and acquires a unique meaning of its own – the mode of address of the film and the spectator behaviour undergo a radical alteration. Therefore, what has been presented as a 'fiction' film is received as if it were a 'documentary'. The same fiction film screened in its own country of origin, however, claims an ideal spectatorship because it is firmly anchored in its own cultural references, codes and symbols. A classic example of how films from one culture can be easily misunderstood and misinterpreted by a viewer from another culture is Glauber Rocha's *The Lion Has Seven Heads* (*Der Leone Have Sept Cabezas*). The film was extensively exhibited in the West, one catalogue compiled in 1974 crediting Rocha with bringing 'the Cinema Novo to Africa for this Third World assault on the various imperialisms represented in its multilingual title. Characters include a black revolutionary, a Portuguese mercenary, an American CIA agent, a French missionary, and a voluptuous nude woman called the Golden Temple of Violence.'[6] Again, a recent compendium of reviews, *Africa on Film and Videotape, 1960–1981*, dismisses the film completely with a one-liner, 'An allegorical farce noting the bond between Africa and Brazil.'[7]

Yet Glauber Rocha, in an interview given to a prominent film historian, Rachel Gerber (author of *Glauber Rocha, Cinema, Politica e a Estetica do Inconsciente*), in Rome, February 1973, and in a discussion with this author at UCLA in 1976, said that the film is a story of Che Guevara who is magically resurrected by Blacks through the spirit of Zumbi, the spiritual name of the late Amilcar Cabral. To Rocha, the film is in fact a homage to Amilcar Cabral. Thus, while the West looks at this film as an offering of clichéd images and an object of curiosity, the film-maker is only trying to affirm the continuity of the Third World's anti-imperialist struggle from Che to Cabral (and beyond), to initiate an awareness of their lives, and the relevance to us today of what they struggled and died for. To the extent that we recognise a history of unequal exchanges between the South and the North, we must also recognise the unequal 'symbolic' exchanges involved. The difficulty of Third World films of radical social comment for Western interpretation is the result a) of the film's resistance to the dominant conventions of cinema, and b) of the consequence of the Western viewers' loss of being the privileged decoders and ultimate interpreters of meaning.

The Western experience of film viewing – dominance of the big screen and the sitting situation – has naturalised a spectator conditioning so that any communication of a film plays on such values of exhibition and reception. The Third World experience of film viewing and exhibition suggests an altogether different route and different value system. For instance, Americans and Europeans hate seeing a film on African screens, because everybody talks during the showings; similarly, African viewers of film in America complain about the very strict code of silence and the solemn atmosphere of the American movie-theatres.

How the system of perceptual patterns and viewing situation varies with conditions of reception from one culture to another, or how changes in the rules of the grammar affect spectator viewing habits, is part of a larger question which solidifies and confirms the issue of cultural relativism and identity.

The confluence of the phases and the constructs also converges on the technologically mediated factors of needed production apparatuses, productive relations and the mechanisms of industrial operations. It needs to be stated outright that 'technology' as such does not in itself produce or communicate meaning; but it is equally true to say that 'technology' has a dynamic which helps to create ideological carry-overs that impress discourse language, i.e. ideological discourse manifests itself in the mechanisms of film discourse. By way of an example, it is possible that a film-maker might have the idea of 'filmic form' before having 'a content' to go along with it. Third World films are heterogeneous, employing narrative and oral discourse, folk music and songs, extended silences and gaps, moving from fictional representation to reality, to fiction – these constitute the creative part that can challenge the ideological carry-overs that technology imposes.

From the needs of Third World film criticism, contemporary film scholarship is criticised on two major fronts: first, contemporary film theory and criticism is grounded in a conception of the 'viewer' (subject or citizen) derived from psychoanalytic theory where the relation between the 'viewer' and the 'film' is determined by a particular dynamic of the 'familial' matrix. To the extent that Third World culture and familial relationships are not described through psychoanalytic theory, Third World filmic representation is open for an elaboration of the relation 'viewer'/'film' on terms other than those founded on psychoanalysis. The Third World relies more on an appeal to social and political conflicts as the prime rhetorical strategy and less on the paradigm of oedipal conflict and resolution.

Second, on the semiotic front, the Western model of filmic representation is essentially based on a literary or written conception of the scenario which implies a linear, cause/effect conception of narrative action.[8] However, Third World oral narratives, founded on traditional culture, are held in memory by a set of formal strategies specific to repeated, oral, face-to-face tellings.

It is no longer satisfactory to use existing critical criteria, which may be adequate for a film practice (Western in this case) now at a plateau of relevance,[9] to elucidate a new and dynamic film convention whose upward mobility will result in a totally new cinematic language. The Third World experience is thus raising some fundamental concerns about the methods and/or commitment of traditional film scholarship. The Third World filmic practice is, therefore, reorganising and refining the pictorial syntax and the position of the 'viewer' (or spectator) with respect to film. The Third World cinematic experience is moved by the requirements of its social action and contexted and marked by the strategy of that action. We need, therefore, to begin attending to a new theoretical and analytic matrix governed by other than existing critical theories that claim specific applications for universal principles.

Cultural contamination is a deeply rooted human fear: it smells of annihilation. Spiritual and traditional practices have a terrific hold on the Third World rural populace. This reminds us of the maxim which was enunciated by Confucius in the sixth century BC and still prevails: 'I'm a transmitter, not an inventor.' To the Third World, spirits, magic, masquerades and rituals, however flawed they may be, still constitute knowledge and provide collective security and protection from forces of evil. Unknown forces for the rural community can only be checked or controlled if they can be identified.

One way of readily understanding what Third World culture is, is to distinguish it from what it claims not to be.[10] We call at this juncture for a thorough and comparative analysis of 'oral' or 'folk' art form and 'literate' or 'print' art form to situate the foregoing discussion on critical theory into focused attention. I propose here to examine the centrifugal as well as the centripetal cultural forces that might determine not only film, but also the media, in the Third World. This dialectical, not differential or oppositional, conception of cultural forms takes into account the dynamics of their exchange.

Several factors ensue from the examination of the two modes of cultural expression. While, for instance, the community issue is at the heart of Third World traditional culture, the issue of the individual is at the base of Western or print culture. With regard to performatory stage presentation, a Western actor interacting with the audience breaks the compact or marginal boundary. Because a special kind of magic enters a playing space, Western stage performance does not allow cross-over. While, therefore, a Western person feels his privacy violated with interactive drama, in the Third World context the understanding between the viewer and the performers is that their positions are interchangeable without notice.

Awe for the old in the Third World culture is very much in evidence. Several films reflect it. The old or the aged as repositories of Third World history is well documented in such films as *Emitai* from Senegal, *They Don't Wear Black Tie* from Brazil, *Shadow of the Earth* from Tunisia and *The In-Laws* from the People's Republic of China. The issue of the aged in Third World culture is beautifully illustrated in Safi Faye's film *Fad Jal*, where the opening sequence of the film states: 'In Africa, an old man dying is like a library burning down.'

A major area of misunderstanding (if we take into account the 'Cognitive Characteristics' of the 'Folk/Print Art' dichotomy in Table 1) is the definition and replacement of 'man', the individual, within Third World societies. For any meaningful dialogue centring on Third World developmental schemes the issue of 'man/woman' in a society must be carefully debated. As Julius K. Nyerere of Tanzania puts it, 'The Purpose is Man',[11] and as the Wolof saying goes, 'Man is the medicine of man.'

A cultural orientation of 'man', the individual, as changeable and capable of effecting change is a condition that reverberates in all advanced societies of the world, be they of capitalist or socialist persuasion. The idea that man, both in the singular and in the plural, has the capability of controlling his/her own destiny and effecting change by his/her own will is a dynamic force which can alter both the thought patterns and work habits of a people. This concept, it must be stated, is not the opposite of the Third World ideal of the primacy of the community over the individual. An excellent example is the film *Beyond the Plains* (where man is born) by Michael Raeburn, in which a young man from the Masai tribe in Tanzania was able to change his people's negative attitude towards education by not only doggedly pursuing it to the university level, but also never losing contact with his people. As he grew up he made sure he performed all the customary rites and fulfilled all the obligations demanded by his people, thus demonstrating that Western and tribal cultural education were not incompatible. From this, it can be seen that the major difference between the Third World and the West with regard to changing the community from a passive to a dynamic entity is one of approach. Whereas the former aims at changing the individual through the community, the latter wants the community changed by the individual. Only time will tell which of the two approaches makes for sustained, beneficial social progress.

Table 1

Comparison of Folk and Print Art Forms

Folk (or Oral) Art Form	Print (or Literate) Art Form
Conception of the Value and Evaluation of Art	
Deeper meaning of art held by cultural groups or community. Interpretive device: one needs to belong and/or understand cultural or folk nuances.	Deeper meaning of art held as the sole property of the artist. Interpretive device: the artist proclaims 'it is for me to know and for you to find, or art is what you mean it to be.'
Recognises general level of excellence, hence emphasis on group competence in the aesthetic judgment of art.	Recognises exceptions, hence emphasis on individual achievement and individual responsibility.
Master artist concept – gifted but normal, and so conforms to the group.	Master artist concept – gifted but eccentric and essentially nonconformist.
Art as occasion for collective engagement.	Art as occasion for 'escape' from normal routine.
Emphasis on contextual relevance.	Emphasis on conceptual interpretation.
Art defined in terms of context.	Art defined in terms of aesthetic.
Performatory Presentation	
Held in fluid boundaries, churchyards, fields, marketplaces – operating in a 360° dimension.	Boxed-in theatres and elevated to a stage – operating in a 180° dimension.
A scene flows into another. Cyclical progression linked thematically.	Each scene must follow another scene in linear progression.

	Performatory Effect
Expects viewer participation, therefore arouses activity and prepares for and allows participation.	Discourages viewer participation. Puts an end to activity. Inhibits participation.
Multiple episodes that have their own centres.	Singular episode extended through detail.

Cognitive Characteristics

Man defined as 'unchangeable' alone. Change emanates from the community.	Man defined as 'man', changeable and, by virtue of his person, capable of effecting change and progress.
Individual interlinked with total social fabric. Concept of human rather than concept of 'man' as such.	Individual perceived primarily as separated from general social fabric.
Strong tradition of suggestion in the cultural symbol and in the use of linguistic formulae.	Strong tradition of detail and minute (graphic) description.
Time assumed to be a subjective phenomenon, i.e. it is the outcome of conceptualising and experiencing movement.	Time assumed to be an 'objective' phenomenon, dominant and ubiquitous.
Wisdom is a state of intellectual maturity gained by experience. Cumulative process of knowledge, derived from the past. Characterised by slowness to judgment.	Wisdom is characterised by high degree of specialisation in a particular field or discipline. Characterised by quickness of judgment based on a vast accumulation of data and information.
Earth is not a hostile world; e.g. the cult of the ancestors is an attempt at unification with the past, present and future.	Earth is a hostile world and has to be subdued. Paradise is in the future or elsewhere.

Manipulation of space and time in cinema

A child born in a Western society is encased, from the initial moments of birth, in purposive, man-made fabricated objects. The visual landscape he experiences is dominated by man-made forms. Even the child's dolls reflect the high technology of the environment. Nowadays, a child who is beginning to learn to spell can have a computer that can talk to him and interact with him in a human way. All of these developments are based on the insistence of a society that puts a high price on individualism, individual responsibility and achievement as most necessary.

A child in a rural Third World setting is born in an unrestricted natural landscape. From the day he/she is born the child is dominated by untampered natural forms. Even the interior of the dwelling where the child is born is made to look like the natural environment: it is not unusual to see fresh grass and flowers lending nature's colour to the child's initial world setting. The child grows in this vast universe where his place within the family and in nature is emphasised. A child born and raised in this situation is taught to submerge his individuality and show responsibility to his extended family and his community. His accomplishments are measured not only by his individual achievements but by the degree to which they accomplish and contribute to the social good.

Culture, the terms on which films are based, also naturally grows from these environmental factors. An examination of oral and literate culture in terms of film brings to light two very crucial elements of cinema, namely the concepts of 'space' and 'time'. All cinema manipulates 'time' and 'space'. Where Western films manipulate 'time' more than 'space', Third World films seem to emphasise 'space' over 'time'. Third World films grow from folk tradition where communication is a slow-paced phenomenon and time is not rushed but has its own pace. Western culture, on the other hand, is based on the value of 'time' – time is art, time is money, time is most everything else. If time drags in a film, spectators grow bored and impatient, so that a method has to be found to cheat natural time. In film, this is achieved in the editing. It is all based on the idea that the more purely 'non-dramatic' elements in film are considered 'cinematic excess,' i.e. they serve no unifying purpose. What is identified as 'excess' in Western cinematic experience is, therefore, precisely where we locate Third World cinema. Let me now identify those essential elements of cinematic practice that are considered cinematic excess in Western cinema but which in the Third World context seem only too natural.

The long take: It is not uncommon in Third World films to see a concentration of long takes and repetition of images and scenes. In the Third World films, the slow, leisurely pacing approximates the viewer's sense of time and rhythm of life. In addition, the preponderance of wide-angle shots of longer duration deal with a viewer's sense of community and how people fit in nature. Whereas when Michelangelo Antonioni and Jean-Luc Godard use these types of shot it is to convey an existential separation and isolation from nature and self.

Cross-cutting: Cross-cutting between antagonists shows simultaneity rather than the building of suspense. The power of images lies not in the expectation we develop about the mere juxtapositions or the collision itself, but rather in conveying the reasons for the imminent collision. Where, therefore, conventional cinema has too often reduced this to the collision of antagonists, on a scale of positive and negative characters, Third World films doing the same thing make it more explicitly an ideological collision.

The close-up shot: A device so much in use in the study of individual psychology in Western film-making practice is less used in Third World films. Third World films serve more of an informational purpose than as a study in 'psychological realism'. The isolation of an individual, in tight close-up shots, seems unnatural to the Third World film-maker because (i) it calls attention to itself; (ii) it eliminates social considerations; and (iii) it diminishes spatial integrity.

The panning shot: Since a pan shot maintains integrity of space and time, the narrative value of such a shot renders the 'cut' or editing frequently unnecessary. The emphasis on space also conveys a different concept of 'time', a time which is not strictly linear or chronological but co-exists with it. My own observation indicates that while Western films tend to pan right on a left-right axis, Middle Eastern films, for instance, tend to pan generally toward the left, as in *Alyam Alyam* (Morocco) and *Shadow of the Earth* (Tunisia). It is quite possible that the direction of panning toward left or right might be strongly influenced by the direction in which a person writes.

The concept of silence: The rich potential for the creative interpretation of sound as well as the effective use of its absence is enormous in Third World films. For instance, in *Emitai* there are English subtitles for drum messages, and a rooster crows as Sembene's camera registers a low-angle shot of a poster of General de Gaulle. A neat visual pun! Silence serves as an important element of the audio track of the same film. It is 'a cinema of silence that speaks'. Silences have meaning only in context, as in the Ethiopian film *Gouma* and the Cuban film *The Last Supper*, where they contribute to the suspension of judgment which one experiences in watching a long take. Viewers wonder what will happen, accustomed as they are to the incessant sound and overload of music of dominant cinema.

Concept of 'hero': Even if a Western viewer cannot help but identify and sympathise with the black labour leader in *They Don't Wear*

Table 2
Comparison of Filmic Conventions
(These are tendencies, not absolutes)

	Western Dominant Conventions	Non-Western Use of Conventions
Lighting	High contrast and low key, mostly Rembrandt lighting in drama while comedy uses low contrast and high-key lighting.	Lighting as a convention in Third World films is less developed, with the exception of Cuban films, whose use of lighting as a language is manifest in *Lucía* and *The Last Supper*.
Camera Angle	Mostly governed by eye-level perspective which approximates to our natural position in the world. Use of angle shots primarily for aesthetic look.	Deliberate choice of low/high-angle shots for purposes of political or social comment. Low/high-angle shots show dominance and power relations between the oppressed and oppressing classes.
Camera Placement	Distance varies according to the emotional content of the scene. Emotion, e.g. anger, is portrayed in close-up.	There is minimal use of the convention of close-up shots. This is perhaps due to lack of emphasis on psychological realism.
Camera Movement	Mostly a fixed perspective (tripod operation), promoting exposition and understanding. Often the camera moves to stay with the individual to study character development and psychological state.	Fixed perspective in African films. A moving perspective (hand-held camera in Latin American films promotes experiential involvement and dramatic identification. If the camera moves it is to contain a scene or a sequence as a unit and not in response to individual psychology.

Set Design

A studio set. Tightens manipulatory controls, enhances fictional reality.	A location set. Location shooting relaxes manipulatory controls, and enhances documentary reality.

Acting

A Hollywood convention, actor as icon.	Mostly non-actors acting out their real-life roles.

Parallel Montage

Shows the relations of conflicting characters/forces for dramatic and expository narrative purposes, i.e. suspense.	Cross-cutting serves an ideological purpose and denotes ironical contrast and class distinction. Consider the film *Mexico: The Frozen Revolution*.

Point of View

Actors avoid looking directly at the camera. Actors are usually positioned or blocked so that their emotional state is easily observed by the camera.	It is not uncommon to see a look directed at the camera, hence a direct address to the audience. A shift to the conventions of oral narrative is evident. Consider the Algerian film *Omar Gatlato*.

The sum total of what is listed above as technique or elements of the film-making process is what expresses ideology. Films that hide the marks of production are associated with the ideology of presenting 'film as reality', the film that announces its message as an objective reflection of the way things are; whereas films which do exhibit the marks of production are associated with the ideology of presenting 'film as message'. Predominant aspect or point of view in Third World film is film announcing itself as a polemic comment on the way things are in their 'natural' reflection.

Films, therefore, in their point of view and stylistic choices, are structured to evoke a certain ideology in their production. A consequence of this, quite logically, is their different use of the conventions of time and space in cinema.

Black Tie, the lunatic in *Harvest: 3000 Years*, the crazy poet in *The Chronicle of the Years of Ember* and the militant party member in *Sambizanga*, the films nevertheless kill those characters. This is because wish-fulfilment through identification is not the films' primary objective; rather, it is the importance of collective engagement and action that matters. The individual 'hero' in the Third World context does not make history, he/she only serves historical necessities.

In summary, Table 2 brings into sharper focus the differences between the film conventions of the Third World and the West and shows the dynamics of their cultural and ideological exchange.

Conclusion

The spatial concentration and minimal use of the conventions of temporal manipulation in Third World film practice suggest that Third World cinema is initiating a coexistence of film art with oral traditions. Non-linearity, repetition of images and graphic representation have very much in common with folk customs. Time duration, though essential, is not the major issue because in the Third World context the need is for films, in context, to touch a sensitive cultural chord in a society. To achieve this, a general overhaul of the parameters of film form is required. Should the reorganisation be successful and radical enough, a rethinking of the critical and theoretical canons of cinema would be called for, leading to a reconsideration of the conventions of cinematographic language and technique. The final result would tend towards a statement James Potts made in his article, 'Is there an international film language?':

> So, far from there being an international language of cinema, an internationally agreed UN charter of conventions and grammatical rules, we are liable to be presented, quite suddenly, with a new national school of film-making, which may be almost wholly untouched by European conventions and will require us to go back to square one in thinking about the principles and language of cinematography.[12]

Film-makers in the Third World are beginning to produce films that try to restructure accepted filmic practices. There is now a distinct possibility of James Potts' perceptive remarks coming true, and it is in anticipation of the emergence of the 'new national school of film-making … untouched by European conventions' that this paper has been written.

Already, certain reactions from film critics may be regarded as a sign of this 'emergence'. For example, a general criticism levelled at Third

World films is that they are too graphic. This spatial factor is part of a general rhythm of pictorial representation in most Third World societies. It is, therefore, precisely because graphic art creates symbols in space that it enables Third World viewers to relate more easily to their films. In the Chinese case, for example:

> The spiritual quality achieved in the supreme Chinese landscape and nature paintings is a feeling of harmony with the universe in which the inner psychic geography of the artist and the outer visual reality transcribed are fused through brush strokes into a new totality that ... resonates with the viewer.[13]

Both the Chinese contemporary photographers and cinematographers have attempted to create similar syntax and effects to enhance the people's appreciation of their art.

Again, the most inaccessible Phase III film, the one African film that drops a curtain in front of a Western audience, and at the same time a most popular and influential film in Africa, is *Emitai* ('The Angry God'). Shot in social space by the Senegalese film-maker Sembene, the film explores the spiritual and physical tension in a rural community. To begin with the film carries its viewers into the story without any credits, only for the entire credit to be provided some twenty-five minutes later. Spectators have been known to leave the screening room at this point, conditioned to read the credits as signalling the end of the film. What Sembene has provided before the credits is essentially the preface of the story like an African folktale. In addition, the ending of the film an hour and a half later is anticlimactic and this occurs at the moment the film is truly engaging – the film simply stops – what we hear is the staccato of bullet sounds against a screen gone dark. In this film the film-maker is forcing us to forget our viewing habits and attend to the film in context instead of the experienced, framed as artistic package. A lesson is thus learned; concern should be with the language of the 'film text' in its own terms and not with the skeletal structure and chronology of the film.

Cinema, since its creation, has beguiled spectators by its manipulation of time – it expands, contracts, is lost and found, fragmented and reassembled. The resultant multiple time-perspectives have conditioned film appreciation as pure entertainment. There is perhaps some justification for this objective in a society whose stabilising conditions can afford the use of the film medium solely for entertainment. The Third World, on the other hand, is still engaged in a desperate struggle for socio-political and economic independence and development and cannot afford to dissipate its meagre resources and/or laugh at its present political and historical situation.

The Combative Phase, in which the historical determinants of Third World culture occur, provides us with the final horizon of a cinema oriented toward a peaceful coexistence with folk-culture. That oral tradition reasserts itself in a new medium is a contribution not only to Third World societies but to the cinematic world at large.

Film is a new language to the Third World and its grammar is only recently being charted. Its direction, however, seems to be a discursive use of the medium and an appeal for intellectual appreciation. Tomás Gutiérrez Alea perhaps best exemplifies the new awareness when he says:

> ... if we want film to serve something higher, if we want it to fulfil its function more perfectly (aesthetic, social, ethical, and revolutionary), we ought to guarantee that it constitutes a *factor in spectators' development*. Film will be more fruitful to the degree that it pushes spectators toward a more profound understanding of reality and, consequently, to the degree that it helps viewers live more actively and incites them to stop being mere spectators in the face of reality. To do this, film ought to appeal not only to emotion and feeling but also to reason and intellect. In this case, both instances ought to exist indissolvably (*sic*) united, in such a way that they come to provoke, as Pascal said, authentic 'shudderings and tremblings of the mind'.[14]

Notes

1. F. Fanon, *The Wretched of the Earth*, New York, Grove Press, 1963, pp. 207–48. See also A. Cabral, *Return to the Source*, New York, African Information Service, 1973, pp. 42–69.
2. J. DeOnis, ' "Pixote" role proves all too real', *Los Angeles Times*, 5 June 1984.
3. J. Espinosa, 'For an imperfect cinema', in M. Chanan (ed.), *Twenty-five Years of the New Latin American Cinema*, London, BFI/Channel 4 Television, 1983, pp. 28–33.
4. R. Gerber, *Glauber Rocha, Cinema, Politica e a Esthetica do Inconsciente*, Brasil, Editore Vozes, 1982, p. 34 and *passim*.
5. G. Rocha, *Revolucão do Cinema Nôvo*, Rio de Janeiro, Alhambra/Embrafilme, 1981, p. 467.
6. From a film catalogue entitled *Films about Africa available in the Midwest*, Madison, African Studies Program, University of Wisconsin, 1974, p. 37.
7. *Africa on Film and Videotape, 1960–81: A Compendium of Reviews*, East Lansing, Michigan, African Studies Center, Michigan State University, 1982, p. 219.
8. It must be freely acknowledged that the future of art criticism and appreciation no doubt lies in the domain of semiotic inquiry. Presently, while its greater virtue lies in the attention it gives to the role of the reader, its greatest weakness is its cultural fixation with Western thought. Third World aesthetics and cultures have been ignored, making it impossible for it to occupy its premier place in a unified human science. Since the works of Lévi-Strauss and various essays and a book by Roland Barthes nothing of substance regarding semiotic inquiry into cultural studies has been offered. For a general reading on the topic, see Edith Kurzweil, *The Age of Structuralism: Lévi-Strauss to Foucault*, New York, Columbia University Press, 1980, and R. Barthes, *Mythologies*, translated by Annette Lavers, New York, Hill and Wang, 1970. For the various contending factions in the semiotic camp – structuralists, deconstructionists, reader-response critics, theories of intertextuality and narratology – the following books will serve as introductions: R. Scholes, *Semiotics and Interpretation*, New Haven, Yale University Press, 1982, and J. Culler, *The Pursuit of Signs*, Ithaca, Cornell University Press, 1983.
9. Recently Western film-makers, in a bid to revitalise their film world, have made 'realistic' forays into Third World themes: *Gandhi* on India's struggle for independence, *The Year of Living Dangerously* on Sukarno's fall from power, *Under Fire* on the Sandinista revolution in Nicaragua, and *Circle of Deceit* on the Lebanese civil war. The statement by one of the characters in *Circle of Deceit* – 'We are defending Western civilisation' – is an ironic but true epigram for all the films. Far from being radical or new, therefore, these productions give us no more than Hollywood's version of the Third World. For an illuminating discussion on this recent fascination with 'the other', see John Powers, 'Saints and Savages', *American Film*, January-February 1984, pp. 38–43.
10. Various sources were consulted, including but not limited to H. Arvon's

Marxist Esthetics, Ithaca, Cornell University Press, 1973, p. 71 and *passim*, and K. Gotrick, *Apidan Theatre and Modern Drama*, Gothenburg, Graphic Systems AB, 1984, pp. 140–63. For an elaboration of culture in the context of Third World films, see my book *Third Cinema in the Third World: The Aesthetics of Liberation*, Ann Arbor, Michigan, UMI Research Press, 1982.

11. J.K. Nyerere, *Ujamaa: Essays on Socialism*, London, Oxford University Press, 1968, pp. 91–105.

12. J. Potts, 'Is there an international film language?', *Sight and Sound*, vol. 48, no. 2, Spring 1979, pp. 74–81.

13. A. Goldsmith, 'Picture from China: the style and scope of photography are changing as outside influences mix with traditional values', *Popular Photography*, February 1984, pp. 45–50, 146 and 156.

14. T.G. Alea, *Dialéctica del Espectador*, Ciudad de la Habana, Sobre la presente edición, 1982, p. 21. The first part of the book has been translated by Julia Lesage and appears under the title 'The viewer's dialectic' in *Jump Cut 29*, February 1984, pp. 18–21, from which this quotation is taken.

Third Cinema as Guardian of Popular Memory: Towards a Third Aesthetics

Teshome H. Gabriel

In an interview given to the *New Left Review*, the Cuban novelist Alejo Carpentier relates an anecdote about a small fishing village in Vene-zuela where all the inhabitants are black. As he got to know the village people, they often told him about the Poet who enjoyed a great deal of prestige among them. The Poet had been away for quite a while, and they missed him. One day the Poet, a colossal man, reappeared. That night by the sea all the villagers, from children to old folk, gathered to hear him recite. With a ritual gesture and deep voice, he told the story of Charlemagne, in a version similar to that of the 'Song of Roland'. 'That day,' Carpentier says, 'I understood perhaps for the first time that in our America, wrongly named Latin, an illiterate man, descendant of the [slaves], recreated the "Song of Roland" in a language richer than Spanish, full of distinctive inflections, accents, expressions and syntax.'

This Poet, in a sense, replicates the anonymous legendary storytellers of traditional times. The peasant, the tiller of the soil, the traveller, the explorer and the hunter all combine the lore of the past with the lore of faraway places, to conserve and deposit into popular memory what has transpired in life and in everyday social existence.

Once memory enters into our consciousness, it is hard to circumvent, harder to stop, and impossible to run from. It burns and glows from inside, causing anguish, new dreams and newer hopes. Memory does something else beside telling us how we got here from there: it reminds us of the causes of difference between popular memory and official versions of history.

Official history tends to arrest the future by means of the past. Historians privilege the written word of the text – it serves as their rule of law. It claims a 'centre' which continuously marginalises others. In this way its ideology inhibits people from constructing their own history or histories.

Popular memory, on the other hand, considers the past as a political

53

issue. It orders the past not only as a reference point but also as a theme of struggle. For popular memory, there are no longer any 'centres' or 'margins', since the very designations imply that something has been conveniently left out. Popular memory, then, is neither a retreat to some great tradition nor a flight to some imagined 'ivory tower', neither a self-indulgent escapism nor a desire for the actual 'experience' or 'content' of the past for its own sake. Rather, it is a 'look back to the future', necessarily dissident and partisan, wedded to constant change.

Folklore as popular memory

As popular memory is the oral historiography of the Third World, folklore is an account of memories passed from generation to generation. Because the promise of freedom and the recovery of autonomy of identity lingers in memory, folklore offers an emancipatory 'horizon' – a liberated and alternative future. In a world where 'logic' and 'reason' are increasingly being used for 'irrational' purposes and aims, folklore attempts to conserve what official histories insist on erasing. In this sense, folkloric traditions of popular memory have a rescue mission. They wage a battle against false consciousness and against the official versions of history that legitimate and glorify it.

Folklore is an all-embracing phenomenon which comes from people's primary relation to the land and community. It comprises the popular expression and interest of 70 to 75 per cent of the Third World population. The closer to the land, the greater the volume and activity of folkloric material. Folklore is thus grounded in the notion of balance and harmony between nature and humanity.

In this conceptual framework, the struggle between good and evil acquires a unique symbolic significance. For instance, in some specific forms of ritual dance in Africa the dancer representing evil is normally quarantined behind stick fences or is physically guarded. The removal of the one possessed by evil from the fellowship of the community is, in a sense, tantamount to death. However, once rid of the possession, the redeemed one may rejoin the group.

This notion of controlling evil, putting it in its place rather than destroying it, is in a way a critique of Western dichotomies. In the Western conception, reason is expected to dominate nature, whereas in other traditions reason is not seen outside the scheme of nature. In the Western conception, positive and negative, self and other, subject and object are seen as distinct and separate, with no possibility of concentricity. Folkloric thinking, which collapses opposites into a unit, encourages us to be prepared for and to accept even the reality of death, because it is not considered to be outside of life. In folkloric

54

logic, what appears to be outside of existence is always seen to be, in fact, at the very core of existence itself.

The dynamic of this logic lies in its ability to make the memory of events accessible through some form of mythification. In this way, with each passing generation, it renews and authenticates itself through popular mandate.

Third Cinema as popular memory

These, then, are the most predominant aspects of the communicative modes within the Third World. Third World cinema is only a further illustration. Third World cinema does not, therefore, have an independent existence. It is merely an index of a general cultural and historical trend in which film-makers can find their role and serve as caretakers of popular discourse in cinema.

My intention here is not to give a unitary definition of 'Third Cinema' which can be brandished at other cinemas and other people. There can be several kinds of Third Cinema depending on the prevailing social order. On the other hand, I do believe that there are still power struggles going on, in the Third World as well as in the West. Independent film-makers seeking representation through filmic discourse need access to power to express them. Somewhere between this access to power and representation lies the battle between history and popular memory, between cinemas of the system and Third Cinema.

As originally conceived, the impetus of Third Cinema was and continues to be participatory and contributive to the struggles for the liberation of the peoples of the Third World. At present, these struggles are of two types. In those regions of the Third World where 'the battles for history and around history' are ever more intensified, the original manifesto of 'camera as a gun' still holds. The films coming out of El Salvador, South Africa and Palestine, to mention a few, are eloquent testimonies. This was perhaps beautifully illustrated in *El Salvador: The People Will Win*, where a fighter emerges from the jungle into a small clearing and exchanges a gun for a camera – then both protagonists clear the premises and go their separate ways. In fact the manifesto of Palestine cinema, as the original manifesto of 'Third Cinema', explicitly calls for 'the establishment of cadres capable of using a camera on the battlefield beside the gun'. In such instances, Third Cinema is a soldier of liberation.

In those other regions where the major battles have moved into the cultural front, including the efforts of minorities and progressives in the West, the conjunction of cinema and struggle takes on a new dimension. Nonetheless, in whatever form, this retains similar strategies both to recover popular memory and to activate it. For this is the passion which fires Third Cinema of various types. We can therefore understand when

55

Ousmane Sembene says of his current project, 'If I die before making *Samore Toure*, please tell the world that I died a very unhappy man.'

Progressive film-makers all over the Third World have expressed a passion for defining their role as custodians of popular expression. Whether it is Fernando Birri of Argentina or Octavio Gómez of Cuba, they have not only expressed but have also shown cinematically a pronounced sensitivity to popular culture. From Julio García Espinosa of Cuba to Ousmane Sembene of Senegal, from Miguel Littin of Chile to Haile Gerima of Ethiopia, the most persistent call has been sounded: that the future of cinema depends on popular culture and popular memory.

What I suggest here about popular memory in film seems to apply equally in Third World literature as well: Gabriel García Márquez of Colombia, Carlos Fuentes of Mexico, Ngugi wa Thiong'O of Kenya and Ousmane Sembene of Senegal largely base their work on collective memory. In fact, all of these distinguished Third World writers have either written about films or have made their own, heralding the emergence of a new kind of cinematic discourse in which film and literature are brought together as a form of collective expression. This expression suggests that one can read literature as one reads film, just as one can read film as one reads literature. Carlos Fuentes, in a foreword to Omar Cabeza's book *Fire From the Mountain: the Making of a Sandinista*, says the following:

> There is a strong sense of cinema in Cabeza's writing. At times I felt I was seeing one of the great Rossellini films in the streets of the open city ... with a handheld pen doing the work of the bumpy, free, gritty, handheld camera of Italian neo-realism. The liberation through language is also a liberation through images.

The degree of consistency of interest in and veneration of popular memory and its manifestation in Third Cinema films is striking. *Letters from Marusia* by Miguel Littin is a film about the massacre at Marusia, Chile in 1907. It depicts an event not found in any official Chilean records or histories. But what happened in the saltpetre mining town eighty years ago persists in oral tradition. The film-maker draws upon these traditional memories, utilising the portrayal as an allegory for present-day Chile.

Similarly, Susan Muñoz and Lourdes Portillo's *Las Madres: the Mothers of the Plaza de Mayo* vividly demonstrates the contradictions between official history and collective memory in its moving account of the testimonies of mothers of the disappeared children in Argentina. Clearly, it is through attempts such as theirs that what is repressed in official versions of history is kept alive through collective accounts.

Carlos Diegues' *Quilombo* is a film also inspired by such popular accounts, in this case of the history of a black free nation, the Republic of Palmares. This film is bracketed around the 'Goddess of the Sea', a popular mythological figure in black folklore. The 'Goddess of the Sea' signifies African peoples' return to identity and dignity. They came by sea and will eventually sail again, both as repositories of past events and as tenacious guardians of popular memory. The 'Goddess of the Sea' therefore marks a place of meaning. It helps stimulate the hushed memories of the homeland and calls for the exiles' complete return.

Whether it is Nelson Pereira dos Santos' *Memories of Prison*, Tomás Gutiérrez Alea's *The Last Supper*, Ousmane Sembene's *Ceddo*, Antonio Ole's *Pathway to the Stars*, Med Hondo's *West Indies*, or Miguel Littin's *The Promised Land* and his more recent film *Acta general de Chile* – all delve into the past, not only to reconstruct, but also to redefine and to redeem what the official versions of history have overlooked.

Towards a Third Aesthetics

In order to explain the ways in which Third Cinema is able to challenge official versions of history, I now turn to a discussion of Third Cinema aesthetics as an alternative to Western classical norms. Let me say a little about narrative as a mode of relation in popular memory. This perhaps might account for the character of the aesthetic factor involved.

Take a hunter and a game. In the Western-style movie, the depiction of the hunt would focus upon the ultimate act of the hunter bagging his game. In the Third World context, the interest would be in depicting the relationship of the hunter to the natural environment which feeds his material and spiritual needs and which, in fact, is the source of the game. Here we are dealing with an unresolved situation, with no closure.

Consider a film that was well received by all sectors of the Cuban populace, Octavio Gómez's *Now it's up to you*. The film was based on the public trial of four counter-revolutionaries who committed sabotage. Both the trial and the film end when a character says, 'Bueno, compañeros, you have seen the facts. Now you have the floor. It's up to you to decide where the responsibility lies.' These words are intended as much for the audience in the theatre as for the jury at the trial, thus conflating the film's text with the everyday reality of the spectator. In this sense, the film makes pertinent and highlights the contradictory situations of everyday life and provides a model for negotiating it. In contrast, closure in Western films contains and separates the work from everyday life.

Even those films in Third Cinema (such as Nelson Pereira dos Santos' *Memories of Prison* and Tawfiq Saleh's *The Duped*) that do contain

57

closure are of a different nature. Their purpose is not simply a call for action, but rather an invitation to consider one alternative among many. In this way they engage and entice us with historical memories, authenticating the causes of conflict, of failure, and of difference.

Another form of Third Cinema narrative – the autobiographical narrative – illustrates this point. Here I do not mean autobiography in its usual Western sense of a narrative by and about a single subject. Rather, I am speaking of a multi-generational and trans-individual autobiography, i.e. a symbolic autobiography where the *collective* subject is the focus. A critical scrutiny of this extended sense of auto-biography (perhaps hetero-biography) is more than an expression of shared experience; it is a mark of solidarity with people's lives and struggles.

Let me take as an example the film *Acta general de Chile*, a recent [1985] and passionate instance of Third Cinema. Exiled Chilean direc-tor Miguel Littin characterises this work as a testimony to the struggle of the people of Chile against Pinochet's repressive regime. Because of his status as a marked person by Pinochet even after twelve years of exile, Littin was forced to shoot the film clandestinely, disguised as a Uruguayan businessman. The film is organised around 'collective' instead of 'individual' points of view through which notions of subjecti-vity collapse. What we get instead is a blurring of identities where the addresser and the addressee are engaged in a ceaseless exchange of roles. Although Littin chooses to include himself as another persona in his own film, he can only do so in disguise, both as the film-maker and as a participant. Metaphorically, there is a sense of irony and sadness about the self-identity of the Chilean people today in that he, a Chilean, had to take on a disguised identity to visit his own country.

Nursing his own memories, Littin muses at the crossroads of dis-course not so much as an 'author', but as a witness. His narration of the film is as much a question to himself and other Chileans as it is addressed to the viewers:

> Are they [Chileans] closer to emotions than ideas today? I think about the man who on September 11 faced his solidarity destiny in order to leave his people a flag ... Does Allende live, I ask myself, in the memory of the Chilean people? Does his thought, his action, his consistency live in the memory of the people: ... it will be necessary to scratch the earth's surface to find the soul.

His personal reflection, blended with interviews and historical footage, becomes a collective testimony to the Chilean struggle, and gives a greater dimension of popular memory than is true of purely historical treatment of such issues. While in the Western documentary the individual and the social are of typically separate realms, in *Acta general de Chile* they are integrated to produce images of popular expression. What distinguishes this narrative structure from Western forms is its use of multiple points of view – in the process of making the film as well as in the delivery of its subject matter. The film thus stands in for a memory deferred by official history, which demands of us a new form of political awareness.

Indeed, the film stands as both a representation of popular memory and as an instance of popular memory itself. Its elaboration of several elements provides us with a quite distinct form of historical narrative, which blends typically disparate categories along three axes: 1) the constitution of the subject which is radically different from a Western conception of the individual; 2) the non-hierarchical order, which is differential rather than autonomous; 3) the emphasis on collective social space rather than on transcendental individual space. I believe that these axes, which predominate in popular memory, resonate the cultural expression indigenous to most of the Third World today.

Furthermore, the process of making the film itself was in fact an integrated and highly collaborative endeavour. Littin organised five different crews of various nationalities, none of whom knew of the existence of the others. Each worked separately in Chile, officially sanctioned to do films which were in fact cover-ups for their actual purpose. For instance, the Italian crew was shooting a film on architecture (which gained them entry into the Italian-designed Presidential Palace), while the French crew pretended to be doing a commercial for perfume and the Danish crew was engaged in an ecological film. Footage from each crew's film was later incorporated in the overall work, providing sufficient material to produce a four-hour television programme in Europe and the two and a half-hour documentary *Acta general de Chile*.

This collective nature extends as well to Gabriel García Márquez's book, *Miguel Littin Clandestino en Chile*, on the making of the film. Márquez builds on, adds to, and becomes part of the collective enterprise by giving it his aesthetic literary form. In a similar way, film viewers, whether Chilean exiles or ourselves, are also introduced to the collective autobiography of events in Chile, and are urged to interact with it. This spectators' position thus defies notions of passive viewing and celebrates direct participation. In this sense the film enters the spectator's own autobiography, awakening a reconstituted identity which allows for the sharing in and acknowledgment of the collective struggle of the Chilean people. One can imagine, then, that when the hour finally strikes – the fall of the Pinochet regime – all those who have collaborated with, commented on, and witnessed the film will realise and reflect upon their part in the making of history.

Here, therefore, is the emergence of a new cultural discourse, epitomising the concept of 'memories of the future', which is a predominant discursive strategy in Third World film and literature today. Generally speaking, this phenomenon, by which we collectively place our signature on historical change, can also be discussed as the emergence of a Third Aesthetics, which in my previous work I have touched on from the perspective of Third Cinema.

We are talking here of 'activist aesthetics' and 'critical spectatorship'. The relationship between the two has a distinctive form which accounts for the character of the aesthetics of Third Cinema. These aesthetics are, therefore, as much in the after-effect of the film as in the creative process itself. This is what makes the work memorable, by virtue of its everyday relevance. In other words, within the context of Third Cinema, aesthetics do not have an independent existence, nor do they simply rest in the work *per se*. Rather, they are a function of critical spectatorship. We consider, therefore, the aesthetic factor of Third Cinema to be, above everything else, extra-cinematic.

In contrast, the aesthetic form of the narrative in Western film culture is the aesthetic of the hero – it starts with a hero, develops with a hero and ends with a hero. This is as natural a style as breathing. Every shot and sequence of shots is governed and orchestrated around this principle. Any other character, place or decor is recognised and made visible only in relation to the hero. The hero occupies the foreground and hovers over the background – the entire screen is his or her domain. This centrality and separation of the hero is what makes him or her a 'star' or a 'super-star'. If Third Cinemas are said to have a central protagonist, it is the 'context' of the film; characters only provide punctuation within it.

Of course, there have been attempts toward collective heroism in Western films, but these have mostly tended to be stories of individual heroes who somehow affect each other by fate or by accident. This kind of cultural identity, of separateness and of isolation, privileges the individual over the social and the collective. It is, in fact, the fundamental basis of difference between Western and Third World discourses. In the contemporary Western movie the theme of the story is the style of the form; in other words, these are the tools – the camera and the sets – that move the story around, instead of the story moving the tools. The shooting of the story is but a pretext for shooting the form. On the other hand, Third Cinema film-makers rarely move their camera and sets unless the story calls for it. Here, style grows out of the material of the film.

Most Third Cinema films focus on the story as opposed to action. This deliberate choice is their identifiable quality. When there is dramatic action it operates within the broader scheme of the story

60

rather than for the mere exultation of tempo and movement. Third Cinema films work with a sense of place and with fluidity of perspective. If they have any mood at all, it is that of a ritual or a carnival. Their meaning, however, resides in the relation of the work to its situation. Besides, the open-ended nature of the films, which accounts for the consideration of everyday life, also helps compose its aesthetic. The memorability of the work has much to do with our intellectual stimulation as well as with our sense of what is emancipatory aesthetics.

Take for example Med Hondo's *West Indies*. This carnival of cinema is without a hero. Its story leaps back and forth in historical time. We as witnesses are not only caught up with a reshuffling of historical documents but also, and more importantly, with the history of resistance itself. Here the camera and the sets are partners in the festive call to revolution. The film thus recognises and dismisses us as spectators at the same time. We are recognised in so far as we respond to the festivities as a call for revolt; we are dismissed if we merely cheer and celebrate its dance and song as vicarious entertainment.

The aesthetics of criticism

Today, some critics dwell on the role of mediation in criticism and claim to occupy the centre of discourse, marginalising all others just as official histories do. But there cannot be mediation without ideology, or criticism without consensus. It is futile to skirt this issue. We know that every spectator mediates a text to his or her everyday situation. Attempts to homogenise difference by networks of mediation are therefore doomed to failure.

It is clear that what is central to mainstream criticism is that other alternative discourses, particularly those considered 'marginal', might reveal the ideological undercurrents that critics are trying to conceal. They insist upon erasing alternative discourses with one purpose only – to maintain their power of domination. But the distinction between 'centre' and 'margin' is no longer relevant when these critical practices are understood to be merely one of various alternative discourses.

Under the structuralist-semiotic impulse the diachronic study (the study of art-works over time) has fallen into eclipse. Structuralism and semiotics offer a synchronic account of the internal structure of the text without its relation to the generic tradition in which it is situated. In other words, the semiotic-structuralist impulse represents an abstraction and rarely does address the question of reception (i.e. how the work appears to spectators). Rather, it seems only to address the text. Thus this kind of criticism describes the features of the story or the text as organised by its formal elements, separating the work from its social context. This minimalises and diffuses the political nature of the text and, therefore, allies itself with official histories.

What then should be the role of criticism in all the interlocking phenomena of Third Cinema and its aesthetics? To answer this question we need to go back to the logic of the folkloric manifested in the interaction between the performers and the listeners, which accounts for a unique cultural and aesthetic exchange. While the performers, at any given time, hold sway, it is in fact the listeners who have the power of criticism in the aesthetic judgment of art and performance. These artist-critics are both the producers and the consumers of the work.

What then is the role of criticism regarding Third Cinema aesthetics today? I believe that there is a significant continuity between forms of oral tradition and ceremonial story-telling and the structures of reception of Third Cinema. This continuity consists of a sharing of responsibility in the construction of the text, where both the film-maker and the spectators play a double role as performers and creators. Together, they construct an ongoing consensus of cultural confirmation through the affirmation of shared memory.

What is a critic anyway, except a story-teller? The only difference is that while story-telling in the traditional sense is more oblique, the critic's discourse is didactic and self-professed by a commitment to a position. In any case, the critic does not necessarily have a privileged access; but he or she is certainly interpellated by ideology.

A critic who is sensitive to the form and meaning of Third Cinema and aesthetics must be aware of the relationship between the work, the society and the popular memory that binds them together. Aesthetic judgment is a consensus between the critic and the audience. Thus critics who are mindful of the relationship of works to the people must seek a liberated future and necessarily take up another, more subversive position.

Let me take such a position to reintegrate a classic screen figure into the social and political context of popular memory. Recall Mantan Moreland, the black man who was well known for his gleaming teeth, his popping eyes and his quivering legs, and who has been labelled 'the accepted USA idea of the Negro clown supreme'. Who was this Mantan Moreland? Official film histories give us no clue beside the label they have attached to him. But long before he became a household Hollywood stereotype, Moreland was a young man living in Monroe, Louisiana, a state where white terror was rampant. When he was only seven years old, he had seen his shoeshine friend hung from a nearby post, his uncle's burnt body dragged down the street, and five black bodies hung dead. So at an early age his eyes rolled and his legs trembled, not because he thought one day Hollywood would discover him, but because he lived in an atmosphere of terror.

The animal that Hollywood tried to create was simply a confirmation of their racism, and the spectators' laughter at the very creation of their own myth was no less than a fulfilment of their racial fantasies. But viewing it as we are now, the spectacle, stripped naked and revealed, can be seen as finally turning upon itself – the fiction thus becomes non-fiction. And the spectacle, by trying to make 'beautiful' and 'lasting' the actual substance of a nightmare, *itself* becomes the nightmare.

Once the mask is removed, Moreland's identity is put in place and regains in death what was denied him in real life. His private life, now shedding the screen persona, is introduced into the social body. This, then, is one of the ways popular memory is made to carry out its rescue mission.

Conclusion

Between the popular memory of the Third World and the wilful forgetting of the West, the gate-keepers of the corridors of discourse cannot be but men and women of courage and of conscience, committed to an urgent, activist cinema – in a word, Third Cinema.

In a recent film, *Witness to Apartheid* by Sharon Sopher, we have an account of tortured bodies as memories. The film portrays excessive violence and brutality on the part of the South African police. In several telling sequences young South Africans show body wounds that were stitched *without* anaesthetic, as a form of torture. In one instance a young man was even able to move the skull-plate on the top of his head, which had been broken by the police.

These violated and tortured bodies, more than any written form, reveal the law of the land. But in another sense they mark the index of a world yet to come. For the flip-side of such memory, born out of suffering and pain, is ferocious and unyielding. These young South Africans, though physically brutalised, openly confess their determination to fight back even if it means joining the ranks of those who have already fallen. We are thus witnessing the re-emergence of new persons in Africa, who perhaps represent the climax of a long struggle that began with the invasion of the continent, and the kidnapping of her sons and daughters to faraway places, five hundred years ago.

This example makes abundantly clear that it is perhaps time to re-think and re-evaluate our understanding of our intellectual activity. The intellectuals are our neglected poets, film-makers, historians and anonymous fighters, who have shown that the true slums and ghettos of the world are not those we define economically, but rather those in the minds of us who lose sleep because of the fear of the hungry and the dispossessed.

The 'wretched of the earth', who still inhabit the ghettos and the barrios, the shanty towns and the madinas, the factories and working districts, are both the subjects and the critics of Third Cinema. They have always '[smelled] history in the wind'. Third Cinema, as guardian of popular memory, is an account and record of their visual poetics, their contemporary folklore and mythology, and above all their testimony of existence and struggle. Third Cinema, therefore, serves not only to rescue memories, but rather, and more significantly, to give history a push and popular memory a future.

Triangular Cinema, Breaking Toys, and Dinknesh vs Lucy[*]

Haile Gerima

I Triangular Cinema: Community, Storyteller, Activist

First, I must make it clear that I am a citizen of Ethiopia and am presently a migrant worker in the USA. The following presentation is my own personal observation of the struggle for independent cultural expression of the African American. My only credential is that I am an African by birth, living and working among the African American community. What has personally attracted me towards this community, beside the obvious, are its historical credentials of revolt and struggle for a democratic world. Besides adopting me as one of their own, this community has been an inspiration and encouragement in my own development as a film-maker. I will concentrate particularly on the cinema movement for social change within the African American community. This personal observation of this community, I must remind you, is limited and dictated by my own ideological point of view.

In my view, throughout history African American people have been a people of never-ending struggle. This precipitated a particular historic experience. The community is one that gives a superficial impression of seeming to succumb to the oppressive nature of the dominant power, while historically it has left a series of testimonies that identify it as a race that has rebelled and insisted on challenging and dismantling the oppressive aspects of the USA. As a result, the community has always been prohibited from fully asserting and realising its capacity, not only

* The three parts of this essay were originally three different lectures: Parts I and II were delivered at the Third Cinema conference in Edinburgh in 1986, Part III the following year at the Third Cinema Forum in Birmingham. Wherever it was possible to do so without significantly interrupting the flow of the argument, repetitions have been deleted.

65

on the cultural level but also on the economic and political levels of this country.

Because of the dominant power structure's use of the mass media intensely to assault African people and their history – its routine depiction of them as clowns, tap dancers and savages; its constant ridicule of the African American's militant desire for change – the African American has been left without any choice but to create and develop a viable cinematic expression in order to combat and counter-balance this oppressive cultural climate. In the world of music and literature, for example, this community has been militant, having a long tradition of cultural protest which has in some instances provoked revolutionary action. Though fully defined and assertive in music and literature, the African American community has not been successful in its attempts to ingrain its aesthetic value on a continual basis in the art of cinema. Intermittent film-aesthetic upsurges have occurred, using striking visual codes. But they have been totally ignored, neglected and omitted, though at times, ironically, they have even been incorporated into the so-called melting pot of the dominant power structure. This shortcoming, a result of primarily economic reasons, has been a point of concern to a great many of its community members and it constantly remains debated. However, these discussions are spontaneous, devoid of concrete and critical analysis.

In light of this negative environment, the African American community must forge a cinema that is combative, innovative and visionary. The African American community's inability fully to realise an organised and coherent cinema movement for social change is in the final analysis central to any form of rectification. Therefore, the critical examination of the internal dynamics of African American cinema in its historical context is decisive and necessary.

Financial backing from the level of commercial investments to that of state and federal grants is crucial to the realisation of any cinema. However, these institutions, which have sponsored some of these productions, play a major role in suppressing aesthetic identities that would otherwise have emerged under different circumstances. Most of the time, the power structure that sits on the funding panels serving as judge and jury in the awarding of these grants also consciously and unconsciously dismisses as 'primitive' and 'unartistic' any form of African American visual identity. The dependency relationship that emerges as a result of this patronage in the long term snuffs out vibrant, burning aspects of this cinema movement. In so doing, they censor the emergence of content and form that are uniquely African American. The relationship that most Third World film-makers in the US have with the dominant power structure ends up arresting artistic temperament and the development of any viable form of creative artistic movement.

Equally, if not more devastatingly, there has been a lack of meaningful, counter-cultural awareness organisations, film appreciation clubs or societies that can strengthen the individual film-maker and intensify the communities' collaborative film-making effort. If such a collaborative process were to establish itself, however, it could work towards overcoming the political and economic obstacles faced by the respective communities in film production. Their realm of operation could be endless, extending to distribution, exhibition, etc. The absence of true, honest and critical strategies to intensify and transform the issues of film production aesthetics, the lack of awareness of the responsibilities and duties of the artist to experiment, all hamper any form of tangible development. The scattered existence of most of the African American film-makers, disconnected from the targeted community, creates a vacuum and destabilises any attempt to approach the crisis with a united front. Though the African American community does not truly control capital (i.e. banking, science and technology), it can still develop realistic and innovative cinema movements that are capable of responding to its own needs.

However, without realising the pitfalls and stereotypes of the dominant spectacle cinema, even these alternatives are incomplete and futile. Through years of mental colonisation, escapist conventional cinema has ingrained its own disruptive stereotypes and, as a result, has perverted and corrupted societal perceptions of cinema. Fundamentally deformed film grammar has historically been taught and dictated to alienate and prevent the emergence of any cinema that may require a whole different set of relationships between the important parties that make up the event of cinema.

First, let's look at the pitfalls of conventional and exploitation cinema that prevent progressive inter-relationships from taking place. The conventional film-maker is by and large egotistical, psychologically deformed and individualistic, incapable of introducing the necessary historic vision that can activate the progressive cultural energy of the masses of people. This commercially proclaimed 'artist' is disconnected from any community of people, deceivingly parading as if he or she were introducing a new vision, when in actuality he or she is perpetuating and reincarnating old stereotypical models, wrapped up in unliberated conventional narrative, exhausted subject-matter disguised in special effects and technological voodoo. This film-maker is without any sense of accountability; he or she is isolated, mystified, and takes the mass of people to be childlike, brainless and incapable of engaging in any meaningful relationship. This traditional film-maker knows what the people want, knows what the people liked yesterday/yesteryear, and continues to feed them that same junk. Appearing in other mass media outlets, surrounded by star entourages, he or she perpetuates the myth of the film-makers by claiming it as his or her birthright: 'I was born to be a film-maker'. Such a film-maker is antagonistic towards any constructive criticism, with no consistent, traceable style to be found from film to film, erratic at best.

But what about the conventional audience? By and large this audience is the by-product of the exploitation commercial film industry: it is colonised by and immersed in conventional film language, has been made to believe in its lack of intellectual need, and has abdicated to junk expressions, at the mercy of spectacle cinema. Castrated of their own potential to be human beings, they are full of self-hatred; constantly wishing for some kind of miraculous alteration of their nose, their lips, their hair, hoping to turn overnight into models of what they see in commercial cinema. These audiences are stranded and are held hostage to predetermined film formulas whose taste and appreciation, in the final analysis, is disfigured. This conventional audience arrived at this sorry state of cultural affairs through years of brainwashing.

In the midst of this decadence, the conventional critic is at best a paid mercenary, swordsman or modern samurai for the highest bidder. Mr Know-it-all, nothing to learn, armed with shallow, trite and nebulous vocabularies such as 'superb', 'magnificent', 'must see', etc. (who, while in school, majored in film clichés, in most cases having an Oedipal obsession with one of the so-called stars in the old movies). These classifiers and compartmentalisers of film relegate cultural outputs to the level of Campbell's soup. Any subversive action or deviation by any film-maker outside of this plantation school mentality is chopped up, smeared, degraded or dismissed as non-existent. Out of these deformed conventional relationships, it is impossible to forge a transformed cultural phenomenon in the African American film community.

Therefore, I contend that the major factor in this crisis is the absence of new, constructive, progressive relationships between the three critical elements of the community that can strengthen and transform the cultural cinema movement. These vital and principal players comprise 1) the audience/community, 2) the film-maker/storyteller, and 3) the activist/critic.

In this epoch, we live where the battle for ideas and values must be waged through the intensification of complementary critical and analytical cultural interaction that links the artist (in this case the film-maker), the audience/community, and the activist/critic. Herein I will refer to these three groups as storyteller, audience and activist, respectively. This interaction is triangular in nature, with all three parts being equally significant. It is crucial that all parties be non-antagonistic, using constructive dialogue, motivated by a genuine desire to effect the transformation of a given society. This triangular relationship best functions through constant critical and innovative deliberation that includes an analysis of the history and practice of conventional cinema. In this process, all inevitable, spontaneous, aesthetic outbursts take motion, becoming organised, coherent, dynamic and vibrant cultural movements.

Until this relationship is realised by all concerned parties and the link is forged through constructive struggle, the achievements of the sporadic, spontaneous creative outburst of the 60s and the early 70s will be endangered, becoming static, without any guarantee of their perpetuation. There cannot exist an African American cinema aesthetic without the realisation of this evolutionary dynamic, and without any dialectical relationship between storyteller, audience and activist. This triangular interaction, in my opinion, is critical and historic.

In order for the profession to be placed in its cultural and historic role, we must understand that the storyteller has to be able to explore and experiment in order to achieve a higher aesthetic transformation. His or her visual narrative must invoke the conditions of communal visual theatre in order to arrive at and synthesise a collective, communal cinema language. The audience, on the other hand, provoked by a given visual arrangement, has to struggle to understand and to help transform the storyteller as well as itself. To bridge the gap, mediating between storyteller and audience, the activist emerges, setting in motion an active, vibrant and living cinema. This triangular relationship enables the communities to complement each other in their respective transformations and set in motion dynamic and innovative cultural inter-relationships. In this process, the aesthetic transformation takes place in a dialectical and revolutionary process, becoming, as a by-product, national and universal in character.

African American film-makers whose main interest is the advancement of visual culture intended for social change must create a new relationship between all parties concerned in the triangular interest groups. If a new relationship is to emerge, when the opportunity arrives to congregate within the confines of a theatre the very structure of a given film should skilfully invoke collective, active participation, instead of passive resignation. Underneath this form of constructive struggle emerges a common visual language. This collective experience should be carefully studied, discussed and debated by skilfully creating the conditions through the agency of the activist. This process will be realised further if a community journal lends a hand as a catalyst and as a decoder for the emerging collective cinematic language. Without fostering this kind of relationship, the primary level of what I call 'the period of the spontaneous outburst' cannot be channelled to make any impact. The bits and pieces of scattered, spontaneous African American cinematic experiences converge through the proposed triangular relationship between film-maker, audience and activist.

We have witnessed in past years audiences that have been exposed to films such as *Soleil Ô*, *The Hour of the Furnaces*, *Xala* and *Memories of Underdevelopment* slowly developing a higher sense of film appreciation, while simultaneously developing a critical and at times antagonistic relationship to exploitation establishment cinema, and making critical demands of film-makers. To accentuate these kinds of contradiction, and to help transform the African American film experience, there needs to emerge a national film association that is committed to defending and encouraging an African American film movement. Through this association it is possible to create avenues to get the African American community involved in the low-budget production of African American films. There needs to be a united approach in the pricing and marketing of these film products. Through these associations, simple measures can be instigated such as converting existing community centres into audio-visual centres, coupled with printing handbooks and manuals with discussion topics.

For quite some time now, attempts to unite the African American film-making community have by and large failed. African American cinema in the community is presently viewed as individual experiences rather than as a collective experience that can be linked by the support and participation of the community. As demonstrated by history, individual film-makers, regardless of their fantasy, cannot survive without this cultural and political interaction with the community from whom they seek support. Their very declaration of an independent African American cinema strongly implies a deliberate and calculated separation from the established film industry.

Time and time again, it has been said that the industry as it is constructed now is incapable of responding to the cultural needs not only of the African American but of all Third World people in the United States. Therefore, this contradiction cannot be cured without creating the conditions that are capable of agitating for and propagating the changing of the system. Even if one fails to be motivated by the larger societal oppressive conditions, there are enough obstacles against the African American film-maker to begin to entertain drastic measures against the existing system by all aspiring film-makers. We need to intensify the call for better ideological clarity among the African American film community, to ask them to investigate their commitment and reaffirmation to film for social change in the tradition of Paul Robeson: 'The artist must elect to fight for freedom or for slavery. I have made my choice. I had no alternative.'

II Breaking Toys: the demystification of imaginary lines

They are poisoning the human mind in incredible doses through commercial cinematography, grossly commercial, and I believe that these questions have to be a real concern for all people who feel or think properly. I am sure that any politician with a sense of responsibility has to worry about increasing alienation, that unceasing intoxication their countries' masses are suffering from. They must understand that all canned propaganda, which comes from the empire through transnationals, is anti-education, deforming, degenerating. They must realise that this is like bacteriological warfare.

This war is worse than bacteriological warfare. It is more humiliating, more degrading, more unbearable. The new Latin American cinema offers other kinds of material, of a different quality. For me this struggle, this film movement, constitutes a great battle, a great battle of enormous transcendence, not just for our identity but for liberation, freedom and survival, because if we do not survive culturally we will not survive economically or politically. This is one of the factors that multiplied my interest in this topic and in this movement. A great struggle is developing, a great struggle for our survival, for our liberation. We cannot believe that under these economic, social and cultural conditions, under these political conditions, we are free.

Fidel Castro
1985 Havana Film Festival closing address

As we approach the 21st century, the ideological mystification and domestication of society by the commercial motion picture industry has come to be accepted by the mass of human beings around the world. The escapist world outlook presented by this dominant medium finally conventionalised its language, establishing itself as the universal standard. It parades itself unabated, presenting the most unnatural as natural; a colonial language invented only to benefit in all its aspects the Eurocentric world order. These unnatural human values are manufactured by a commercially controlled industry that transmits its demented ideological cultural values through seemingly universal characters like cultural soldiers. These sugar-coated models – seemingly harmless in appearance, but in their essence devastating – are presented in film after film, passing verdicts on universal manhood, universal womanhood, universal childhood, universal romance, universal good and universal evil, universal time/structure/rhythm. The representatives, the culture

71

carriers, the agents of this industry are the so-called 'stars'. These stars invented by the exploitative industry are the false superhuman models about whom all human beings on earth should fantasise. These are the soldiers of cultural imperialism. Effective mercenaries advertised with millions of dollars are dispatched throughout the world into many dark theatres to steal our hearts and minds. In order for this glamorous commercial cinema successfully to colonise, imperialise and lobotomise the minds of millions of people all over the world, it must reduce the world population to little children. In this uneven struggle for ideas, these stars, these models, these toys, daily insensitively trample around the world in a seemingly silent battle, dementing and at times replacing any kind of national or cultural identity. The term 'toys', in this case, is used to link to the most profound statement of Hegel when he asserted that the most important act a child can engage in is the breaking of his/her toys.

In order to combat this form of cultural colonialism, our first battle zone must lie in determining the method to destroy the very toys of mystification. However, in this period the counter-struggle to turn this phenomenon around is in its embryonic stage. These very cultural models mentioned above have by and large pacified our basic human need for change. Any struggle for transformation has been made to appear as the most unnatural behaviour. To dare to change the very condition of humanity as presented by this cultural phenomenon is viewed as unnatural. Selfishness, greed, false individualism, sexual obsession, violence and the theme of fear are the most widely consumed supposedly natural ingredients of this industry. Through its cultural expression, we are forced day and night to accept the artificial reality presented by this industry as the law of nature and therefore eternal. It is in this epoch that the cultural toys have made a drastic inroad into our central nervous system, governing and fashioning our behaviour – our minds are occupied territory. The motive for this mental occupation is the subjugation of our labour, our land, and our raw materials.

This epoch is the most important and critical period since the birth of cinema. Especially in the case of the Third World countries, exploitation cinema has effectively alienated a whole generation of spectators, a generation who watches false history as it is constructed and reorganised by the West. The phenomenon is compounded by the emergence of video and the installation of advanced satellite communications weaponry. In whatever form this cultural incursion takes place, the most decisive aspect of the struggle remains diffused. Effective counter-attack organisations at this point are not fully developed. Cultural activists with the necessary political insight are rare. As a result, the incursion continues to trample unchallenged over our cultural, political vision.

As a result of colonialism and neo-colonialism, the intellectual class that has been historically capable of providing the necessary leadership has been rendered ineffective, and has itself been nurtured by the cultural diet of the coloniser and its licensed intellectuals. This unfortunate intellectual class, effectively armed by and with the cultural models of Western literature, is incapable of committing the necessary act towards liberation: to divorce itself from these dominant models, to cut its umbilical cord attached to these early ingested alien models/toys – from Homeric literature all the way to Greta Garbo and James Dean. This class is attracted to an outmoded world outlook, incapable of transforming its own society in the journey towards a new humanity.

This so-called developed society has its own population in a state of siege, preventing any consciousness from sprouting as a result of these cultural weapons – the industry of mass thought-control. This fear-centred cultural domination ensures the repression of any instinctual desire for change on the part of the dominated. Parading as horror, pseudo-science fiction, cops and robbers etc., they bombard us daily, intensifying the antagonistic relationship between human beings and their environment, disarming human beings' capacity to understand nature by filling the environment with alien and fearful imaginations, turning masses of people into tortured souls and walking zombies.

Daily, glamorised and sensationalised violent characters are imposed in movie after movie, in simplistic terms that romanticise and popularise the culture of violence. Muscle-headed characters are the staple heroes. Intellect is the most unattractive subject-matter, giving way to trigger-happy killers. Daily, we see the complex issues of the world reduced to simple resolutions as a result of violent brute acts. This simplistic but violent cultural phenomenon is devastating the most vulnerable segment of society, i.e. the young people. Fear and violence, attractively presented through the agents of cultural models, consumed daily and digested by masses of people, have successfully created self-destructive human beings. Motion pictures that are socially concerned are classified as boring, too taxing, too long – meaning, 'there's not enough action, violence, car accidents, brutal acts against Third World people, against women'. Motion pictures that are capable of introducing sober emotional as well as intellectual issues are dismissed and prevented from reaching masses of people by the power structure that bestowed upon itself the responsibility of dictating the best cultural menu to the whole world.

Let's pause for a second to look critically at the world and the shape it is in. The reality we face is that:

1. Communications in all their forms that shrink the world are no longer a factor.

2. We live in a world of diminishing resources in relation to the rapidly growing population. Even resources taken for granted such as air and water are now threatened.

3. The colonial legacy of violence is still with us and intensifying.

4. The threat of war for world abomination by the superpower is eminently active in all the social, psychological, economic, political and, last but not least, cultural manifestations.

Given some of these critical realities, we should ask what kinds of cultural expression are capable of confronting and resolving the needs of this complicated world. What kind of humanity is capable of designing and struggling for democratic solutions to this planet's problems? What kind of human models do we want to illustrate and confront contradictory phenomena? Is it the rugged, selfish individual, the cowboy, who only understands resolutions in physical terms without the intellect being involved? Or is it the so-called masses of people that are hostages of the cultural phenomenon of fear, whose very actions are dictated by this power that controls their value system, mentality and response?

The image and, as a consequence, the status of Third World people in commercial cinema is one of stereotypical characterisations, a backdrop for the dominant Euro-American groups. It is comparable to the status of the fly on our planet. We always see flies around waste, hovering over garbage, hunting for left-overs, predetermined from creation to be miserable, identity-less from the individual to the collective, always ready to be slaughtered by apparently invincible abominations from Hollywood heroes ranging from John Wayne to Clint Eastwood and the modern Tarzan, Rambo. How many people care about the history of flies, the genealogy of flies, the grandparents, the fathers and mothers of flies, all but created to be killed at a whim? Who cares to be bothered by the theme of love, that is, of flies? Who cares about the concerns and visions of a fly regarding the status of the planet?

Flies might be interesting for those obsessed with overpopulation, for they are a danger and threat to the privileged, 'developed' society. You can't count them. They don't have names. Who cares to speak their language? If they care to live on this planet, they have to study ours. Who takes their life seriously? Only Western life. Culture? Good for the background, for the exotic. They will be Native Americans, Arabs, Africans and Asians. When they charge toward the Anglo-Saxon hero and heroine, they fall and die well, they know how to get beaten up and

74

killed. For heaven's sake, who goes to see flies talk and debate about love and hate, their desires and dreams of changing the world?

This is the reality of the out-of-context people whose life is an inhuman life, whose death is non-human, whose marriage and birth is non-human. These types of reality, often illustrated in film, are especially exemplified by a film entitled *Missing*. *Missing* is a typical motion picture of the kind that deceives Third World people by letting us appear but denying in essence our very existence by its deeper testimony. Throughout the film, we witness a graphic depiction of masses of faceless, nameless Third World people in the background, while in the foreground we are skilfully manipulated and emotionally tormented by one American character who is missing. The agenda is set for us. We are subliminally made to believe in the value of the Gods, the stars, the models, the toys. The disappearance and mutilations of Third World peoples in the midst of the drama and romance of the stars is insignificant. The film illustrates the human value of the European American, while simultaneously devaluing other human beings, specifically Third World people. This value is illustrated daily by the mass media of the dominant world in its highlighting the value of Westerners over and above Third World people. We are told again and again that in order to make the world understand our cause it must be endorsed by the stars of the West playing our experiences for us. Through this technique, we will attract sympathy and solidarity to further communicate to all human beings our existence. Personally, if it has to take the stars and the toys of cultural domination to depict my grandmothers, my fathers and mothers, I call this dictatorship, obscene and unacceptable.

Any sympathy or solidarity acquired as a result of this tragic misrepresentation is a travesty of the truth. It only reinforces a dominance which in the end is illegitimate and corrupt. It is psychologically devastating in the long run. If we cannot achieve our desired objectives by presenting our human dilemma, interacting as we are, the cycle of dependency will only intensify the self-destructive aspect of this planet. Human beings should be able to receive the emotional as well as the intellectual message of my film expression, apparent in the eyes, face, posture and essence of my own grandmother. I should never be forced to replace my own kind for irrelevant and extraneous considerations. This will only continue to exaggerate, spoil, corrupt and delude the Western people. No wonder they go around invading countries, assassinating visionaries and replacing governments as part of their quest to rearrange the world. No wonder the world is divided between human beings that are dispensable and those that are indispensable. These kinds of consideration feed into the already bad state of the planet. This is what is called silent violence.

Can you imagine how obscene it would have been to have Ann-Margret and Ricardo Montalban cast as principal characters in *Blood of the Condor*, or Steve McQueen or Dustin Hoffman playing *The Jackal of Nahueltoro*? Oh yes, in this age of cultural imperialism, masses of people are guaranteed to turn out to celebrate our own destruction. Chewing popcorn and drinking Coca-Cola, our hearts throbbing like a dance of death. This is equally true in content and form. Had *Soleil Ô* and *Memories of Underdevelopment* taken the journey of that *Taxi Driver* or *ET*, how tragic it would have been. How much of the temperament would we have missed had *The Hour of the Furnaces* taken shape in the convention and passivity of Flaherty? Imagine for a second Yves Montand, Catherine Deneuve and Katharine Hepburn in *Xala*. All would have been commercial box-office successes. Can you imagine how much humanity would have missed? The point is that the melodies and essences of other types of human beings that do exist and do have a right to be preserved on celluloid get abandoned. I don't know how many of you will submit to this form of silent, violent censorship and cultural domination.

I clearly remember, as a young man in my country [Ethiopia], an uppity American jumping into the River Nile and being consumed by a hungry crocodile. The world, including my own country, was made to mourn this episode. This was at the time that many Ethiopians and people all over the world were dying from a host of other factors. I also remember, as a university student, watching Western news covering a war incident in Africa. Camera, panting and heaving, searches for the dead and selectively skips, jumps and zooms past many African black bodies to a white body. Camera holds, mourns, sheds tears and undulates. Composition: control focus in the foreground, white body. In the background, out of focus, dead, faceless, nameless, identity-less African bodies, the flies. This form of illustration of human values takes place daily in South Africa, Nicaragua, Chile, Libya, Grenada, Angola, Mozambique etc., ingraining in our heads what they deem to be of special human value and that the good things of the world belong to these special, white people.

Third World cinema cannot establish itself in this tradition of mystification, but must be a cinema of demystification. Third World cineastes must take a deliberate and active role that is intellectual as well as physical. The inherent vision and the logical aesthetic by-product must not be a cinema of passivity, but a combative cinema; a cinema of long-term objectives to change, if necessary to rearrange our disgraceful existence. Each search to harmonise sight and sound as we recognise our long-term vision must be assertive and defiant, because it is through cultural militancy and interaction that we will be able to ascertain the logical as well as the uncertain cultural and aesthetic dynamics.

Part of the legacy of colonialism and the practical reality of neo-colonialism is the stigma that is attached to technological know-how. Especially in the world of cinema, the typical discussion of the know-how camouflages the fundamental confusion between mechanical applications of the techniques and the aesthetic and cultural aspects of that technology. As it is, aspiring cineastes of the Third World are the most denied and barred group of people in the struggle to acquire technological know-how. However, cultural identity – a fundamental and crucial ingredient in the formation of the cineaste – is confused in this struggle. In this period, a great number of Third World people join the casualties of neo-colonialism, allowing themselves to confuse the know-how with the aesthetic essence. Storytellers, in this instance via cinema, are equally governed by the cultural/national identity. This cultural/national identity, which is the critical linguistic and visual accent, is compromised. Under the scrutiny and supervision of neo-colonialism, imposed by the value judgment of the Western cultural barometer, most fall prey to an exhausted convention of Eurocentric cinema language.

In the struggle to reverse this trend, continual cultural and aesthetic dialogue between Third World people will provide the edge. Third World people, for quite some time, have consistently struggled for the right to define their own spaces and identities. In order to accomplish this cinema, we have to intensify concrete, constructive cultural criticism and analysis. We have to take the lead in breaking down the grammatical syntax of our sight and sound expression. This cannot be left to other self-appointed shapers and definers/moulders of our reality. For we can learn to drive the car, fly the airplane without turning into or becoming the monster.

We are fortunate to have inherited a long history of films for social change from Africa, South and Central America, Cuba and Asia. These socially relevant films have set in motion a progressive tradition of cultural debate. The process of breaking the toys of mental and cultural colonialism has shown successful results in certain segments of our societies, likewise setting in motion the process of audience-building. We should be grateful to the earlier cultural pioneers who began this process of audience-building when it was considered subversive, unpopular cinema. The audience we have inherited was built slowly, painfully stacking up person by person. In this epoch, we have no right to be disillusioned, for we have inherited better times as a result of past struggles.

The historic creative tasks of Third World people cannot be accomplished without venturing into bold and honest experiments. In order to harmonise the storyteller with the mode of instruments that transmit his or her imagination, every new technology has to be tailored to that end.

77

Cinema should be put under that service and should constantly be moulded, developed and transformed towards that objective. It would be a cultural scandal in the world of cinema to submit as imitators rather than innovators. Here again, I am not advocating experiment for experiment's sake, or art for art's sake, but an experiment that is grounded in a genuine and honest search for ways to express our essence, our temperament and our accents in sight and sound.

To further illustrate this thought, we can look at the example of a wooden tree trunk before the sculptor's axe. It has its own inherent content and form. The duty of the sculptor is to violate that primary status for a higher aesthetic expression. A weapon in the form of an axe is introduced; every careful stroke chipping away at the wooden trunk is a dialectical and artistic journey towards the artist's imagination. Therefore, the primary content and form throughout the creative process enters a higher or a new state of content and form. Likewise, in cinema, we should struggle to transform our creative imaginations, in order to harmonise sight and sound.

From the germination of ideas to the final product we need to structure and restructure laboriously, in order to discover and transform our aesthetic identity, to preserve the footprints of our journey toward that fulfilment. The process of assembling and reassembling our creation in sight and sound is a constant and intense exploration for a higher societal aesthetic gratification. It is our historic responsibility and duty. This struggle can be observed in the two distinct gestures of Third World cinema in the form of neo-colonial and decolonised cinema: the struggle between the imitators and the innovators. In the innovative cinema, you find the introduction of vibrant aesthetics into the veins of film history in the way that content and form are organised, time, space and rhythm are structured. On the other hand, the cinema of imitation in the Third World is as rampant as the imitation of Coca-Cola.

With an equal intensity we have to concern ourselves with production/exhibition/distribution issues inside the borders of Third World cinema. In some Third World countries the status of distribution and exhibition is a scandal: it is still controlled and managed by colonial and neo-colonial forces. In other countries, under the pretext of national policies, bureaucratic states in oppressive, uncreative environments prevent the realisation of progressive films. All these and other conditions have to be fought by clearly identifying their respective particularities in order to change and transform Third World cinema. We have to struggle for a progressive and democratic national film policy, including independent and alternative cultural expressions. National policy in cinema should free and unleash the imprisoned creative cinematic temperament of the Third World people. Every film production has to be used to create an economic and political climate that will ensure the perpetuation of our cinema movement.

While we should be pleased with the growing interest shown by the progressive, international community in our cinema movement, we need to be concerned with the distribution and exhibition aspects of our creative outputs. We have to restore dignity to and for our films, we have to fight against the free exhibition of our culture. We must receive economic as well as political return for our labour, as part and parcel of our struggle for legitimate cinema. This will prevent the tendency to relegate our culture to the world of the exotic – even by those who should know better, our friends in Europe and in the West who insist on the free exhibition of our product under the pretext of introducing or exposing our culture to their society, thereby becoming familiar with our culture for future consumption. The fact of the matter is that the Western world has been exposed to our culture since it set foot in Alexandria, followed by Marco Polo and Vasco da Gama, all the way down to Livingstone and Stanley. I must add, the world is still paying the penalty for that past and present uneven relationship that has made a grotesque, dependent, false co-existence.

In the coming years, Third World cinema has a two-pronged responsibility: 1) to be an active catalyst in instigating the revolutionary uplifting of the masses of Third World people from the gutter to the level of equal partnership – the birthright of all human beings – and to struggle to bring about the total removal of the above- and below-the-line distinctions of existence; and 2) to be a catalyst, directly or indirectly, in demystifying the superiority of the developed countries. This demystification can only take place through the decoding of the deemed superiority of the West. This will create some form of parity that will contribute to a better climate and democratic existence for all human beings. In other words, our cultural contribution to the West will be to bring them a little bit down into the human orbit.

In the final analysis, the most difficult duty of Third World cinema is the replacing of the toys. They have to be broken, they have to be torn down. Their 'childness' and their 'nothingness' has to be exposed. These toys that are controlling and manipulating the exported behavioural patterns of our people have to be destroyed through profound and skilfully structured counter-film expressions, i.e. guerrilla cinema, however imperfect. There can never be a peaceful film existence with these colonial models occupying our optic nerve. The Tarzans, the John Waynes, the James Deans, the Marilyn Monroes and the Mickey Mouses have to be torn down. Without this primary concern, there can never be any development of cinema. Every frame and every take, every shot and every sound must be able to enter into the different compartments of our brains the way a guerrilla engages in hand-to-hand combat. All these thousands of so-called heroes and heroines of mankind, all those so-called stars and false human models, all those Indian killers, African exterminators, Arab and Asian destroyers have to be erased and eliminated from within our mentalities. With this act we should celebrate our humanity, honestly expressing our essence and our vision of a democratic world where all human beings, by right, express their cultural and national existence. To fall short of participating and agitating in the bridging of this gap will only contribute to the already lopsided dictatorial cultural grammar, and will result in more suffering and violence in the world. After all, this imaginary line is man-made.

'Nothing is more logical amongst us than a racist humanitarianism. Since the European has only been able to become a man by creating slaves and monsters, Comrades, let us not honour Europe by creating states, institutions and societies in its image. Humanity expects more from us than this caricatural and generally obscene imitation.'

Frantz Fanon

III   Dinknesh* vs Lucy: Bone of contention

Censorship
Capital in the form of finance, technology and human resources is the foundation of the realisation of any motion picture project. Since the African American community does not control the banking system it is the most powerless segment of the United States, uninvolved in any meaningful fashion in the decision-making process of a film production. The expression and manifestation of a film project is determined by one's access to the bank. One cannot easily use films as a means of expression without the sanction of those who control capital. Therefore one's lack of access to finance is a form of censorship.

Unlike societies which openly declare ideological censorship, a capitalist society such as the US disguises the reality of censorship under the guise of a free society, but in fact daily applies censorship in a more insidious way. In these so-called open societies, artists who uphold the status quo are provided with the means to express themselves, and are subservient to those who control the economics. Those who control capital determine the allocation of these resources. All the tools of expression in mass media are at the disposal of the dominant group of

* Dinknesh is a 3.5 million-year-old (estimated) Ethiopian woman whose bones were discovered by a European archaeologist who named her Lucy. Ethiopians insist upon referring to her by her Ethiopian name.

that society. Their cultural perspective and their cultural needs become the order of the day.

The power structure finances all cultural activities on the basis of its own notions and its own criteria of aesthetics. Their bias becomes a standard. Nevertheless, bold individuals have miraculously completed film projects outside the establishment without the sanction of that establishment. Such is the case of the independent African American cinema in the United States. So far, the very fact of completion of most African American films defies the basic logic of film production. Despite the odds, they intermittently emerge without a trace of any preconceived formula for their success, taking their society by surprise.

Emerging artists of any society are in most cases immersed in historic challenges created by the objective and subjective conditions of their own community. Since film-makers usually emerge unaware of their realities, they are usually free from the social pitfalls and obstacles awaiting them. The few film projects that are completed by the African American film community reflect immense talent and creativity, exhibiting great ability in content and form. Any survey will find that most African American films are innovative and reflect their communities' aesthetic aspirations as well as confidence, explosive energy, assertiveness and originality. Most of these works exemplify a film aesthetic that is a germinating agency towards self-definition and independence. Social fluctuations within African American communities, be they rebellious or dormant, serve to charge and inspire film-makers. This is visibly apparent in completed film projects as well as in thousands of unrealised film scripts and film ideas. This historic state brings us into direct contradiction with the demands and expectations of the Eurocentric dominant group.

In a racially polarised state of existence a highly sophisticated form of censorship proceeds surgically to prevent these creative productions from developing into a film movement, while the African American film community is in the process of formulating its possible expansion into the film profession. In any artistic movement this is a critical period. It is the process of evolution. The cruel interjection of the power structure imposing its own concept of the African American reality contrary to the will of that society is a total violation of the artistic instincts of the African American community. We can identify at least three side-effects or typical patterns resulting from these contradictions.

Pattern 1: This is the stage where for lack of finance, an African American film-maker begins to feel like an illegitimate film-maker. In other words, the foundation of any artist, which is a sense of self-confidence, begins to erode. His or her confidence, an absolutely necessary ingredient in the journey of the creative process, is arrested, confused or negated.

81

Pattern 2: This is a group which under the stated circumstances begins to submit to the dictates and desires of the dominant Eurocentric concepts of the world. Here the artist dishonestly accepts the prescription of the dominant group. As a result of this unholy marriage, he or she is thrown into a psychological orbit of self-denial, a state of unnaturalness. To accept the Eurocentric cultural aesthetics as the order of the day and to be an instrument for that end has its own crippling consequences. Here again, in an assimilated environment, the artist's development is arrested and eroded.

Pattern 3: This group is defined by the beliefs and ideas of resistance that have been passed from generation to generation within the African diaspora. In this category of film-makers, the dominating thought and the energy required for existence spring from a desire to be an independent institution. Under this economic, political and cultural arrangement, the African American film-maker feels that he/she should not have the illusion of any fairness. He/she proclaims that as it exists now the system is incapable of responding to his/her cultural needs. Therefore, one has to create alternative institutions to respond to those needs. He/she considers these contradictions to be historic, having to be fought against; considers these abnormal arrangements to be alienating and unacceptable; and declares the cultural war to be a battle for ideas, a struggle for which the camera should be of service as a weapon. Though this posture is correct, if one is not in a position of access to the necessary capital, the lack of a financial base makes it impossible to pursue this battle. Though different from the other two crisis patterns, the group of artists in this category are still forced to gyrate in an orbit of ideas without the material base to realise them. This prolonged search for an alternative equally contributes to the retardation and arrest of the creative process.

In all three crisis stages, African American cinema enters into a confusing and devastating existence. These oppressive conditions destroy cadres of film artists as well as dissipate the communities' creative energy, like pregnancy after pregnancy without a birth. These are the three identifiable side-effects which plague the African American community. A film-maker of a given society, born at a given historic moment, fortunately or unfortunately chooses the most expensive weapon to express historic and cultural concerns. This is the contradiction.

History
Any society fighting for the cause of truth is in my view engaged in a natural struggle. This contradiction is eternal and is a law of nature, even if it is not accomplished in one's own lifetime. However, racism is dropped into this normal struggle for truth, causing it at this point to

become a very unnatural contradiction. For racism is the most crippling and vicious poison. In a racially polarised society such as the United States, where the different national groups are daily brainwashed and fashioned to submit to the dictates and the gratifications of Eurocentric cultural domination, African American artists are choicelessly engaged in responding to the very abnormal ills of that society. This contradiction manifests itself physically, as well as sociologically and pscyhologically. It throws many non-European nationals into the incurable disease of self-hatred and self-degradation. This condition affects not only African Americans, but other Third World nationals. This racist society insults their look, their way of speaking, their aspirations, their cultural notions. It turns them into victims and puts them against the wall, making them apologise for who they are and beg for a prescribed aesthetic surgery on themselves. It relegates its artists to the work of roaming around funding agencies, as legitimate as vagabonds and pimps ... all this for the crime of wanting to express their own humanity. This is history and history is used as censorship.

The consequence of our history is the very foundation of this contradiction. Our lives are divided into two historic reflections, two reflections that determine our daily struggle, wherever we may be:

1) If you take our faces, our external manifestations, we are a series of blackboards on which a consequence of certain historic experiences is written. In the first instance, this fundamentally serves the oppressor in being able to identify who we are, our movements and locations. Our mere existence can't help but haunt the European world. Though they would like us to be non-existent in the memory of history, we continue to exist. We remain, pointing an accusing finger at the guilt-ridden conscience of the dominant society. This transaction takes place without a single bullet fired, before a single finger is actually pointed, simply by walking in the streets. The representational role of Black people is that they daily remind the false historians of Eurocentric history that we've come into contact with them at a given stage of history. We therefore are the conscience of history. Every social explosion in all parts of the world directly invokes a silenced memory, pointing to where things went wrong. Consequently, development and growth is denied to any African American artist who may stray from the support of his or her community. For they are in fact considered dangerous as a result of their chosen profession. Therefore, silent censorship is imposed upon them for being a physical reminder of history.

2) The second and most crucial cutting edge of this history is the artists, the film-makers themselves. They are choicelessly obsessed by history. For they see the answer inseparably linked to history. They proclaim that, to rectify the problem, exorcism within the annals of history is

necessary; they point out the significance of finding oneself. They are engaged in inner monologues: 'Why am I interested in history?', 'Why is there a need for redefinition of oneself?' There is a need for history and the redefinition of oneself because of the existing misrepresentations of history that cripple one's development and growth. The misnamings, renamings of Third World people's history is crucial. One stumbles into a series of these examples: 'Lake Victoria', 'South Africa', 'Lucy' instead of 'Dinknesh'. The configurations, balkanisations of Third World people, past and present, make one hold history as a key to liberation, to self-reliance and independence, and therefore as a target of the silent censorship, the classification of non-existence in cinema.

As a consequence of history, our ideas, our vision remind them of the crimes, the colonialism, the slavery, the Hiroshima, the Nagasaki, the Zulu War, the many so-called anti-Christ African sculptures they have burned and disfigured, or the war they have waged to exterminate Third World people; and you are not supposed to address it or even recall it in your memory. The European says, 'Be a buffoon!', 'Be a clown!', 'Be a freak!', but don't use history. 'I'll finance you as long as you remain a freak/a clown, but don't remind us of history.'

The violence of renaming

The reason why we are obsessed with history is because we have been renamed. Our ancestors have been renamed, our mountains, our rivers, our hills, our whole being have all been renamed to fit a Eurocentric world. So the first step as a cultural activist is wanting to rename ourselves into our original names. This whole period unleashes all sorts of reactions for us, the colonised people. In this process, as a result of the study of history, we not only find ourselves renamed but devastatingly misrepresented, deformed and omitted from history.

At this critical juncture, we enter a new consciousness of wanting to change the very society that renamed us. So now our first engagement is to struggle against the history that renamed us. Thus any subject-matter, any content and form that obsesses us, as Third World film-makers, becomes a popular memory that the dominant society wants to erase, forget and accept as a non-existent entity, though there is no single day without their teaching us about 'St Aristotle', 'St Shakes-peare', 'St Hamlet', 'St Dickens' etc. – cultural soldiers that continue to revitalise European history in mass media. And then the dominant power structure consciously or unconsciously asserts further that the world will know nothing of you, making sure you are perceived as being non-existent. Hollywood says, 'O.K., you want to make a film about Malcolm X, Angela Davis, Steve Biko, Gandhi, Shaka, Nelson Mandela, Denmark Vessy, Tedros, Nat Turner or Sojourner Truth; but I will make it for you.' Their access to power enables this abnormal proposal to be a reality. Even though they lose a war in the actual battlefield, they reward themselves by the illusion of winning in cinema: the US loses the war in Vietnam, but it wins on the Hollywood screens. If they lose in the boxing ring to Muhammad Ali, they win on the screen, in the illusion of Hollywood cinema, by creating Rocky I, II, III, IV and V. So the Rockies and the Rambos, and their progenitors John Wayne and Audie Murphy, were created to compensate for their losses in reality. Movies continue to glorify old glories of erroneous history.

The power that makes them a dominant group is their capacity to define, create and legitimise a new dictionary. Third World people – politically, sociologically, psychologically – are immersed in and brainwashed by the dictionary of this 'ethnocentricity'. This is the level of racism daily confronted whenever the African in the diaspora or in Africa is not allowed to make his or her own history without the scrutiny and permission of Europe. Any issue that African Americans hold as precious could be made into a movie via a White film-maker. Black people are considered to be too reactionary and emotional, without the artistic integrity to tackle such subject-matter! This is the statement productions such as these make. So what happens is that they stifle the development of the artistic community within Black America, and they redefine history according to their personal perceptions.

Soliloquy of a film-maker
Without any formula or power of finance, you have completed one or two films. Those films have never brought in a revenue significant enough to recycle into the production of more films. They have been shown at many film festivals, community centres, most of the time at no charge. Much praise, many reviews and even awards have been received by these films. Presently, you have several scripts but in order to produce any one of them you roam the world in search of finance. You've been in several compromising and humiliating positions and slowly two personalities emerge from inside you, one real, one false.

The real self is always asking the false self to go in front in order to hide its true face. The real self observes and passes judgment over the false self. The false self, characteristically placed in the firing line, humbly fires off many false 'hellos' projecting the false, humble figure that quickly agrees and nods without challenging the typically stupid, ignorant, racist statements of people sitting in powerful positions. To them every film subject-matter is exhausted, except their own particular obsessions framed by their own immature concepts of reality. Meanwhile, the real self in you, hiding behind the false self, keeps secret the true content and objective of your project. At times, however, the real self is compelled to push aside the false self and emerges to expose your true colours. In the aftermath of such an outburst of honesty, during the never-ending street-walks, the false and real selves debate who was responsible for screwing up, only to be awakened from this tumultuous inner dialogue by a near-hit from a passing car.

All this struggle waged in the wrong territory. The real self asks, 'Where are the people I made the films for?' Well, they have seen your films for free, praised you, hugged you, cried and even written poetry inspired by your work. But powerless people cannot go beyond 'I like your film', and on another occasion 'I liked your film', and on another occasion 'What is your next film about, are you working on a new film?' Fade. Five years later the same people ask you 'What are you doing these days?' Thinking you've run out of topics, they're quick to offer ideas, from police brutality to science-fiction, unaware that all of this contributes to the further deterioration and loss of confidence of the film-maker. The real self continues to ask, 'And what of the critics who praised me, who could have played a major role in intensifying the contradictions that have prevented the making of new films, who could have publicised and exposed the problem, coming up with new answers to old questions?' And of course the answer is that they are continuing to praise films done ten to fifteen years ago. Like vultures, jumping and irrationally grabbing films that are miraculously completed, never getting themselves involved in the real problems of the recycling of films of the Black community.

When a piece of film drops like meat from the sky once in a blue moon everybody is thrown off base, including the audience; some are emotional and overly protective, while others respond by being irrational and too negative. The film-maker him- or herself (who may also be trying to be a family person) is subjected to such irrational feedback as, 'I think you should make a "real" film, a film that can be shown in real theatres and on real TV ...'

'And what about the community of film-makers?' asks the real self. Immersed in animosity and negative competitiveness, it is a back-biting community, targeting the existence of another film-maker as the source of his or her problem, overshadowing the systemic problem, thereby disrupting the creative process and destroying each other's support base.

Umbilical tie

Independent African American cinema is without foundation if organised outside of the African American community. It must be umbilically linked to the community from which it comes. Outside of its community it is dispersed, detested and feared. Therefore, it is powerless, a vagabond cinema.

There are organisations which have approached Hollywood producers to finance Black films. If I were a Hollywood producer, and my motive was to make money using the backdrops of my own White history, when a Black or a Native American walks into my office, their very physical presence would remind me of a history I do not want to remember. My main preoccupation would be to try to make money and perpetuate my own culture. On top of that, your request is too unrealistic, you are demanding that I put my own money into your history. It becomes a very surreal expectation, the classic case of a dependent people. Therefore, it becomes a futile struggle, not directed towards a resolution of the crisis.

Then what do you do? The alternative is to develop an independent cinema. But independent cinema doesn't mean that you ask the very system that denies you the tools and finances to make films against itself. This is a double standard. I think implicit in independent cinema is the idea that the very system that denies you also forces you to begin the germs and the seeds of personal, individual industry which will allow you to develop your own independent institutions.

If film culture is to develop within the African American community, then African American cinema must ground itself within the community it claims to come from. If you claim to be a representative or the by-product of the Black community, then you have to ask that community why it is not amassing all its capabilities behind you to make that motion picture project possible. Which means that there is a need for something along the lines of a community policy for cinema, whereby a community is involved in the making, distribution and exhibition of films. We need to make proposals, create organisations, initiate activities to respond to and tackle this problem, instead of marching into some Hollywood producer's home or office with unrealistic expectations. It is better to march in the Black community on Black people who have the resources and who need to be shown the importance of cultural nutrition for the future of their children. Wherever the African American community happens to congregate, it should be a place where marches take place, where people organise some kind of innovative and creative way of filling the gap created by the absence of relevant images and visual expressions from the Black community. To me, this is a very important dialogue. To mobilise an organisation that will respond to the very crisis of independent film-makers; to regroup and reorganise them in order to give them some anchor within the Black community.

One thing that we have to recognise is that over the years millions of tax dollars are given for artistic expression within the United States. African Americans and other Third World groups have to organise to address the sharing of this financial resource, as a means of developing a self-reliant and independent infrastructure in the long run. Of course, the problem with grant agencies as they now exist is that the preliminary grant examiners – the employees of the National Endowment of the Arts and the National Endowment for the Humanities, the Corporation for Public Broadcasting etc., which were created under a liberal charter to support alternative expression – nevertheless operate with mainstream grammar. Thus proposals are subjected to the same standards of aesthetic measurement – in terms of both content and form – by these so-called alternative institutions as they are by the mainstream industry. The struggle here is to have an input into the development of new criteria or a new grammar, and to put in place people who will understand the divergent points of independent film-makers.

While Hollywood produces by and large escapist spectacle, commercial and emotionally exploitative cinema, independent cinema, hopefully, produces a rational, pedagogical alternative that seeks to meet the particular needs of the community. Whatever the reason, there is a basic code, grammar and signature, signifying points of separation. Those points have to be understood so that the granting agencies do not operate with a predefined, demented grammar, a yardstick handed down from a very backward industry. Otherwise, one would better spend one's time waiting for a lottery, or knocking on the doors of Hollywood, than using the alternative institutions. The alternative institutions are, after all, supposed to be alternatives. Independent film-makers would better spend their time making sure these codes of measurement are changed in the so-called national cinema policy in America. People have to discuss, understand, and be clear why there is an independent cinema. It is not just because Hollywood would not let you in. Some people are outside because they choose to be outside. The funding agencies' lack of understanding of the aesthetic departure is the biggest tragedy of funding for independent cinema in the United States.

Independent cinema needs to invent and develop alternative forms of production, distribution and exhibition. In production, it is crucial to collaborate with a large sector of the community, in terms of economics and human resources. It is equally important to share skills and creativity and to create an information centre pertaining to innovative approaches to national and international co-production possibilities. This would include information about equipment and crew sources. This form of collaboration will result in a culture of low-budget productions in keeping with our reality. In distribution, there must be the encouragement of institutions and infrastructures that will assume collective distribution responsibilities. To maximise economic returns it is important that practical research concerning alternative distribution outlets is undertaken. It should be stressed that collective distribution minimises cost and maximises profit. In exhibition, we must introduce innovative outlets. It should be noted that presently established theatre owners, even those located within the African American community, have refused to show African American works. Since it is important to build an African American audience, it is critical that we devise creative ways of reaching this community. Those theatres located within the Black community must be confronted in an organised manner. If necessary, we should rent exhibition facilities, sharing the costs.

In order to promote most effectively our exhibitions, alternative ways of advertising must be devised. This can be realised even by simply standing on street corners and in churches distributing leaflets, displaying posters, etc. In order to build audiences we need to participate in community workshops, film festivals and panel discussions. We need to produce collective handbooks with information on national and international film festivals, identifying their advantages and disadvantages in terms of promotion and economic returns.

All societies learn to speak by learning the letters, learning how to accumulate them, to gather them, to spell, make words, make passages, make full essays and books, etc. A normal society allows these stages of development. The African American is expected to know how to make a perfect film without having made a film, while the Anglo-Saxon within America has grown from film to film, tolerantly received by the community, to evolve and become grandiose, spectacle film-makers. This stage-by-stage developmental process is denied to the African race in America, which makes one unable ever to learn how to spell in motion pictures. So that whenever by mere accident a film project does fall into the lap of an African American film-maker, he or she is under so much scrutiny and pressure that the film becomes a failure and the film-maker is proved to be a failure, because that film-maker has not progressed from film to film, step by step. You live or die by one project. It's almost like Russian roulette.

The mandate faced by Third World film-makers, for the sake of ourselves, our children and the reproduction of Third World film-makers, is with deliberate determination to do all that we can to create an environment in which we can speak on behalf of ourselves. We should fight tooth and nail to paint our own concepts of ourselves, our own vision, in the final analysis our own humanity, and be fully accountable for our failures and successes. We owe it to our ancestors, who left us monumental footprints, from the Nubian and Axum all the way to the Zimbabwean civilisations.

Three and a half million-year-old Dinknesh, our oldest known mother, will disown us if we stand by and let modern missionaries call her 'Lucy' and make a movie called 'Lucy'. She would curse with such strength that the earth would split open into the second phase of the Rift Valley, burying us without a trace. And if we are still alive, in the heart of the earth we would be tried by the oldest skeletons of humanity for the crime of neglect and betrayal of our history.

Black Cinema in the Post-aesthetic Era

Clyde Taylor

I think, therefore I am.
René Descartes

A person is a person only because of other people.
Xhosa proverb, a favourite of Archbishop Desmond Tutu

The situation of black people in the image hierarchy is framed by the ideological contours of representation, or what Michel Foucault calls 'power/knowledge'. The effectiveness of repressed people in the communications struggle, either as senders or receivers through systems influenced by this hierarchy, depends on their realisation of the obsolescence of the contest over the nature of truth beside the contest over the control of truth, and the irrelevance of 'beauty' beside the power to choose and name beauty.

From the beginning the question of aesthetics is always a non-dialogue between those who subscribe to the conditioned world order and those who stand to gain from a reconstructed forum. The first question must always be whether blacks are to be allowed a vision of themselves mediated through cinema technology and practices. The conditioned world order pressures discussion to table this imperative in favour of distracting arguments about 'art', 'the humanities', 'competence', 'marketability'. Even among their victims these ideological masks continue to appear in varied disguises.

Discussions about cinema and black people – whether they are portrayed accurately, which films are 'positive', how films made by blacks fare beside others – reproduce false consciousness until they are grounded in knowledge of how the overwhelming experience of African people with this apparatus of representation has been as a mechanism of domination. Dialogue about which film is better or more authentic than which may already be hopelessly entrenched within the favoured discourse of cultural imperialism. Its bias is already satisfied by the pragmatic concern with individual cases rather than with the network of relationships that makes social expressions possible or impossible, with advantageous use of genres rather than the service done to constituted authority by the fragmentation of perception through genre demands. The next stage in such a dialogue is picking a top ten, and the next, trivia contests. The magnetic direction of aesthetic discourse orients toward passive consumption, toward competitive, hierarchical recognition, acceptance and collection of what has been offered, and therefore toward the social system that has provided it.

Nietzsche's well-founded suspicion that the genealogy of moral categories roots back to their foundation in ancient class divisions between the aristocracy and the lower orders (as in the etymology of designations such as *noble* and *vulgar* or *villainous*) applies equally to the eighteenth-century invention of aesthetics and the service of many of its categories, if not its whole enterprise, to class and racial stratification. Nietzsche's genealogy reminds us that such formations of power/knowledge are not limited to the modern European middle class.[1] Yet the Greek root of *aesthetics* reflects the deliberate appropriation by the emergent dominating bourgeoisie of a past associable with classical beauty and aristocratic connections in which only the posture of barbarian and savage would be left for lower strata contemporaries.

The strict constructionist interpretation of aesthetics refers it to the pleasurable appeal to the senses. But to this orientation we must ask Teshome Gabriel's question: whose pleasure? Consideration of the sensory/organisational pleasure of the dominated is disallowed or devalued in aesthetic analysis. Are not the interpretations of the dominated debased by animalised sensitivity, bruised with rage, discoloured by pain and protest, and thereby rendered unrepresentative? The normative ideal subject of the aesthetics shaped by its creators in neo-classical Europe would be the bourgeois gentleman in good health. From the very beginning, the concept was historically determined and class-bound.

Post-Cartesian aesthetics is a late humanist system taken over by the bourgeoisie from aristocratic beginnings for the control of knowledge, specifically of the 'beautiful'. As such, it is a 'key instance in the formation of the bourgeois subject and in the constitution of subject positions from which first world domination is effected and reproduced.'[2] The central mental operation of aesthetics became the objectification of sense experience through the bracketing of an aesthetic attitude, disposition, experience, gaze. Increasingly, as in its Kantian formulation, the aesthetic experience is distinguished by its disinterestedness, its purity from contamination by moral and political considerations. It is in this definitive claim as value-free, trans-ideological, universally applicable cognitive knowledge that the discourse of aesthetics is being exposed as a product of ideology.[3]

The evolution of several post-60s discourses has created the conditions for a decisive interrogation of aesthetics and an exposure of its factitiousness. The sociology of knowledge and of art, neo-Marxist reconsiderations of ideology, symbolic anthropology, Foucauldian archaeology, post-structuralism, the challenge to formalism from hermeneutic modes of critical interpretation, feminism and the Black Aesthetic have each in their turn eroded and exposed the shaky foundations of this pseudo-science of the beautiful. It remains to continue the critique that each has organised, recognising what few of them have acknowledged, that aesthetics as a system is obsolescent and bankrupt.

The self-ascribed capacity for aesthetic appreciation, placing a priority on form over function, is, as Bourdieu notes in his compendious analysis,[4] a disposition affordable by those individuals who have lifted themselves above the imperatives of necessity and survival – indeed is celebrated as a sign of that deliverance. The aesthetic disposition functions as a base for the concoction and appreciation of countless social distinctions between the haves and the have-nots (or the have-less) through what Baudrillard calls a 'political economy of signs'. Grounded in this base is the mechanically reproduced, normative superiority of bourgeois knowledge, experience and practice.

From its beginnings, the pseudo-science of aesthetics played a major role in the concordance between Western organisation of knowledge and visually centred racism. In a period when the concept of art and artist had not been separated from notions of scholarship, knowledge and science, visual artists such as Petrus Camper and Johann Lavater invented racially based schemes of physiognomy that were incorporated into the developing science of natural history.[5] In classical thought of the 18th century, in which aesthetics played a contributing role, natural history, elaborating the theory of the great chain of being, sought to establish a knowledge-grid that left no gaps or spaces unaccounted for. In this system, black became the no-colour, the absence of colour that established the presence of all other hues. Concordantly, for many, African people occupied the place of the otherwise missing link in the great chain of continuity from God and man at the top down to the animal kingdom. What is remarkable about this system of knowledge in the present context is the regularity with which aesthetic attitudes and ascriptions were incorporated among other data by which the 'races' of mankind were catalogued and classified. So that when avowedly racist theorisers like Gobineau introduced aesthetic criteria of racial designation – in which blacks were inscribed by characteristics of ugliness, malformation, moral degeneration synonymous with

92

chaos, etc. – they seemed to make explicit judgments that were implicitly accommodated by the extensive practice of racial classification and stratification. The kind of visual stereotyping that frequently takes place between endogamous and exogamous communities in many societal settings was systematised and codified in Europe by the 'scientific' establishment. Thus was mounted the condition of impossibility for black beauty and creativity.

Looking at the paradox of the Enlightenment producing modern, 'scientific' racism, Richard Popkin comes to perceptions similar to that of Cornell West, that 'authority of science, undergirded by a modern philosophical discourse guided by Greek ocular metaphors and Cartesian notions, promotes and encourages the activities of observing, comparing, measuring, and ordering the physical characteristics of human bodies.'[6] For West, these mental postures, companions to a 'normative gaze' hypothetically reconstructed from classical antiquity, 'secrete' notions of white supremacy that became conventional in Western racism. The commonness of the idea of white (over black) supremacy in core Western philosophical discourse is confirmed in utterances of Locke, Berkeley, Hume, Montesquieu, Voltaire, Franklin, Jefferson, Kant, Buffon, Hegel and Linnaeus. The normative, neoclassical gaze of eighteenth-century aesthetics, adjoined to this practice of observing, comparing, measuring and ordering, supported such nineteenth-century 'sciences' as phrenology, craniology, Lombroso's 'psychological' classification of 'criminal' types, crypto-Darwinism and social Darwinism; isolated blacks, Jews and the working classes as forms of 'degeneracy'; and led to the rationales for the 'final solution' in this century.[7]

The scramble of power/knowledge has determined several modifications of the concept of aesthetics, many of them devised to protect the interests of increasingly marginalised Western artists. But by a remarkable demonstration of the persistence of cultural vision, within all of these transformations, the possibilities of the aesthetic pleasure and judgment of the dominated have remained in internment, as Foucault might say. Romanticism, symbolism, modernism, post-modernism: as aesthetic movements or bodies of theory and criticism, in none of them is there a role for the non-Western Other except as occasional exotic object. 'Why Have There Been No Great Women Artists?'[8] To this question, which in the light of the history of aesthetics is almost self-answering, we might add another paradox. How is it that under the administration of aesthetics, while its laws are taken as being universally applicable, its discourse has reflected the influence of not one non-Western thinker, nor has there arisen within its parameters or in popular imagination a single great or even pivotal non-Western artist (as opposed to performer)?

What more evidence do we need before seeing the concept of aesthetics as irremediable? In a productive gesture of resistance, Afro-American artists and critics in the late 1960s (myself among them) sought to overturn a long history of misrepresentation under the Eurocentric ideology of aesthetics by creating a 'black aesthetic'. The new designation was a short cut which also led the way to many still fertile and valid perceptions. Some noted the saturation of language with associations from a racist cosmology – black sheep, black Friday, black as sin, dark ages, etc. – and some attempted a Manichean upheaval with inverse coinages like 'white-balled' and 'white-listed'. The black aesthetic, through such quick reversals, betrayed some abdication of the tasks of reconstruction, as though merely filling old categories with new content were enough.

The rejection of aesthetics opens the way for new, liberative critical principles, which criterionise the revelation and advancement of the human. The creation of a new science of the human would rejoin the idea of creativity with the holistic apprehension of life that the dichotomising aesthetic category alienated along class-serving, fraudulently humanist lines. But the project of reconstruction must face the challenge of self-transforming, continually reviving Eurocentrisms, as in deliberations about 'post-humanism'. As post-structuralism decentres the human subject, and along with it the humanism based on individualism, some questions need to be asked from other quarters. Is it humanism that is bankrupt and exhausted, or merely Euro-American humanism? Might not grounds be found for other, non-Western humanising principles in the Xhosa proverb cited as epigraph, the antithetical and corrective answer to Descartes' *cogito*? In place of a black cinema aesthetic, the appropriate goal would be a cinema in which a revitalised struggle for human creativity can take place.

II

The plausibility of such a redirection gains credence from the formulations of Sylvia Wynter toward the construction of a new science of the human.[9] In her analysis, contemporary society is characterised as passing through a crisis of knowledge, demanding for its solution a radical rewriting of historical experience. One of the principal signs of this crisis is the recognition of a transitional action among the overload of contradictions, in Hans Blumberg's terms a 'phase of Objectification'. This is a historical moment in which events and their functioning spin out of the control of human motivation and purpose and a kind of new authoritarianism is introduced to reassert control. The Middle Ages produced one phase of objectification accompanied by a theological Absolutism; in the current crisis, the Absolutism is furnished by technological rationality.

That earlier crisis was negotiated through the construction of Renaissance humanism and its heretical elaboration of a new knowledge. A key role in this reconstructed new knowledge was played by Rhetoric, out of which was shaped an act of symbolic self-representation. A new human Self, self-imaging, self-troping, 'came to function as the Final/Formal cause which determined behaviour for the human, as the mode of genetic speciation had determined behaviours for other biological organisms'. What happens with these rhetorical-figurative systems of group-bonding and self-definition is central in Wynter's reading of history. Among the essential phenomena here are the replacing of biological inheritance with cultural inheritance and the employment by group systems of a Same/Difference methodology of identification/exclusion, or boundary maintenance, in which some other group necessarily figured as corresponding chaos to identifying order.

The oppositional structural codes of Same/Difference that operate to motivate behaviour in all societies around different Life/Death criteria are further reflected as Culture/Safety vs Nature/Danger. In the medieval period, the Order/Chaos opposition came to figure as celestial/earthly and as Divine Man/Natural Man. The rewriting of knowledge subversively accomplished by Humanism overturned this last pair of oppositions, moving the ordering system of recognitions from religio-aesthetic modes into the 'new profane narrative representations that we have come to call "literature".'[10]

A controlling manoeuvre of Renaissance Humanism was the projection of the new European man as man-in-general; his reasoning process was portrayed as being isomorphic with reason-in-general. And in the new power orientation of knowledge a governing discrimination of Same/Difference sought to privilege reason-in-general against alternative modes of reasoning. Hence followed a sequence of what Foucault called 'internments', such as the isolation of 'the Mad', or, adds Wynter, of New World peoples in encomienda systems, followed by the general internment of African peoples.

As she observes the framing of a new structural bond between self-imaged Self and its necessary Other during this new 'regime of truth' where European ratiomorphic behaviour was established as normative, Wynter arrives at the juncture where Popkin, West and Mosse also note the confluence of Western aesthetics and European racism. The effort to authorise the Aryan or Indo-European as isomorphic with Being itself demanded a bio-ontological principle that refused to perceive blacks except as 'the Ultimate Chaos'. This fundamental error is symptomatic of the distortive, anti-humanistic behaviour arising out of the 'ratiomorphic apparatus', and resulting in the massacres of the colonial era and the genocides of Auschwitz, the Gulag, and Cambodia.

The contemporary crisis of knowledge was advanced during the appearance of revolt on university campuses in demand of Black studies. Perhaps more revealing than the revolt was its reward in the form of 'the proscription of the financially starved Black Cultural Center, always a whitewashed rotting house to be reached by a scramble up a muddy bank, mainly always on the nether edge of campus' (Wynter, p. 40). Within the drama of metaphors Wynter re-enacts at this point, what is decisive is the recognition by the recipients of this gift of the regularities involved in the response to their presence. Among these regularities was the familiar employment of the out-group as the markers of the boundary-keeping system. We should recognise again the persistence amid reform in the new situation which nevertheless managed to maintain 'American fiction' courses that included Hemingway, Hawthorne and Fitzgerald, but implicitly excluded Hurston, Richard Wright and Ralph Ellison.

The new studies, which were soon to include Chicanos, Women, Asian Americans, and to be signally illuminated by Said's *Orientalism*, at first expressed the Jester's heresy, parallel to that of the Renaissance Humanists. Wynter notes that 'because of our non-consciousness of the real dimensions of what we were about, we asked at first only to be incorporated into the normative order of the present organisation of knowledge, as add-ons, so to speak. We became entrapped, as a result, in Bantustan enclaves labelled "ethnic" and "gender" and/or "minority studies".' The self-definition of 'the black aesthetic', I might add, demonstrates a similar add-on entrapment: when what was newly made possible and necessary was another heretical rewriting of knowledge, 'a science of human systems'.

Wynter's arguments constitute a forceful historical allegory. In the similitude between the period when Euro-humanism extricated itself from the medieval world-view and the insoluble crush of present-day knowledges lies an explanatory power that convenes and entertains troublesome contradictions and mobilises scattered resurgences. Among the most promising options for rewriting human experience made possible by this historical trope, I would argue, are those which focus on the dogmas of Euro-humanist aesthetics as a repressive, secular theology that must be rejected and replaced, much as emergent humanism arose to displace and transform the socio-religious energies of the European Middle Ages.

III

The present crisis of knowledge, of competing inscriptions of the human, is reflected on a lower level in the crisis of aesthetics and its increasingly problematical legitimation, and more concretely still in the chasm between over-developed cinema's portrayal of black people and their portrayal in black cinema. The birth of black cinema takes place in the context of the struggle between a dying concept of the human and an emerging one. If black cinema is to evolve as a significant player in this critical historical juncture, it will do so through predications outside 'aesthetics', rewriting its version of humanity while passing through a hypothetical zero aesthetic point.

The crisis, then, has created the conditions of possibility for a post-aesthetic perspective from which repressed dimensions of the human can be recovered. The appropriate first response of this perspective is to direct towards the Western patriarchal effort to colonise human creativity a vigorous nihilism in the overly maligned original sense of that revolutionary notion. ('Here is the ultimatum of our camp: what can be smashed should be smashed; what will stand the blow is good; what will fly into smithereens is rubbish; at any rate, hit out right and left – there will and can be no harm from it.')[11]

Yet it would be self-defeating to attempt to dismiss a concept of mythic proportions already deeply ensconced in institutionalised practice and powerfully exerting its influence in systems of domination. The post-aesthetic perspective requires a re-examination of the 'something' that aesthetics unquestionably points to, though doubtless misnaming, misclassifying and misappropriating its substance. What is dictated is a return of the repressed in the form of a broad, unclassified, unspecified category such as human creativity. Thereafter there is possible a consideration of the various redistributions of creative energies in formulations that run at variance with the canons of aesthetic discourse. Jacques Maquet, whose anthropological groundings nevertheless leave him unable to escape the confines of Western aesthetics, speaks of creativity (aesthetics) as having different loci in different societies: thus, bullfighting in Spain, the tea ceremony in Japan, the Christian ritual in medieval Europe. His analysis does not carry him to the point where it becomes clear that the cultural specificity of these forms defeats the search for universal aesthetic principles.[12] But it does go far enough to remind us that creativity is differently located, perceived and valued in varying cultural situations.[13] Post-aesthetics begins with the recognition that the articulation of this wide range of activity as transcribed within the discourse of 'aesthetics' is a primitive foreshortening of human potentiality within the perspective not merely of Western culture at a particular historical pass, but of one class in Western society.

Hence post-aesthetics recognises the local validity of 'pre-aesthetic' creativity, as being at least no more restricted or culture-bound than the 'art' subsequently made under the aesthetic banner. By contrast with creative activity followed outside aesthetic cognition, post-aesthetic perspective must cope with the self-conscious burden of extricating itself from the hegemonic influence of aesthetic discourse. Yet this obligation also provides a necessary opportunity. Since aesthetics as an oppressive ideology demands continual analysis and scrutiny, this analysis may provide materials for a deconstruction that will in turn prepare the reconstruction of post-aesthetic strategies in a dying regime of aesthetic 'truth'.

The primary determinants of the Western aesthetic project are questions of beauty, transcendence, order, perception/reception, the creative principle, principles of criticism, values, authorship (genius), taste, and historical definitions. To examine one of these determinants – order – may be instructive. Nicos Hadjinicolaou, a Marxist theorist, points out 'different spheres or forms of the ideological level: for example, the moral, legal, political, religious, economic, philosophical and aesthetic spheres. The process by which one sphere dominates the others is extremely complex.'[14] Despite this complexity, it is plain to see the role of aesthetics in uniting, rationalising, legitimating, that is, bringing order to these other levels. In the following passage from *The Wretched of the Earth*, Fanon invokes several of these levels and dramatises the role of aesthetics in harmonising them.

> In capitalist societies the educational system, whether lay or clerical, the structure of moral reflexes handed down from father to son, the exemplary honesty of workers who are given a medal after fifty years of good and loyal service, and the affection which springs from harmonious relations and good behaviour – all these aesthetic expressions of respect for the established order serve to create around the exploited person an atmosphere of submission and of inhibition which lightens the task of policing considerably. (p. 31)

Since Fanon's day, technology has rapidly accelerated the aestheticisation of everyday life, leaving the Western citizen of consumption stunned by what DeBord calls 'the society of the spectacle'[15] and what Baudrillard perceives as simulacra boosted into hyper-reality. Fanon goes on to assert that 'when the native hears a speech about Western culture he pulls out his knife – or at least he makes sure it is within reach'. But does he do so when he sees a moped or a portable tape-recorder?

On this plane, the aestheticisation of everyday life, the regularising role of aesthetics as a form of power/knowledge is presented in its most formidable guise. The magnitude of its challenge suggests postpone-ment of a full-scale examination. Appropriate here, however, is the notation that of all the spheres of ideological regulation, the disruption of the aesthetic sphere offers the least material or social disorganisation in the lives of those who would alter the system.

Further, since over-developed cinema is completely embedded in this aestheticisation of daily experience, the post-aesthetic perspective must recognise the futility of challenging the one without challenging the other. The implications of a post-aesthetic analysis suggest that this doubled resistance must become more refined than the inclusion of a few anecdotal references and metaphors thrown at the larger context in the course of resisting the sensory domination of capitalist cinema. In programmatic terms, such a course implies ignoring the artificial, academic separation of film studies from media studies and cultural studies.[16]

From a non-Western standpoint, the post-aesthetic prospect inevi-tably interrogates and rewrites the genre boundaries established by aesthetic discourse. If the category 'art' is mythical, then it must stand that its subcategories are also mythical, and, further, erected through power/knowledge to subdivide and patrol the possibilities of human creativity in encampments beneficial to institutionalised order and in a way that discourages rebellious creative alliances. On the sociological level, the function of genres in legitimating professionalisation and specialisation is reinforced by, and in turn reinforces, the action of genres as abstract ideology.

Except for a few professionalised beneficiaries, the maintenance of the present system of genres, itself a formalistic elaboration of mythic aesthetic 'knowledge', serves only as an obstacle to the creative empow-erment of developing Third World people. To glance at a more pressing instance, the differences in the modes of production of literature and cinema, and the complex needs to preserve the boundaries between these two forms of creativity in the West, carry far less weight in the black world. From the logic of its own development, the appropriate strategy in the black world is to perceive cinema as another, newer literature. Just as, from the logic of Western cultural evolution, it was appropriate to incorporate an equally divergent form, drama, as literature.

Yet another area of productive interrogation is the relation between aesthetics and history, particularly their co-development and eventual fusion in aesthetic historicism. This formulation awaited the subjectivi-sation of history, the construction of the Cartesian subject almost simultaneously with the invention of history and aesthetics. The out-come of these cultural innovations was the aestheticisation of history and the historicisation of aesthetics.

The foundation of aesthetics and historiography were both for-warded through the 17th-century debate of 'the Ancients and the Moderns'. In the 18th century, following Winckelman's rediscovery of the archetypal sources of beauty in ancient Greek example, an immense interest in archaeology and antiquarianism focused on the classical world more concretely furthered the incipient historical discipline. Thereafter, it no longer became possible to perceive an era of human experience as grotesque and backward so long as that era could make some claim to historical continuity with the formation of the revered subjectivity of Western consciousness.

The hothouse environment of aesthetics accounts for the increasing self-referentiality of Western art and literature. The manner in which works refer less to nature or to social reality and more to other works and their traditions can be taken as a sign of a crisis of legitimation. Aesthetics has always functioned as a language into which the given work is encoded. Pierre Bourdieu develops a portrait of this code as a system of cultural inheritance which legitimates its possessors and delegitimates the dispossessed.[17] This self-referential code of 'cultural nobility' and its reliance on a pedigree of historical continuity is such that one cannot speak of aesthetics without considerable knowledge of Western art traditions and their theoretical support systems. No indi-vidual – however creative, I might add – can pretend to hope for acceptance into this cultural nobility lacking this proficiently demon-strated canonical knowledge. Given the class-paternalism of advanced capitalism and the Eurocentrism and xenophobia of the Western cul-tural directorate, recent acceleration in self-referentiality may reflect no more than the frantic display of cultural credentials at a time when the exposure of their arbitrary value is immanent.

The ensuing development of aesthetic discourse incorporated the historicism it had helped to invent by establishing causal connections between aesthetic styles and historical periods. The first aestheticians were unavoidably neo-classicists, who presented themselves as updat-ing the 'aesthetic' principles and practice of the paragonal model of human creativity among the ancient Greeks and Romans. What is remarkable if not scandalous is the subsequent impossibility of escape for those Western elites who came to contest the contours of this paradigm but who were ideologically incapable of questioning its grounds.

If the battle between Ancients and Moderns was the first of Western-rooted 'style wars', that waged by the romantics against the neo-classicists was the first of many over the terrain claimed by the fiction of aesthetics by several camps of Western bourgeois artists, who in their ideological paralysis have been inoculated against transgressions out-side its parameters.

100

Hence aesthetics-based history proceeds through canonical art movements wherein romanticism is followed by the aesthetes of art-for-art's sake, followed by Impressionism to Symbolism and thereafter by Modernism, with its tributaries of Expressionism, Cubism, Surrealism, etc., right into post-modernism. These movements are best understood as ideological rationales of competing Western male elites for preference in the competition to colonise creativity and corner the art market.

The strange career of aesthetics has no more paradoxical chapter than that contributed by one of its Western elite contestants, the Marxist version. Marxist materialist analysis enables some of its proponents to unmask the ideological composition of aesthetics. Almost invariably, however, the Marxist discourse on aesthetics turns toward *correcting* or reforming the concept, to solving its 'problems' from a Marxist viewpoint. Marx, Engels, Lenin, Trotsky and second-ranked figures such as Lukács, Adorno, Marcuse, among many others, allow themselves to get stuck to the aesthetic tarbaby, unable to concede that this is one baby that can conscionably be thrown out with the bathwater.[18] On the question of human creativity and the non-question of 'art', Marxist materialist philosophy falls unabashedly into idealism and essentialism. Moreover, their searches after the essentiality or specificity of art – the Western philosopher's Eldorado – usually end up canonising an anti-popular notion of art reflected in classical bourgeois forms of earlier periods. There lies an instructive warning in this strange history: that these first-world intellectuals were able to manage courageous betrayals of their class in every ideological arena except the aesthetic. A more useful implication, however, is the reminder of the placement of aesthetics at a nexus of capitalist ideology *and* Western (bourgeois) culture.

Marxism offers fertile ground for the reinterpretation of Western art ideologies. But post-aesthetics finds similarly attractive prospects of reinterpretation in one of the style periods of aesthetic history, modernism. Modernism distinguishes itself as the only one of these historical art paradigms that appoints itself, in name and significance, as commensurate with its general historical era, co-equal to its developments in science, technology, economics, politics. The disproportionate ambitiousness of 'modernism', as the cultural-creative situation and solution of an alienated segment of European patriarchy to represent itself as prototype of global experience, recommends that the whole concept of modernity be rejected and rewritten.

From the vantage-point of those who have been the object of modern history and not its subject, the most salient development of the modern era lies in the movement of subjugated peoples away from systems of domination as that movement has been influenced by an industrialising social order and by Western ideological constructs and doctrines (democracy, socialism, communism, etc.) designed to articulate with that order. Modernism, then, reflects a search, worldwide in scope, for democratisation of a social experience within the (relative) control of industrially disempowered groups.[19]

The task here is not to replenish that history, which is a labour already begun with the recent invigoration of popular history,[20] but merely to characterise the means of its existence. For subordinated peoples, the modern era prescribes the removal of populations from the oppressive aspects of feudalism, theocracy and similar regimes. At the same time, the major world development of that era has been the colonisation and subordination of the majority world population by Europe, and the resistance, internal and external, to that subordination. Hence the familiar paradox that the same source of the most crucial domination has also provided, through advanced systems of communication technologies and the example of domestic Eurocentric liberative doctrines, the provocations of the (revised) modernising project.

But while this other modern history takes its incitement from developments in the West, and evolves internally in the West as well as beyond, it nevertheless differs radically from official Western historiography in which 'backward' or 'primitive' peoples, including women and European peasants, experience 'modernisation' and 'civilisation' to the extent that they assimilate the cultural perceptions of Euromodernism. The rhetorical awkwardness of addressing two modernisms – one hierarchical, hegemonic and controlled by the Western bourgeoisie, the other demotic and global – accurately reflects the interpretive challenge of perceiving the simultaneous and interacting development of these two courses of history, magnified by the appropriation of 'knowledge' by the one while the other shapes itself in an epistemological underground.

Programmatically, popular modernism finds its origins spontaneously with the first resistances of traditional cultures to capital-organised industrialisation and imperialism.[21] Hereafter, the corporate experience of such coerced communities enters the modern era; for as in officially sanctioned modernity, the term both merely denotes an era comprehensively by its pivotal features and connotes a valorisation of its most progressive developments; namely, in the instance of popular modernism, the emancipatory. The character of events and movements within the popular modern period are multifold, subject to ideological fragmentation, continuous debate, dialogue and reinterpretation and tormented by regressions into fascism, theocracy, messianism, chosen-people racialism.

The beginnings of this era may be left to the debate of historians. But for black people in the New World, the Haitian Revolution obviously signifies a momentous instance in the arrival of Afro-modernism. In the

102

Afro-modernist humanism of Ousmane Sembene, such resistances are artistic-creative-cultural acts, for 'Man is the symbol of art.... What would be the value of all the arts of the Universe, if the Universe were void of human existence?'[22] Neglecting even a brief sketch of the reinscribed modern era, certain orienting contours emerge as seen glancing back from the perspective of contemporary decolonisation.

Decolonisation represents a heightened consciousness within the Afrocentric modernising process. We might note as one recent marker of that consciousness Chinweizu's *The West and the Rest of Us*, in which the two versions of modern history are contested; and, on a more strictly cultural plane, Ngugi wa Thiongo's *Decolonising the Mind*. Seen as 'the absolute quest for independence; the recuperation of one's cultural patrimony', including the recovery of history, the re-examination of popular culture and a sharpened critique of Western power/knowledge, accretions of decolonisation are landmarked retrospectively in the writings of Fanon, in Negritude, in the Harlem Renaissance, in the thought and writing of Carter G. Woodson, Marcus Garvey, C.L.R. James, W.E.B. DuBois and Edward Blyden.

These arbitrary notations must be supplemented by another series that includes June Jordan's essays *Civil Wars* and *On Call*; Angela Davis' *Women, Race and Class*; the novels of Buchi Emecheta, Toni Morrison and Alice Walker; the writings of Lorraine Hansberry, Margaret Walker, Amy Jacques Garvey, Ida B. Wells, Anna Julia Cooper, Harriet Jacobs and others. For decolonisation theory is malformed if it excludes the complementary labours to de-patriarchalise consciousness.

The break with Euro-modernist power/knowledge simultaneously propels a release from its strictures of authorised expertise and professionalisation, recognising them as agencies of dominant discourse, gatekeeping mechanisms of approved 'knowledges'. Afro-modernist cultural discourse refuses the confinement to detailed study within the established, Eurocentric narrative of human culture and inaugurates the reconstruction of its own. It averts the prohibitions against illegitimate, reboundarised knowledge-paradigms such as Pan-Africanism and the Third World. It quarantines black cultural productions misdirected by the attraction of Western 'great traditions'.

The reconstruction of modernism requires no elaboration of formalising characteristics comparable to the antagonism to traditional forms, dissonance, rejection of photographic realism, by which museum/library modernism is recognised. For emergent popular creativity, the imperative of these formal innovations is mooted: antagonism is cultivated selectively to forms traditional in hegemonic 'art' but not to those of the popular modern community. For related reasons, reconstructed modernism proceeds without the necessity of an 'aesthetic' history, a grid of art movements, a grammar of styles. The founding perceptions of underground modernity, that man is culture, as Sembene asserts, and that creativity is a part of its historic character, embrace without rigorous classification expression as diverse as ex-slave narratives, documentary films, Calypso, critical essays, graffiti, autobiographies.

The arrival of the post-aesthetic era offers the possibility of a reconditioned understanding of these expressions and of black cinema; for post-aesthetics tends to evaporate innocent collaboration with Western aesthetic goals. The post-aesthetic era finds historical antecedents in the Black Aesthetic of the 1960s and 70s, negritude, the Negro Renaissance in the United States, parallel movements in the Caribbean, ultimately to a conjectural point in group self-consciousness when culture was first perceived as a major battleground. This moment may represent a significant caesura in Afro-modernism, since the roots of decolonisation theory may be traced to the same juncture, possibly in the 1880s and 90s, a period when a markable reorientation was attempted in Africa and the diaspora through a movement called Ethiopianism.[23] We can see cultural redefinition asserting itself in Ethiopianism, a movement for an independent Black Christianity, reflected in the slogan 'God is Black'.

If cultural and ideological decolonisation is a specific phase within the larger development of Afro-modernism, itself one dimension of popular modernism globally, then post-aesthetics is locatable as a more recent initiative within decolonisation (and within popular modernism) focused on issues relating to the new humanism and reperceived human creativity. To Richard Wright falls the distinction (until further research proves otherwise) of first articulating and executing a post-aesthetic strategy. Realising that his first volume of fiction produced tears from his readers, he swore that the next book he wrote 'no banker's daughter would weep over'.[24] By choosing for his rhetorical trope a *banker*'s daughter, Wright specifically targets the bourgeoisie, and by forestalling tears he deliberately diverts a typical religio-sentimental response from 'the aesthetic disposition' cultivated by that class. In the text of *Native Son*, moreover, Wright persistently refuses his reader the sympathetic identification with his hero made commonplace in the *bildungsroman*. At its end, he checks altogether the cathartic release that might allow the absorption of the work as an 'aesthetic experience' and impede its reintegration with social reality.

As in the adaptive epistemology of Afro-modernism, post-aesthetics postulates no stringent dogmatics. The most repressive features of aesthetics have been its *a priori* rules for beauty and creativity, producing stifling forms of traditionalism, the academy and its lists of creative desiderata (which have unfortunately been recycled in some Black

Aesthetic theorising). Since post-aesthetic initiative is directed to the creative and the liberative, it must be at liberty to express itself before it is evaluated. Moreover, to impose critical tenets – endlessly verbalising the role of the artist, for instance – short-circuits the dialogic evolution of emancipatory, post-aesthetic process at a time when traditional aesthetic concepts such as the author, the unity of the text, the neutrality of narrative and genre forms are promisingly falling apart under deconstruction.

The avoidance of dogmatics does not mean that post-aesthetics seeks anarchic escape from theory, creative self-direction or considerations of formal presentation. Though Wright's novel and other anti- or post-aesthetic work like Haile Gerima's film *Child of Resistance*, Alice Walker's novel *The Color Purple* or Sembene's films may call up in the mind a hypothetical point of 'zero degree aesthetics', the implausibility and irrelevance of reaching that point is soon apparent. A creative strategy is unavoidably present in a humanly intentioned utterance, observable in *Native Son*'s parody of the popular detective novel genre, for instance, or Sembene's references to griotology. A developmental-critical function is available to post-aesthetics in the tri-part dialogue diagnosed by Haile Gerima among film-maker/storyteller, audience/community and activist/critic. In its early formation, a fertile pre-aesthetic expression like jazz managed to find its critical path to creative criteria through the informal operation of a very similar dialogue.

The conditions of possibility out of which post-aesthetics arises makes valid a reperception of four fundamental postures towards aesthetics as reflected in the Afro-American tradition. These are assimilationist: popular syncretism (as in the blues), where a highly selective adaptation of Western creative precedents is used for ends productive of meanings outside the typical Western 'aesthetic experience'; the ironic, in which Western aesthetics is followed instrumentally but with reservations about its values, or possibly to attack it (Toni Morrison's *The Bluest Eye*; Julie Dash's film *Illusions*; dimensions of Ralph Ellison's *Invisible Man*); or post-aesthetic.

Post-aesthetics implies a conscious realisation of the need to orchestrate one's efforts against cultural imperialism and bourgeois cultural elitism, and therefore against the rationales for these ideological agencies embedded in aesthetics. As it moves into the post-aesthetic era, the creative direction of black cinema, already alert to the dangers of cultural imperialism and dominative elitism, may increasingly avert the seductions of aesthetics in favour of liberative strategies. What these strategies will be can be expected to emerge organically out of the dialogue between theory and practice within the tri-part dynamic just mentioned. Of the many directions possible, however, one appears at this point to recommend itself for privileged attention.

105

Post-aesthetic creative/critical strategies that claim pre-eminence are homologous with the conscious historical development of the liberationist ideologies that give rise to goals beyond aestheticism. In the instance of black cinema, these would be Afro-modernism, popular modernism and gender liberation. These creative/critical practices would prove to be symmetrical with the most promising modes of decolonising thought.

I would argue at this point that this pre-eminent creative/critical principle would be the dialogic mode of discourse. The created text would, given appropriate mediations, reflect the dialogic disposition that mobilises decolonisation theory. The semic references within the text would be intertextual with the social discourse of mental decolonisation. Such a text might articulate an internal heteroglossia; it might elude the mono-glossic identification with a single heroic representative, instead coding its rhetoric to the understanding of the observer viewed as a seeker/sharer in community with local cultural groups in the concrete instance, extending to the range of self-democratising populations. In such a hero-less narrative, the protagonistic centre is the social process dramatically revealed through the internal hermeneutics of the work, not the emotive charge and individualistic gratification of hero-identification.

In place of a schematisation of the possibilities of dialogic discourse, we might note some of these possibilities as imaginatively distributed in a black cinemawork that carries post-aesthetic and dialogic strategy to a high point of sophistication, Ousmane Sembene's film *Ceddo*.[25] Its narrative opens in a vaguely nineteenth-century Western Sudan community at a crucial, synecdochic moment of imperialist-Afro-modernist history. The 'ceddo', the despised common people outside the faith, have risen in desperate revolt by kidnapping the Princess. Thereafter, the multiple sectors of political interest are stirred into action around this crisis. These include the traditionalist royalty and one of its noble sons who claims the Princess' 'hand' as a legitimisation of his claim to the throne. Another, Islamised young noble claims the Princess as a leader of the new faith. Both these claims are rejected by the Imam, who seizes this critical moment to institute a new, repressive Islamic regime and law that invalidates the legitimacy of the traditionalist royalty and the claims to independence of the ceddo. In the margins of this struggle, awaiting its crumbs, a European slaver and a Christian missionary manoeuvre for advantageous position.

Ceddo moves in a post-aesthetic and dialogic zone of creativity by problematising a conflict that rejects simple, dualistic dialectics for a perception of social interaction as a simultaneous struggle among many competing sources of domination that refuse to coalesce into a neat binary opposition, involving plural religions, politics, class, gender and culture. The potential for mechanical allegory is averted by a hetero-glossic exchange among these competing allegiances and the transfor-mations undertaken by the character-representatives who position themselves among these various interests. The film not only establishes a multiplicity of ideological voices (not equally weighted, to be sure) but also a compounding of internal voicings, as in the non-linear, momen-tary (and unstable) confluence of the Princess as at once the triumphant salvation of the traditionalist regime and partisan of the independent-minded ceddo.

Not only is this a hero-less drama, it is also an open narrative, not merely in its refusal of closure at the end, but in the 'open' spaces within the narrative left for the participatory reflection of the viewer. The film is unashamedly partisan in its coding for the self-liberating observer – importantly signalled by the use of a non-canonical speech-language, ancient Wolof, as well as by the cultural identification implied in the music. But this spectator has many spaces left from which to examine the contradictions and extrapolate diverse personally heightened mean-ings. Beneath its surface eventualities lie embedded multiple texts for the viewer's continual re-integration.

Equally important is *Ceddo*'s progressive sense of history, using its setting in the past to embody the understanding that personal/political reality is the result of combined historical articulations. The film refuses the closed historical linearity of commercial film pageants, whose fugitive lessons reflect on a fossilised 'human nature', for a referentiality of contemporary actuality. In one of its violations of historical linearity – the flash forward of the priest's self-exalting reverie – Sembene invokes Western religious-aesthetic disposition only to satirise it. In another – the use of a propulsive jazz score at the climactic moment – this anachronistic intervention serves to underscore the narrative's multiple homologies between the colonised past and the present. The final freeze frame of the Princess walking towards and beyond the viewer not only punctuates the narrative's (history's) openness but allows the viewer to reconsider this instance of the threshold of African modernity.

Among the post-aesthetic strategies of *Ceddo* is the avoidance of anaesthetising music. In its exception to Sembene's well-known suspi-cion of Western film scores, *Ceddo* introduces music as an open, conscious dramatic effect, not as a subliminal caress. Characteristically, Sembene also avoids the folkloric, for him a mode polluted by Western stereotypical precedents and by anthropologism; hence, no dances, no hands beating drums, no colourful rituals. Sembene also uses a minima-lised physical setting lest anything more elaborate might invoke the phony pagan spectacle dear to Eurocentric movies. At the same time this minimalised setting refuses the social distancing of aestheticised historical spectacle. *Ceddo*'s dialogic, progressive hermeneutics, an Afro-modernist mediation of oral tradition, serves a creative strategy at once pre- and post-aesthetic in its management of expressive effects.

The impertinence of aesthetics for the culturally dispossessed, for those excluded from Western subjectivity, should by now be apparent. The Black Aesthetic only half-perceives this irrelevance. Its adaptive motivation (they have an aesthetic that serves them well; why can't we have one of our own) soon shows its limits. To say 'Western bourgeois aesthetics' is to be tautological. There is no other kind – except where independently developed creative/critical systems of other cultural settings allow themselves or are forced to be perceived analogically as 'aesthetics', in deliberate or helpless submission to Western hegemony. Where this acquiescence is conscious, it rehearses the familiar confusion between modernisation and westernisation. Creative-expressive individuals in black and other communities who orient their practices around Western elitist precedents by perceiving these as variant or alternative aesthetics should realise the inevitability of their constructions being contained within the academy's power/knowledge as 'ethno-aesthetics'.

The morbid vitality of aesthetics to attract even those outside its zone of legitimation to its mythology of art, and those outside its aesthetic historicism to its pageant of art movements, is symptomised in the incipient conversion of some blacks, seeking generational groundings, to the apparition of 'post-modernism'. Such self-subversion results from reading another's history as one's own, neglecting the difference between 'modernism' and Afro-modernity. Part of the irony here is that black activist resistances contribute liberally to the social horizon that has driven modernism into its 'post-' phase. To join precipitously the convocation of post-modernism may have for blacks the paradoxical effect of cutting short whatever energies lie in that movement toward ideological realignment with multicultural reality. The historically warranted likelihood, however, is that post-modernism, like its predecessors, will attempt to colonise human creativity through a campaign of art-propaganda.

While blacks and whites in the overdeveloped countries may jointly be confronting the consumerist alienations of late capitalism, their relation to these social contradictions express different historical cruxes in which one group meets these conditions as subject-inheritors and the other as object-victims. From the recognition of the two antagonistic modernisms, it is plain that modernism for blacks is hardly over, has in fact hardly begun. Blacks can only dubiously be post-modernists since they were never permitted to be 'modernists' in the first place.

Notes

1. Friedrich Nietzsche, *The Genealogy of Morals* (New York, 1918).
2. Laura Kipnis, 'Aesthetics and Foreign Policy', *Social Text* (Fall 1986), p. 90.
3. The modern usage of aesthetics was first coined by Alexander Baumgarten in his *Meditationes philosophicae de nonnullis ad poema pertinentibus* (*Reflections on Poetry*, Berkeley, 1954) in 1735. This date is sometimes overlooked in favour of 1750, the date of the German philosopher's more extensive treatment, *Aesthetica*. According to the OED, the term was accepted in English by 1830, but not without reservations and resistances as late as 1842 ('a silly pedantic term') and 1859. See also Raymond Williams' gloss in *Keywords: A Vocabulary of Culture and Society* (London, 1976). Contemporaries may recall that the term found widespread common use among college-trained Americans only since the 1950s.
4. Pierre Bourdieu, *Distinction: A Social Critique of the Judgement of Taste* (Cambridge, Mass., 1984).
5. Stephen Jay Gould, 'Petrus Camper's Angle', *Natural History* (July 1987), pp. 12–18; George L. Mosse, *Toward the Final Solution: A History of European Racism* (New York, 1978), pp. 21–7.
6. Cornell West, *Prophecy Deliverance: An Afro-American Revolutionary Christianity* (Phila., 1982).
7. Mosse, *Toward the Final Solution*.
8. Linda Nochlin, in Thomas B. Hess and Elizabeth C. Baker (eds), *Art and Sexual Politics* (New York, 1971), pp. 1–39; see also Norma Broude, *Feminism and Art History: Questioning the Litany* (New York, 1982).
9. 'The Ceremony Must Be Found: After Humanism', *Boundary 2* (Spring/Fall, 1984), pp. 19–70.
10. Ibid., p. 31.
11. Quoted in Avrahm Yarmolinsky, *Road to Revolution: A Century of Russian Radicalism* (New York, 1959), p. 120.
12. *Introduction to Aesthetic Anthropology* (Malibu, California, 1971); see also his *The Aesthetic Experience: An Anthropologist Looks at the Visual Arts* (New Haven, Conn., 1986).
13. For an elaboration of this point, see Roger Taylor, *Art, an Enemy of the People* (Hassocks, Sussex, 1978), pp. 37–9. The same demonstration of a concept, *art* or *aesthetics*, corresponding to different referents in varied historical epochs is even more applicable when considering different cultures.
14. *Art History and Class Struggle* (London, 1978), p. 12.
15. Guy Debord, *Society of the Spectacle* (Detroit, 1983).
16. One article that successfully overcomes these artificial boundaries is Angela Gilliam's 'African Cinema as New Literature', *Journey Across Three Continents* (catalogue, New York, 1985), pp. 37–40.
17. Bourdieu, *Distinction*, pp. 1–2.
18. Roger Taylor views these contradictions rather brusquely in his chapter 'The Fraudulent Status of Art in Marxism', op. cit.; More sympathetic treatments can be found in Janet Wolff's *Aesthetics and the Sociology of*

Art (London, 1984) and Terry Eagleton, *Criticism and Ideology* (London, 1976). Eagleton's book ends with a testimony of the Euromarxist dependency on bourgeois culture, in the face of a clear understanding of its ideological character (false consciousness): 'The "aesthetic" is too valuable to be surrendered without a struggle to the bourgeois aestheticians, and too contaminated by that ideology to be appropriated as it is. It is, perhaps, in the provisional, strategic silence of those who refuse to speak "morally" and "aesthetically" that something of the true meaning of both terms is anticipated' (p. 187). This dying fall, this Jamesian ambiguity and Joycean silence, cloaking empty resolutions and defeatist quietism, demonstrates all too clearly the damage that aestheticism can do to what might have been a science of liberation.

19. Other views of Afro-modernity can be found in Eleanor Traylor, 'Introduction' to Margaret Walker Alexander, *This is My Century: Black Synthesis of Time* (collected poems); Houston Baker, *Modernism and the Harlem Renaissance* (Chicago, 1987); and Paul Gilroy, *There Ain't No Black in The Union Jack* (London, 1987). 'For whites,' writes Gilroy, 'the aesthetics of modernism may have centred on a "detachment if not revulsion from the human" (Cook, 1984), captured in the image of Gregor Samsa as a beetle and made concrete in Adorno's reflection on the barbarity of writing lyric poetry after Auschwitz. For the African diaspora, constituted for several centuries in a "milieu of dispossession", modernity raised a different set of issues centring on the need to recover and validate black culture and reincarnate the sense of being and belonging which had been erased from it by slavery' (p. 219).

20. See Raphael Samuel (ed.), *People's History and Socialist Theory* (London, 1981).

21. See C.L.R. James, *A History of Negro Revolt* (London, 1938).

22. *Man is Culture*, Sixth Annual Hans Wolff Memorial Lecture, African Studies Program, Indiana University (Bloomington, 1979), pp. 1, 3.

23. Bengt Sundkler, *Bantu Prophets* (London, 1964), relates the effort to establish independent black Christianity in South Africa specifically calling itself Ethiopianism; in *The Redemption of Africa and Black Religion* (Chicago, 1970), St. Clair Drake extends the term and concept to developments across the black world.

24. 'How "Bigger" Was Born', *Native Son* (New York, 1966), p. xxvii.

25. For a fuller discussion of the narrative and its backgrounds, see Françoise Pfaff, *The Cinema of Ousmane Sembene* (Westport, Conn., 1984), pp. 165–77.

The Commitment to Theory

Homi K. Bhabha

There was a damaging and self-defeating assumption circulating at the [1986] Edinburgh 'Third Cinema' Conference – and in many influential places beyond it – that theory is necessarily the elite language of the socially and culturally privileged. It is said that the place of the academic critic is inevitably within the Eurocentric archives of an imperialist or neo-colonial West. The Olympian realms of what is mistakenly labelled 'pure theory' are assumed to be eternally insulated from the historical exigencies and tragedies of the wretched of the earth. I believe it ain't necessarily so. Must we always polarise in order to polemicise? Are we trapped in a politics of struggle where the representation of social antagonisms and historical contradictions can take no other form than a binarism of theory vs politics? Can the aim of freedom or knowledge be the simple inversion of the relation of oppressor and oppressed, margin and periphery, negative image and positive image? Is our only way out of such dualism the espousal of an implacable oppositionality or the invention of an originary counter-myth of radical purity? Must the project of our liberationist aesthetics be forever part of a totalising Utopian vision of Being and History that seeks to transcend the contradictions and ambivalences that constitute the very structure of human subjectivity and its systems of cultural representation?

Deep within the vigorous knockabout that ensued, at times, at Edinburgh, between what was represented as the 'larceny' and distortion of European 'metatheorising' and the radical, engaged, activist experience of Third World creativity,[1] I could see the mirror image (albeit reversed in content and intention) of that ahistorical nineteenth-century polarity of Orient and Occident which, in the name of progress, unleashed the exclusionary imperialist ideologies of self and other. This time round, the term 'critical theory', often untheorised and unargued, was definitely the Other, an otherness that was insistently identified with the vagaries of the 'depoliticised' Eurocentric critic. Was the cause of radical art or critique best served by the fulminating professor of film who announced, at a flashpoint in the argument, 'We are not artists, we are political activists'? By obscuring the power of his own practice in the rhetoric of militancy, he failed to draw attention to the specific value of a politics of cultural production which, because it makes the surfaces of cinematic signification the grounds of political intervention, gives depth to the language of social criticism and extends the domain of 'politics' in a direction that will not be entirely dominated by the forces of economic or social control. Forms of popular rebellion and mobilisation are often most subversive and transgressive when they are created through the identification with oppositional *cultural* practices.

Before I am accused of bourgeois voluntarism, liberal pragmatism, academicist pluralism and all the other -isms that are freely bandied about by those who take the most severe exception to 'Eurocentric' theoretic*ism* (Derrideanism, Lacanianism, post-structuralism ...), I would like to clarify the goals of my opening questions. I am convinced that, in the language of political economy, it is legitimate to represent the relations of exploitation and domination in the discursive division between First and Third Worlds. Despite the claims to a spurious rhetoric of 'internationalism' on the part of the established multinationals and the networks of the new communications technology industries, such circulations of signs and commodities as there are, are caught in the vicious circuits of surplus value that link First World capital to Third World labour markets through the chains of the international division of labour. Spivak is right to conclude that it is 'in the interest of capital to preserve the comprador theatre in a state of relatively primitive labour legislation and environmental regulation':[2] remember Bhopal.

I am equally convinced that in the language of international diplomacy there is a sharp growth in a new Anglo-American nationalism (NATO-nalism?) which increasingly articulates its economic and military power in political acts that express a neo-imperialist disregard for the independence and autonomy of Other peoples and places, largely in the Third World. Think of America's 'backyard' policy towards the Caribbean and Latin America, the patriotic gore and patrician lore of Britain's Falkland Campaign, or the triumphalism of the American and British navies patrolling the Persian Gulf (July 1987). I am further convinced that such economic and political domination has a profound hegemonic influence on the information orders of the Western world, its popular media and its specialised institutions and academies. So much is not in doubt.

What does demand further discrimination is whether the 'new' languages of theoretical critique (semiotic, post-structuralist, deconstructionist and the rest) simply reflect those geopolitical divisions and spheres of influence. Are the interests of 'Western' theory necessarily collusive with the hegemonic role of the West as a power bloc? Is the specialised, 'textualised', often academic language of theory merely another power ploy of the culturally privileged Western elite to produce a discourse of the Other that sutures its own power-knowledge equation?

A large film festival in the West – even an alternative or counter-cultural event such as Edinburgh's 'Third Cinema' Conference – never fails to reveal the disproportionate influence of the West as cultural forum, in all three senses of that word: as place of public exhibition and discussion, as place of judgment, and as market-place. An Indian film about the plight of Bombay's pavement-dwellers wins the Newcastle Festival which then opens up distribution facilities in India. The first searing exposé of the Bhopal disaster is made for Channel Four. A major debate on the politics and theory of Third Cinema first appears in *Screen*. An archival article on the important history of neo-traditionalism and the 'popular' in Indian cinema sees the light of day in *Framework*.[3] Among the major contributors to the development of the Third Cinema as precept and practice are a number of Third World film-makers and critics who are exiles or émigrés to the West and live problematically, often dangerously, on the 'left' margins of a Eurocentric, bourgeois liberal culture. I don't think I need to add individual names or places, or detail the historical reasons why the West carries and exploits what Bourdieu would call its symbolic capital. The condition is all too familiar, and it is not my purpose here to make those important distinctions between different national situations and the disparate political causes and collective histories of cultural exile. I want to take my stand on the shifting margins of cultural displacement – that confounds any profound or 'authentic' sense of a 'national' culture or an 'organic' intellectual – and ask what the function of a committed theoretical perspective might be, once the cultural and historical hybridity of the post-colonial world is taken as the paradigmatic place of departure. . . .

Committed to what? At this stage in the argument, I do not want to identify any specific 'object' of political allegiance – the Third World, the working class, the feminist struggle. Although such an objectification of political activity is crucial and must significantly inform political debate, it is not the only option for those critics or intellectuals who are committed to progressive, political change in the direction of a socialist society. It is a sign of political maturity to accept that there are many forms of political writing whose different effects are obscured when they are divided between the 'theoretical' and the 'activist'. It is not as if the leaflet involved in the organisation of a strike is short on theory, while a speculative article on the theory of ideology ought to have more practical examples or applications. They are both forms of discourse and to that extent they produce rather than reflect their objects of

113

reference. The difference between them lies in their operational qualities. The leaflet has a specific expository and organisational purpose, temporally bound to the event; the theory of ideology makes its contribution to those embedded political ideas and principles that inform the right to strike. The latter does not justify the former; nor does it necessarily precede it. It exists side by side with it – the one as an enabling part of the other – like the recto and verso of a sheet of paper, to use a common semiotic analogy in the uncommon context of politics.

My concern here is with the process of 'intervening ideologically', as Stuart Hall describes the role of 'imaging' or representation in the practice of politics in his response to the British election of 1987.[4] For Hall, the notion of hegemony implies a politics of *identification* of the imaginary. This occupies a discursive space which is not exclusively delimited by the history of either the right or the left. It exists somehow in between these political polarities, and also between the familiar divisions of theory and political practice. This approach, as I read it, introduces us to an exciting, neglected moment, or movement, in the 'recognition' of the relation of politics to theory; and confuses the traditional differences between them. Such a movement is initiated if we see that relation as determined by the rule of repeatable materiality, which Foucault[5] describes as the process by which statements from one institution can be transcribed in the discourse of another. Despite the schemata of use and application that constitute a field of stabilisation for the statement, any change in the statement's conditions of use and reinvestment, any alteration in its field of experience or verification, or indeed any difference in the problems to be solved, can lead to the emergence of a new statement: the difference of the same.

In what hybrid forms, then, may a politics of the theoretical statement emerge? What tensions and ambivalences mark this enigmatic place from which theory 'speaks'? Speaking in the name of some counter-authority or horizon of 'the true' (in Foucault's sense of the strategic effects of any apparatus or *dispositif*), the theoretical enterprise has to represent the adversarial authority (of power and/or knowledge) which, in a doubly inscribed move, it simultaneously seeks to subvert and replace. In this complicated formulation I have tried to indicate something of the complex boundary and location of the event of theoretical critique which does not *contain* the truth (in polar opposition to totalitarianism, 'bourgeois liberalism' or whatever is supposed to repress it). The 'true' is always marked and informed by the ambivalence of the process of emergence itself, the productivity of meanings that construct counter-knowledges *in medias res*, in the very act of agonism, within the terms of a negotiation (rather than a negation) of oppositional and antagonistic elements. Political positions are not simply identifiable as progressive or reactionary, bourgeois or radical, prior to the act of *critique engagée*, or outside the terms and conditions of its discursive and textual address. It is in this sense that the historical moment of political action must be thought of as part of the history of the form of its writing. This is not to state the obvious, that there is no knowledge – political or otherwise – outside representation. It is to suggest that the dynamics of writing – of *écriture* – require us to rethink the logics of causality or determinacy through which we recognise the 'political' as a form of calculation and strategic action dedicated to social transformation.

'What is to be done?' must acknowledge the force of writing, its metaphoricity and its rhetorical discourse, as a productive matrix which defines the 'social' and makes it available as an objective of/for action. Textuality is not simply a second-order ideological expression or a verbal symptom of a pre-given political subject. That the political subject – as indeed the subject of politics – is a discursive event is nowhere more clearly seen than in a text which has been a formative influence on Western liberal democratic and socialist discourse – Mill's essay *On Liberty*. His crucial chapter, 'On the liberty of thought and discussion', is almost entirely an attempt to define political judgment as the problem of finding a form of *public rhetoric* able to represent different and opposing political 'contents' or principles as a dialogical exchange in the ongoing present of the enunciation of the political statement. What is unexpected is the suggestion that it is a crisis of identification initiated in the textual performance that displays a certain 'difference' *within* the signification of any single political system, prior to the substantial differences *between* political beliefs. A knowledge can only become political through an agonistic language-game: dissensus, alterity and otherness are the discursive conditions for the circulation and recognition of a politicised subject and a public 'truth':

> [If] opponents of all important truths do not exist, it is indispensable to imagine them. . . . [He] must feel the whole force of the difficulty which the true view of the subject has to encounter and dispose of; *else he will never really possess himself of the portion of truth which meets and removes that difficulty.* . . . Their conclusion may be true, but it might be false for anything they know: they have never thrown themselves into the *mental position* of those who think differently from them . . . and consequently they do not, in any proper sense of the word, *know the doctrine which they themselves profess.* (My emphases)[6]

It is true that Mill's 'rationality' permits, or requires, such forms of contention and contradiction in order to enhance his vision of the inherently progressive and evolutionary bent of *human* judgment. (This

115

makes it possible for contradictions to be resolved and also generates a sense of the whole truth which reflects the natural, organic bent of the human mind.) It is also true that Mill always reserves, in society as in his argument, the unreal neutral space of the Third Person as the representative of the 'people', who witnesses the debate from an 'epistemological distance' and draws a reasonable conclusion. Even so, in his attempt to describe the political as a form of debate and dialogue – as the process of public rhetoric – that is crucially mediated through this ambivalent and antagonistic faculty of a political 'imagination', Mill exceeds the usual mimetic sense of the battle of ideas. He suggests something much more dialogical: the realisation of the political idea at the ambivalent point of textual address, its emergence through a form of political fantasy. Rereading Mill through the strategies of 'writing' that I have suggested above reveals that one cannot passively follow the line of argument running through the logic of the opposing ideology. The textual process of political antagonism initiates a contradictory process of reading 'between the lines'; the agent of the discourse becomes, in the same time of utterance, the inverted, projected, fantasmatic object of the argument, 'turned against itself'. It is, Mill insists, only by effectively assuming the mental position of the antagonist and working through the displacing and decentring force of that discursive difficulty that the politicised 'portion of truth' is produced. This is a different dynamic from the ethic of 'tolerance' in liberal ideology which has to imagine opposition in order to contain it and demonstrate its enlightened relativism or humanism. Reading Mill against the grain like this suggests that politics can only become 'representative', a truly 'public' discourse, through a splitting in the signification of the subject of representation, through an ambivalence at the point of the enunciation of a politics.

I have chosen to demonstrate the importance of the space of writing and the problematic of address at the very heart of the liberal tradition, because it is here that the myth of the 'transparency' of the human agent and the reasonableness of political action is most forcefully asserted. Despite the more radical political alternatives of the right and the left, the popular, common-sense view of the place of the individual in relation to the social is still substantially thought and lived in ethical terms moulded by liberal beliefs. What the question of writing reveals most starkly are the ambivalent and fantasmatic texts that make 'the political' possible. From such a perspective, the problematic of political judgment cannot be represented as an epistemological problem of 'appearance and reality' or 'theory and practice' or 'word and thing'. Nor can it be represented as a dialectical problem or a symptomatic contradiction constitutive of the materiality of the 'real' whose difference must be sublated in the progress of history or the political science of Marxism. On the contrary, we are made excruciatingly aware of the ambivalent juxtaposition, the dangerous interstitial, invaginated relation of the 'factual' and the 'fantasmatic', and, beyond that, of the crucial function of the fantasmatic and the rhetorical – those vicissitudes of the movement of the signifier – in the fixing of the 'factual', in the 'closure' of the real, in the efficacy and power of strategic thinking in the discourses of *Realpolitik*. It is this to-and-fro, this *fort/da* of the symbolic process of political negotiation, that we are challenged to think in, and through, what I have called a politics of address. The question of writing and address focuses on the necessity of this ambivalent movement in the construction of political authority, in the fixity and fixation of boundaries of meaning and strategies of action. Its importance goes beyond its unsettling, from the point of view of philosophy, of the essentialism or logocentricism of a received political tradition, in the name of an abstract 'free play of the signifier'.

The first principles of a socialist critique will appear contentious and contradictory to a bourgeois humanist reading, as indeed will be the political intentions of the critic. So much is obvious. In the act of the *écriture* or scription of an oppositional reading, however, we must not expect to recognise the *new* political object, or aim, or knowledge, as simply a mimetic reflection of the *a priori* principle or commitment. Nor should we demand of it a pure teleology of analysis or purport whereby the prior principle is simply augmented, its rationality smoothly developed, its identity as 'socialist' or 'materialist' (as opposed to 'neo-imperialist' or 'humanist') consistently confirmed in each oppositional stage of the argument. Such identikit political idealism may be the symptom of great individual fervour, but it lacks the deeper, if dangerous, sense of what is entailed by the *passage* of history in theoretical discourse. The language of critique is effective not because it keeps forever separate the terms of the master and the slave, the mercantilist and the Marxist, but to the extent to which it overcomes the given grounds of opposition and opens up a space of 'translation': a place of hybridity, figuratively speaking, where the construction of a political object that is new, *neither the one nor the Other*, properly alienates our political expectations, and changes, as it must, the very forms of our recognition of the 'moment' of politics. The challenge lies in conceiving of the 'time' of political action and understanding as opening up a space that can accept and regulate the differential structure of the moment of intervention without rushing to produce a dialectical unity of the social antagonism or contradiction. This must be a sign that history is *happening* – within the airless pages of theory, within the systems and structures we construct to figure the passage of the historical.

When I talk of *negotiation* rather than *negation*, it is to convey a temporality that makes it possible to conceptualise the articulation of antagonistic or contradictory elements without either the idealism of a dialectic which enables the emergence of a teleological or transcendent History, or the 'scientism' of symptomatic reading where the nervous tics on the surface of ideology reveal the 'real materialist contradiction' that History embodies. In such a temporality, the act of theory is the process of articulation, and the event of theory becomes the *negotiation* of contradictory and antagonistic instances. These open up hybrid sites and objectives of struggle and destroy those familiar polarities between knowledge and its objects, and between theory and practical-political reason.[7] If I have argued against a primordial and previsionary division of 'right' or 'left', progressive or reactionary, it has been only to stress the fully historical and discursive *différance* between them. I would not like my notion of negotiation to be confused with some syndicalist sense of 'reformism' because that is not the political level that is being explored here. By negotiation I attempt to draw attention to the structure of *iteration* which informs political movements (in both senses of the word) that attempt to articulate antagonistic and oppositional elements without the redemptive rationality of sublation or transcendence.[8]

The temporality of negotiation or translation as I have sketched it has two main advantages. First, it acknowledges the historical connectedness between the subject and object of critique so that there can be no simplistic, essentialist opposition between ideological miscognition and revolutionary truth. The progressive 'reading' is crucially determined by the adversarial or agonistic situation itself; it is effective because it uses the subversive, messy mask of camouflage and does not come like a pure avenging angel speaking the truth of a radical historicity and pure oppositionality. If one is aware of this heterogeneous emergence (not origin) of radical critique, then – and this is my second point – the function of theory within the political process becomes double-edged. It makes us aware that our political referents and priorities – the people, the community, class struggle, anti-racism, gender difference, the assertion of an anti-imperialist, black or third perspective – are not 'there' in some primordial, naturalistic sense. Nor do they reflect a unitary or homogeneous political object. They 'make sense' as they come to be constructed in the discourses of feminism or Marxism or the Third Cinema or whatever, whose objects of priority – class or sexuality or 'the new ethnicity' (Stuart Hall) – are always in historical and philosophical tension, or cross-reference with other objectives.

Indeed, the whole history of socialist thought which seeks to 'make it new and better' seems to be a difficult process of articulating priorities whose political objects can be recalcitrant and contradictory. Within contemporary Marxism, for example, witness the continual tension between the 'English', humanist, labourist faction and the 'theoreticist',

118

structuralist, 'Trotskyist' tendencies. Within feminism, there is again a marked difference of emphasis between the psychoanalytic/semiotic end and those who see the articulation of gender and class as less problematic through a theory of cultural and ideological interpellation. I have presented these differences in broad brush-strokes, often using the language of polemic, to suggest that each 'position' is always a process of translation and transference of meaning. Each objective is constructed on the trace of that perspective that it puts 'under erasure'; each political object is displacing in relation to the other, and displaced in that critical act. Too often these theoretical issues are peremptorily transposed into organisational terms and represented as 'sectarianism'. I am suggesting that such contradictions and conflicts, which often thwart political intentions and make the question of commitment complex and difficult, are rooted in the process of translation and displacement in which the 'object' of politics is inscribed. The effect is not stasis or a sapping of the will. It is, on the contrary, the spur to the 'negotiation' of socialist democratic politics and policies which demand that questions of organisation are theorised and socialist theory is 'organised', *because there is no given community or body of the people, whose inherent, radical historicity emits the right signs.*

This emphasis on the representation of the political, on the construction of discourse, is the radical contribution of the 'translation' of theory whose vigilance never allows a simple identity between the political objective (not object) and its means of representation. This emphasis on the necessity of heterogeneity and the double inscription of the political objective is not merely the repetition of a general truth about discourse introduced into the political field. In denying an essentialist logic and a mimetic referent to political representation it is a strong, principled argument against political separatism of any colour, which cuts through the moralism that usually accompanies such claims. There is literally, and figuratively, no space for the 'unitary' or single political objective which offends against the sense of a socialist *community* of interest and articulation.

In Britain, in the 1980s, no political struggle was fought more powerfully and sustained more poignantly on the values and traditions of a socialist community than the miners' strike of 1984–5. The battalions of monetarist figures and forecasts on the 'profitability' of the pits were starkly ranged against the most illustrious standards of the British labour movement, the most cohesive cultural communities of the working class. The choice was clearly between the dawning world of the new 'Thatcherite' city gent and a long history of 'the working man', or so it seemed to the traditional left and the new right. In these class terms the 'mining' women involved in the strike were applauded for the heroic supporting role they played, for their endurance and initiative.

119

But the 'revolutionary' impulse, it seemed, belonged securely to the working-class male. Then, to commemorate the first anniversary of the strike, Beatrix Campbell, in the *Guardian*, interviewed a group of women who had been involved in the strike. It was clear that their experience of the historical struggle, their understanding of the 'historic' choice, was startlingly different and more complex. Their testimonies would not be contained simply or singly within the priorities of the politics of class or the histories of industrial struggle. Many of the women began to question their roles within the family and the community – the two central institutions which articulated the meanings and mores of the *tradition* of the labouring classes around which ideological battle was enjoined. Some challenged the symbols and authorities of the culture they fought to defend. Others disrupted the homes they had struggled to sustain. For most of them there was no return, no going back to the 'good old days'. It would be simplistic to suggest either that this considerable social change was a spin-off from the class struggle or that it was a repudiation of the politics of class from a socialist-feminist perspective. There is no simple political or social 'truth' to be learned, for there is no unitary representation of a political agency, no fixed hierarchy of political values and effects.

My illustration attempts to display the importance of the 'hybrid' moment of political change. Here the transformational value of change lies in the re-articulation, or translation, of elements that are *neither the One* (unitary working class) *nor the Other* (the politics of gender) *but something else besides* which contests the terms and territories of both. This does not necessarily involve the formation of a new synthesis, but a negotiation between them *in medias res*, in the profound experience or knowledge of the displaced, diversionary, differentiated boundaries in which the limits and limitations of social power are encountered in an agonistic relation. When Eric Hobsbawm suggests in *Marxism Today* (October 1987) that the Labour Party should seek to produce a socialist alliance among progressive forces that are widely dispersed and distributed across a range of class, culture, and occupational forces – without a unifying sense of the 'class for itself' – he is acknowledging, as *historical* necessity, the kind of 'hybridity' that I have attempted to identify as a practice in the signification of the political. A little less pietistic articulation of political principle (around class and nation); just a little more of the principle of political articulation. . . .

This seems to be the theoretical issue at the heart of Stuart Hall's arguments for the construction of a counter-hegemonic power bloc through which a socialist party might construct its majority, its constituency; and the Labour Party might (in)conceivably improve its 'image'. The unemployed, semi-skilled and unskilled, part-time workers, male and female, the low-paid, black people, underclasses:

these signs of the fragmentation of class and cultural consensus represent both the historical experience of contemporary social divisions, and a structure of heterogeneity upon which to construct his theoretical and political alternative. That is, for Hall, the imperative to construct a new social bloc of different constituencies, through the production of a form of symbolic identification that would result in a collective will. The Labour Party, with its desire to reinstate its traditionalist image – white, male, working-class trade-union based – is not 'hegemonic enough', Hall writes. He is right; what remains unanswered is whether the rationalism and intentionality that propel the 'collective will' are compatible with the language of 'symbolic image' and fragmentary identification which represents, for Hall and for his 'hegemony'/'counter-hegemony', the fundamental political issue. Can there ever be hegemony 'enough', except in the sense that a two-thirds majority will elect us a socialist government?

It is in intervening in Hall's argument that the necessities of 'negotiation' are revealed, in my attempt to foreground his analytic of fragmentation. The interest and excitement of Hall's position lie in his acknowledgment, remarkable for the British left, that, though influential, 'material interests on their own have no necessary class belongingness'.[9] This has two significant effects. It enables Hall to see the agents of political change as discontinuous, divided subjects caught in conflicting interests and identities. Equally, at the historical level of a Thatcherite 'population', he asserts that divisive rather than solidary forms of identification are the rule, resulting in undecidabilities and aporia of political judgment:

> What does a working woman put first? Which of her identities is the one that determines her political choices?

The answer to such a question is defined, according to Hall, in the ideological definition of materialist interests; a process of symbolic identification achieved through a political technology of 'imaging' that hegemonically produces a social bloc of the right or the left. Not only is the social bloc heterogeneous but the work of hegemony – as I see it – is itself the process of iteration and differentiation. It depends on the production of alternative or antagonistic images that are always produced side by side and in competition with each other. It is this side-by-side nature, this partial presence or metonymy of antagonism, and its effective significations, that give meaning (quite literally) to a politics of struggle *as the struggle of identifications* and the war of positions. It is therefore problematic to think of it as sublated into an image of the collective will.

Hegemony requires iteration and alterity to be effective, to be pro-

121

ductive of politicised populations: the (non-homogeneous) symbolic-social bloc needs to represent itself in a solidary 'collective' will – a modern image of the future – if those populations are to produce a progressive government. Both may be necessary but they do not easily follow from each other, for in each case the mode of representation and its temporality are different. The contribution of negotiation is to display the 'in-between' of this crucial argument that is *not* self-contradictory, but significantly performs, in the process of its discussion, the problems of judgment and identification that inform the political space of its enunciation.

For the moment, the act of negotiation will only be interrogatory. Can such split subjects and differentiated social movements, which display ambivalent and divided forms of identification, be represented in a 'collective will' that distinctively echoes Gramsci's enlightenment inheritance and its rationalism?[10] How does the language of the will accommodate the vicissitudes of its representation, which is its construction through a symbolic majority where the have-nots identify themselves from the position of the haves? How do we construct a politics based on such a displacement of affect or strategic elaboration (Foucault), where political positioning is ambivalently grounded in an acting-out of political fantasies that require repeated passages across the differential boundaries between one symbolic bloc *and an other*, and the positions available to each? If such is the case, then how do we fix the counter-image of socialist hegemony to reflect the divided will, the fragmented population? If the polity of hegemony is, quite literally, *unsignifiable* without the metonymic representation of its agonistic and ambivalent structure of articulation, then how does the collective will stabilise and unify its address as an agency of *representation*, as representative of a 'people'? How do we avoid the mixing or overlap of images, the split screen, the failure to synchronise sound and image? Perhaps we need to change the ocular language of the image in order to talk of the social and political identifications or representations of a 'people' – it is worth noting that Laclau and Mouffe have turned to the language of textuality and discourse, to *différance* and enunciative modalities, in attempting to understand the structure of hegemony.[11] Paul Gilroy also refers to Bakhtin's theory of narrative when he describes the performance of black expressive cultures as an attempt to transform the relationship between performer and crowd 'in *dialogic* rituals so that spectators acquire the active role of participants in collective processes which are sometimes cathartic and which may symbolise or even create a community' (my emphasis).[12]

Such negotiations between politics and theory make it impossible to think of the place of the theoretical as a metanarrative claiming a more total form of generality. Nor is it possible to claim a certain familiar 'epistemological' distance between the *time and place* of the intellectual and the activist, as Fanon suggests when he observes that 'while politicians situate their action in actual present-day events, men of culture take their stand in the field of history'.[13] It is precisely that popular binarism between theory and politics, whose foundational basis is an epistemological view of knowledge as totalising generality and everyday life as experience, subjectivity, or false consciousness, that I have tried to erase. It is a distinction that even Sartre subscribes to when he describes the committed intellectual as 'the theoretician of practical knowledge' whose defining criterion is rationality and whose first project is to combat the irrationality of ideology.[14] From the perspective of negotiation and translation, *contra* Fanon and Sartre, there can be no final discursive *closure* of theory. It does not foreclose on the political, even though battles for power-knowledge may be won or lost to great effect. The corollary is that there is no first or final act of revolutionary social (or socialist) transformation – just as, in Lacan's account of the process of subjectivity in language, there is no fixed point of identity, for the 'signifier represents a subject for another signifier'.

I hope it is clear that this erasure of the traditional boundary between theory/politics, and my resistance to the en-*closure* of the theoretical whether it is read negatively as elitism or positively as radical suprarationality, do not turn on the good or bad faith of the activist agent or the intellectual *agent provocateur*. I am primarily concerned with the conceptual structuring of the terms – the 'theoretical'/the 'political' – which inform a range of debates around the place and time of the committed intellectual. I have therefore argued for a certain relation to knowledge which I think is crucial in structuring our sense of what the *object* of theory may be in the act of determining our specific political *objectives*.

II

What is at stake in the naming of critical theory as 'Western'? It is, obviously, a designation of institutional power and ideological Eurocentricity. Critical theory often engages with Third World texts within the familiar traditions and conditions of colonial anthropology either to 'universalise' their meaning within its own cultural and academic discourse, or to sharpen its internal critique of the Western logocentric sign, the idealist 'subject', or indeed the illusions and delusions of civil society. This is a familiar manoeuvre of theoretical knowledge, where, having opened up the chasm of cultural 'difference' – of the indeterminacy of meaning or the crisis of representation – a mediator or metaphor of 'otherness' must be found to contain that 'difference'. In order

123

to be institutionally effective as a discipline, the knowledge of cultural difference must be made to 'foreclose' on the Other; the 'Other' thus becomes at once the fantasy of a certain cultural space or, indeed, the certainty of a form of theoretical knowledge that deconstructs the epistemological 'edge' of the West.

More significantly, the site of cultural difference can become the mere phantom of a dire disciplinary struggle in which it has no space or power. Montesquieu's Turkish Despot, Barthes' Japan, Kristeva's China, Derrida's Nambikwara Indians, Lyotard's Cashinahua 'pagans' are part of this strategy of containment where the Other text is forever the exegetical horizon of difference, never the active agent of articulation. The Other is cited, quoted, framed, illuminated, encased in the shot/reverse-shot strategy of a serial enlightenment. Narrative and the *cultural* politics of difference become the closed circle of interpretation. The Other loses its power to signify, to negate, to initiate its 'desire', to split its 'sign' of identity, to establish its own institutional and oppositional discourse. However impeccably the content of an 'other' culture may be known, however anti-ethnocentrically it is represented, it is its *location* as the 'closure' of grand theories, the demand that, in analytic terms, it be always the 'good' object of knowledge, the docile body of difference, that reproduces a relation of domination and is the most serious indictment of the institutional powers of critical theory.

There is, however, a distinction to be made between the institutional history of critical theory and its conceptual potential for change and innovation. Althusser's critique of the temporal structure of the Hegelian-Marxist expressive 'totality', despite its functionalist limitations, opens up the possibilities of thinking the 'relations of production' in a time of differential histories. Lacan's location of the signifier of desire, on the cusp of language and the law, allows the elaboration of a form of social representation that is alive to the ambivalent structure of subjectivity and sociality. Foucault's archaeology of the emergence of modern, Western 'man' as a problem of finitude, inextricable from its afterbirth, its Other, enables the linear, progressivist claims of the social sciences – the major imperialising discourses – to be confronted by their own historicist limitations. These arguments and modes of analysis can be dismissed as internal squabbles around Hegelian causality, psychic representation, or sociological theory. Alternatively, they can be subjected to a translation, a 'transformation of value' as part of the questioning of the project of modernity in the great, revolutionary tradition of C.L.R. James – *contra* Trotsky or Fanon, *contra* phenomenology and existentialist psychoanalysis. In 1952, it was Fanon who suggested that an oppositional, differential reading of Lacan's Other might be more relevant for the colonial condition than the Marxisant reading of the master-slave dialectic.

124

It may be possible to produce such a translation or transformation if we understand the tension within critical theory between its institutional containment and its revisionary force. The continual reference to the horizon of Other cultures which I have mentioned earlier is ambivalent. It is a site of 'citation', but it is also a sign that such critical theory cannot forever sustain its position in the Western academy as the adversarial cutting edge of Western idealism. What is required is to demonstrate another territory of translation, another testimony of analytical argument, a different engagement in the politics of and around cultural domination. What this other site for theory might be will become clearer if we first see that many of these post-structuralist ideas are themselves opposed to Western Enlightenment humanism and aesthetics. They constitute no less than a deconstruction of the moment of the modern, its legal values, its literary tastes, its philosophical and political categorical imperatives. Secondly, and more importantly, we must rehistoricise the moment of 'the emergence of the sign', or 'the question of the subject', or the 'discursive construction of social reality', to quote a few popular topics of contemporary theory. And this can only happen if we relocate the referential and institutional demands of such theoretical work in the field of cultural difference – *not cultural diversity*.

Such a reorientation may be found in the historical texts of the colonial moment in the late 18th and early 19th centuries. For at the same time as the question of cultural difference emerged in the colonial text, discourses of 'civility' were defining the doubling moment of the emergence of Western modernity. Thus the political and theoretical genealogy of modernity lies not only in the origins of the *idea* of civility, but in this history of the colonial moment. It is to be found in the resistance of the colonised population to the Word of God and Man – Christianity and the English language. The transmutations and translations of indigenous traditions in their opposition to colonial authority demonstrate how the 'desire of the signifier', the 'indeterminacy' of intertextuality, is deeply engaged in the struggle against dominant relations of power and knowledge. In the following words of the missionary master we hear, quite distinctly, the oppositional voices of a culture of resistance; but we also hear the uncertain and threatening process of cultural transformation. I quote from A. Duff's influential *India Missions* (1839):

Come to some doctrine which you believe to be peculiar to Revelation; tell the people that they must be regenerated or born again, else they can never 'see God'. Before you are aware, they may go away saying, 'Oh, there is nothing new or strange here; our own Shastras tell us the same thing; we know and believe that we must be born again; it is our fate to be so.' But what do they understand by the expression? It is that they are to be born again and again, in some other form, agreeably to their own system of transmigration or reiterated births. To avoid the appearance of countenancing so absurd and pernicious a doctrine, you vary your language, and tell them that there must be a second birth – that they must be twice-born. Now it so happens that this, and all similar phraseology, is preoccupied. The sons of a Brahman have to undergo various purificatory and initiatory ceremonial rites, before they attain to full Brahmanhood. The last of these is the investiture with the sacred thread; which is followed by the communication of the Gayatri, or most sacred verse in the Vedas. This ceremonial constitutes, 'religiously and metaphorically, their second birth'; henceforward their distinctive and peculiar appellation is that of the twice-born, or regenerated men. *Hence it is your improved language might only convey the impression that all must become perfect Brahmans, ere they can 'see God'.* (My emphasis)

The grounds of evangelical certitude are opposed not by the simple assertion of an antagonistic cultural tradition. The process of translation is the opening up of another contentious political and cultural site at the heart of colonial 'representation'. Here the word of divine authority is deeply flawed by the assertion of the indigenous sign, and in the very practice of domination the language of the master becomes hybrid – neither the one thing nor the other. The incalculable colonised subject – half acquiescent, half oppositional, always untrustworthy – produces an unresolvable problem of cultural difference for the very address of colonial cultural authority. The 'subtile system of Hinduism', as the missionaries in the early 19th century called it, generated tremendous policy implications for the institutions of Christian conversion. The written authority of the Bible was challenged and together with it a post-Enlightenment notion of the evidence of Christianity and its historical priority, which was central to evangelical colonialism. The Word could no longer be trusted to carry the truth when written or spoken in the colonial world by the European missionary. Native catechists therefore had to be found, who brought with them their own cultural and political ambivalences and contradictions, often under great pressure from their families and communities.

This revision of the history of critical theory rests, I have said, on the notion of cultural difference, not cultural diversity. Cultural diversity is an epistemological object – culture as an object of empirical knowledge – whereas cultural difference is the process of the *enunciation* of culture as 'knowledge*able*', authoritative, adequate to the construction of systems of cultural identification. If cultural diversity is a category of comparative ethics, aesthetics, or ethnology, cultural difference is a process of signification through which statements *of* culture or *on* culture differentiate, discriminate, and authorise the production of fields of force, reference, applicability, and capacity. Cultural diversity is the recognition of pre-given cultural 'contents' and customs; held in a time-frame of relativism it gives rise to anodyne liberal notions of multiculturalism, cultural exchange, or the culture of humanity. Cultural diversity is also the representation of a radical rhetoric of the separation of totalised cultures that live unsullied by the intertextuality of their historical locations, safe in the Utopianism of a mythic memory of a unique collective identity. Cultural diversity may even emerge as a system of the articulation and exchange of cultural signs in certain early structuralist accounts of anthropology.

Through the concept of cultural difference I want to draw attention to the common ground and lost territory of contemporary critical debates. For they all recognise that the problem of the cultural emerges only at the significatory boundaries of cultures, where meanings and values are (mis)read or signs are misappropriated. 'Culture' only emerges as a problem, or a problematic, at the point at which there is a 'loss' of meaning in the contestation and articulation of everyday life, between classes, genders, races, nations. Yet the reality of the limit or limit-text of culture is rarely theorised outside of well-intentioned moralist polemics against prejudice and stereotype, or the blanket assertion of individual or institutional racism – that describes the effect rather than the structure of the problem. The need to think the limit of culture as a problem of the enunciation of cultural difference is disavowed.

The concept of cultural difference focuses on the problem of the ambivalence of cultural authority: the attempt to dominate in the *name* of a cultural supremacy which is itself produced only in the moment of differentiation. And it is the very authority of culture as a knowledge of referential truth which is at issue in the concept and moment of *enunciation*. The enunciative process introduces a split in the performative present of cultural identification; a split between the traditional culturalist demand for a model, a tradition, a community, a stable system of reference, and the necessary negation of the certitude in the articulation of new cultural demands, meanings, strategies in the political present, as a practice of domination, or resistance. The struggle is often between the historicist teleological or mythical time and narrative of traditionalism – of the right or the left – and the shifting, strategically displaced time of the articulation of a historical politics of negotiation which I suggested above. The time of liberation is, as Fanon powerfully evokes, a time of cultural uncertainty, and, most crucially, of significatory or 'representational' undecidability:

127

But [native intellectuals] forget that the forms of thought and what [they] feed ... on, together with modern techniques of information, language and dress, have dialectically reorganised the people's intelligences and *the constant principles (of national art)* which acted as safeguards during the colonial period are now undergoing extremely radical changes.... [We] must join the people in that fluctuating movement which they are *just* giving a shape to ... which will be the signal for everything to be called into question ... it is to the zone of *occult instability* where the people dwell that we must come. (My emphases)[15]

The enunciation of cultural difference problematises the division of past and present, tradition and modernity, at the level of cultural representation and its authoritative address. It is the problem of how, in signifying the present, something comes to be repeated, relocated, and translated in the name of tradition, in the guise of a pastness that is not necessarily a faithful sign of historical memory but a strategy of representing authority in terms of the artifice of the archaic. That iteration negates our sense of the origins of the struggle. It undermines our sense of the homogenising effects of cultural symbols and icons, by questioning our sense of the authority of cultural synthesis in general.

This demands that we rethink our perspective on the identity of culture. Here Fanon's passage – somewhat reinterpreted – may be helpful. What is implied by his juxtaposition of the constant national principles with his view of culture-as-political-struggle, which he so enigmatically and beautifully describes as 'the zone of occult instability where the people dwell'? These ideas not only help to explain the nature of colonial struggle. They also suggest a possible critique of the positive aesthetic and political values we ascribe to the unity or totality of cultures, especially those that have known long and tyrannical histories of domination and misrecognition. Cultures are never unitary in themselves, nor simply dualistic in relation of Self to Other. This is not because of some humanistic nostrum that beyond individual cultures we all belong to the human culture of mankind; nor is it because of an ethical relativism which suggests that in our cultural capacity to speak of and judge Others we necessarily 'place ourselves in their position', in a kind of relativism of distance of which Bernard Williams has written at length.[16]

The reason a cultural text or system of meaning cannot be sufficient unto itself is that the act of cultural enunciation – the *place of utterance* – is crossed by the *différance* of writing or *écriture*. This has less to do with what anthropologists might describe as varying attitudes to symbolic systems within different cultures than with the structure of symbolic representation – not the content of the symbol or its 'social function', but the structure of symbolisation. It is this 'difference' in language that is crucial to the production of meaning and ensures, at the same time, that meaning is never simply mimetic and transparent.

The linguistic difference that informs any cultural performance is dramatised in the common semiotic account of the disjuncture between the subject of a proposition (*énoncé*) and the subject of enunciation, which is not represented in the statement but which is the acknowledgment of its discursive embeddedness and address, its cultural positionality, its reference to a present time and a specific space. The pact of interpretation is never simply an act of communication between the I and the You designated in the statement. The production of meaning requires that these two places be mobilised in the passage through a Third space, which represents both the general conditions of language and the specific implication of the utterance in a performative and institutional strategy of which it cannot 'in itself' be conscious. What this unconscious relation introduces is an ambivalence in the act of interpretation. The pronominal I of the proposition cannot be made to address – in its own words – the subject of enunciation, for this is not 'personable', but remains a spatial relation within the schemata and strategies of discourse. The meaning of the utterance is quite literally neither the one nor the Other. This ambivalence is emphasised when we realise that there is no way that the content of the proposition will reveal the structure of its positionality; no way that context can be mimetically read off from the content.

The implication of this enunciative split for cultural analysis that I especially want to emphasise is its temporal dimension. The splitting of the subject of enunciation destroys the logics of synchronicity and evolution which traditionally authorise the subject of cultural knowledge. It is often taken for granted in materialist and idealist problematics that the value of culture as an object of study and the value of any analytic activity that is considered cultural lie in a capacity to produce a cross-referential, generalisable unity that signifies a progression or evolution of ideas-in-time, as well as a critical self-reflection on their premises or determinants. It would not be relevant to pursue the detail of this argument here except to demonstrate – via Marshall Sahlins' *Culture and Practical Reason* – the validity of my general characterisation of the Western expectation of culture as a disciplinary practice of writing. I quote Sahlins at the point at which he attempts to define the difference of Western bourgeois culture:

> We have to do not so much with functional dominance as with structural – with different structures of symbolic *integration*. And to this gross difference in design correspond differences in symbolic performance: between an *open*, *expanding* code, responsive by *con*-

129

tinuous permutation to events it has itself staged, and an apparently *static* one that seems to know not events, but only its own preconceptions. The gross distinction between 'hot' societies and 'cold', development and underdevelopment, societies with and without history – and so between large societies and small, expanding and self-contained, colonising and colonised. (My emphases)[17]

The intervention of the Third Space of enunciation, which makes the structure of meaning and reference an ambivalent process, destroys this mirror of representation in which cultural knowledge is customarily revealed as an integrated, open, expanding code. Such an intervention quite properly challenges our sense of the historical identity of culture as a homogenising, unifying force, authenticated by the originary Past, kept alive in the national tradition of the People. In other words, the disruptive temporality of enunciation displaces the narrative of the Western nation which Benedict Anderson so perceptively describes as being written in homogeneous, serial time.[18]

It is only when we understand that all cultural statements and systems are constructed in this contradictory and ambivalent space of enunciation, that we begin to understand why hierarchical claims to the inherent originality or 'purity' of cultures are untenable, even before we resort to empirical historical instances that demonstrate their hybridity. Fanon's vision of revolutionary cultural and political change as a 'fluctuating movement' of occult instability could not be articulated as cultural *practice* without an acknowledgment of this indeterminate space of the subject(s) of enunciation. It is that Third Space, though unrepresentable in itself, which constitutes the discursive conditions of enunciation that ensure that the meaning and symbols of culture have no primordial unity or fixity; that even the same signs can be appropriated, translated, rehistoricised, and read anew.

Fanon's moving metaphor – when reinterpreted for a theory of cultural signification – enables us to see not only the necessity of theory, but also the restrictive notions of cultural identity with which we burden our visions of political change. For Fanon, the liberatory 'people' who initiate the productive instability of revolutionary cultural change are themselves the bearers of a hybrid identity. They are caught in the discontinuous time of translation and negotiation, in the sense in which I have been attempting to recast these words. In the moment of liberatory struggle, the Algerian people destroy the continuities and constancies of the 'nationalist' tradition which provided a safeguard against colonial cultural imposition. They are now free to negotiate and translate their cultural identities in a discontinuous intertextual temporality of cultural difference. The native intellectual who identifies the people with the 'true national culture' will be disappointed. The people are now the very principle of 'dialectical reorganisation' and they construct their culture from the national text translated into modern Western forms of information technology, language, dress. The changed political and historical site of enunciation transforms the meanings of the colonial inheritance into the liberatory signs of a free people of the future.

> I have been stressing a certain void or misgiving attending every assimilation of contraries – I have been stressing this in order to expose what seems to me a fantastic mythological congruence of elements. . . . And if indeed therefore any real sense is to be made of material change it can only occur with an acceptance of a concurrent void and with a willingness to descend into that void wherein, as it were, one may begin to come into confrontation with a spectre of invocation whose freedom to participate in an alien territory and wilderness has become a necessity for one's reason or salvation.[19]

This meditation by the great Guyanan writer Wilson Harris on the void of misgiving in the textuality of colonial history reveals the cultural and historical dimension of that Third Space of enunciation which I have made the precondition for the articulation of cultural difference. He sees it as accompanying the 'assimilation of contraries' and creating that occult instability which presages powerful cultural changes. It is significant that the productive capacities of this Third Space have a colonial or post-colonial provenance. For a willingness to descend into that alien territory – where I have led you – may reveal that the theoretical recognition of the split-space of enunciation may open the way to conceptualising an *inter*national culture, based not on the exoticism or multi-culturalism of the *diversity* of cultures, but on the inscription and articulation of culture's *hybridity*. To that end we should remember that it is the 'inter' – the cutting edge of translation and negotiation, the *in-between*, the space of the *entre* that Derrida has opened up in writing itself – that carries the burden of the meaning of culture. It makes it possible to begin envisaging national, anti-nationalist histories of the 'people'. It is in this space that we will find those words with which we can speak of Ourselves and Others. And by exploring this hybridity, this 'Third Space', we may elude the politics of polarity and emerge as the others of our selves.

Notes

1. See Clyde Taylor, 'Eurocentrics vs new thought at Edinburgh', *Framework* 34 (1987), for an illustration of this style of argument. See particularly footnote 1 (p. 148) for an exposition of his use of 'larceny' ('the judicious distortion of African truths to fit western prejudices').
2. Gayatri C. Spivak, *In Other Worlds* (London: Methuen, 1987), pp. 166–7.
3. See Teshome H. Gabriel, 'Teaching Third World cinema' and Julianne Burton, 'The politics of aesthetic distance – Sao Bernardo', both in *Screen*, 24, 2 (March-April 1983), and Ashish Rajadhyaksha, 'Neo-traditionalism: film as popular art in India', *Framework* 32/33 (1986).
4. Stuart Hall, 'Blue election, election blues', *Marxism Today* (July 1987), pp. 30–5.
5. Michel Foucault, *The Archaeology of Knowledge* (London: Tavistock, 1972), pp. 102–5.
6. J.S. Mill, *On Liberty* (London: Dent & Sons, 1972), pp. 93–4.
7. For a significant elaboration of a similar argument see Ernesto Laclau and Chantal Mouffe, *Hegemony and Socialist Strategy* (London: Verso, 1985), ch. 3.
8. For a philosophical underpinning of some of the concepts I am proposing here see Rodolphe Gasché, *The Tain of the Mirror* (Cambridge, Mass.: Harvard University Press, 1986), especially ch. 6: 'The Otherness of unconditional heterology does not have the purity of principles. It is concerned with the principles' irreducible impurity, with the difference that divides them in themselves against themselves. For this reason it is an impure heterology. But it is also an impure heterology because the medium of Otherness – more and less than negativity – is also a mixed milieu, precisely because the negative no longer dominates it.'
9. Hall, op. cit., p. 33.
10. I owe this point to Martin Thom.
11. Laclau and Mouffe, op. cit., ch. 3.
12. Paul Gilroy, *There Ain't No Black in the Union Jack* (London: Hutchinson, 1987), p. 214.
13. Frantz Fanon, *The Wretched of the Earth* (Harmondsworth: Penguin, 1967 [1961]), p. 168.
14. Jean-Paul Sartre, *Politics and Literature* (London: Calder & Boyars, 1973 [1948]), pp. 16–17.
15. Fanon, op. cit., pp. 182–3.
16. Bernard Williams, *Ethics and the Limits of Philosophy* (London: Fontana, 1985), ch. 9.
17. Marshall Sahlins, *Culture and Practical Reason* (Chicago: Chicago University Press, 1976), p. 211.
18. Benedict Anderson, *Imagined Communities* (London: Verso, 1983), ch. 2.
19. Wilson Harris, *Tradition, the Writer, and Society* (New Beacon: 1973), pp. 60–3.

Outside In Inside Out

Trinh T. Minh-ha

An objective constantly claimed by those who 'seek to reveal one society to another' is 'to grasp the native's point of view' and 'to realise *his* vision of *his* world'. Fomenting much discord, in terms of methodology and approach, among specialists in the directly concerned fields of anthropology and ethnographic film-making in the last decade, such a goal is also diversely taken to heart by many of us who consider it our mission to represent others, and to be their loyal interpreters. The injunction to see things from the native's point of view speaks for a definite ideology of truth and authenticity; it lies at the centre of every polemical discussion on 'reality' in its relation to 'beauty' and 'truth'. To raise the question of representing the Other is, therefore, to reopen endlessly the fundamental issue of science and art; documentary and fiction; universal and personal; objectivity and subjectivity; masculine and feminine; outsider and insider.

Knowledge about often gives the illusion of knowledge

Zora Neale Hurston wrote years ago how amazed she was by the Anglo-Saxon's lack of curiosity about the internal lives and emotions of the negroes, and more generally of any non-Anglo-Saxon peoples. Although this still largely holds true today, one is more inclined to restate this differently by saying that one is presently more amazed by the general claim of Western 'experts' to be interested just in that aspect of the Other's life and in not much else. The final aim now is 'to uncover the Javanese, Balinese or Moroccan sense of self', supposedly through the definitions they have of themselves. Things often look as though they have radically changed, whereas they may have just taken on opposite appearances, as they so often do, to shuffle the cards and set people on a side-track. The move from obnoxious exteriority to obtrusive interiority, the race for the so-called *hidden* values of a person or a culture, have given rise to a form of legitimised (but unacknow-

133

ledged as such) voyeurism and of subtle arrogance – namely, the pretence to see into or to *own* the others' *mind*, whose *knowledge* these others cannot, supposedly, have themselves; and the need to define, hence confine, providing them thereby with a standard of self-evaluation on which they necessarily depend. Psychological *conflicts*, among other idiosyncratic elements, are thus equated with *depth* (a keyword of Occidental metaphysics), while *inner* experience is reduced to subjectivity as *personal* feelings and views.

'How it Feels to Be Colored Me'[1]
How Does it Feel to Be White You?

A good, serious film about the Other must show some kind of conflict, for this is how the West often defines identities and differences. To many scientifically oriented film-makers, seeing ironically continues to be believing. Showing is not showing how I can see you, how you can see me and how we are both being perceived – the encounter – but how you see yourself and represent your own kind (at best, through conflicts), the Fact by itself. Factual authenticity relies heavily on the Other's words and testimony. To authenticate a work, it becomes therefore most important to prove or make evident how this Other has participated in the making of his/her own image; hence, for example, the prominence of the string-of-interviews style and the talking-heads, oral-witnessing strategy in documentary film practices. This is often called 'giving voice', even though these 'given' voices never truly form the Voice of the film, being mostly used as devices of legitimation whose random, conveniently given-as and taken-for-granted authority often serves as compensation for a filmic Lack (the lack of imagination or of believability, for example). Power creates its very constraints, for the Powerful is also necessarily defined by the Powerless. Power therefore has to be shared ('shared anthropology' is a notion that has been tossed around for a try), so that its effect may continue to circulate; but it will be shared only partly, with much caution, and on the condition that the share is *given*, not taken. A famed anthropologist thus voiced the crisis existing in his field when he wrote: 'Where are we when we can no longer claim some unique form of psychological closeness, a sort of transcultural identification with our subjects?'[2] Surely, the man has to keep his role alive. And after all, there is always some truth in every error.

> the matter is one of degree, not polar opposition ... Confinement to experience-near concepts leaves an ethnographer awash in immediacies, as well as entangled in vernacular. Confinement to experience-distant ones leaves him stranded in abstractions and

smothered in jargon. The real question, and the one . . . in the case
of 'natives', you don't have to be one to know one, is what roles
the two sorts of concepts play in anthropological analysis.[3]

However, 'to put oneself into someone else's skin' is not without difficulty. The risk the man fears for himself as well as for his fellow men is that of 'going over the hill'. For this, he takes on the task of advising and training his followers for detachment in the field so that they may all remain on the winning side. Giving, in such a context, should always be determined 'with reference to what, by the light of Western knowledge and experience tempered by local considerations', *We think is best for them.*[4] Thus, make sure to take in Their secrets, but don't ever give up Ours.

> *The trick is not to get yourself into some inner correspondence of*
> *spirit with your informants. Preferring, like the rest of us, to call*
> *their souls their own, they are not going to be altogether keen*
> *about such effort anyhow. The trick is to figure out what the devil*
> *they think they are up to.*[5]

The natural outcome of such a rationale is the arranged marriage between 'experience-distant' and 'experience-near', between scientist's objectivity and native's subjectivity, between outsider's input and insider's output. To get at the most intimate, hidden notions of the Other's self, the man has to rely on a form of (neo-)colonial interdependency. And since sharing in this framework always means giving little and taking more than little, the need for informants grows into a need for disciples. We have to train Insiders so that they may busy themselves with Our preoccupations, and make themselves useful by asking the right kind of Question and providing the right kind of Answer. Thus, the ideal Insider is the psychologically conflict-detecting and problem-solving subject who faithfully represents the Other for the Master, or comforts, more specifically, the Master's self-other relationship in its enactment of power relations, gathering serviceable data, minding his/her own business-territory, and yet offering the difference expected.

THE 'PET' NEGRO SYSTEM
(by Zora Neale Hurston)

And every white man shall be allowed to pet himself a Negro. Yea,
he shall take a black man unto himself to pet and to cherish, and
this same Negro shall be perfect in his sight. Nor shall hatred

135

among the races of men, nor conditions of strife in the walled cities, cause his pride and pleasure in his own Negro to wane.[6]

when everything is discounted, it still remains true that white people North and South have promoted Negroes – usually in the capacity of 'representing the Negro' – with little thought of the ability of the person promoted but in line with the 'pet' system.[7]

Apartheid precludes any contact with people of different races which might undermine the assumption of essential difference.[8]

An Insider's view: the magic word that bears within itself a seal of approval. What can be more authentically 'other' than an otherness by the other him/herself? Yet every piece of the cake given by the Master comes with a double-edged blade. The Afrikaners are prompt in saying, 'You can take a black man from the bush, but you can't take the bush from the black man.'

The place of the native is always well-delimited. 'Correct' cultural film-making usually implies that Africans show Africa; Asians, Asia; and Euro-Americans . . . the World. Otherness has its laws and interdictions. Since 'you can't take the bush from the black man', it is the bush that is consistently given back to him, and as things often turn out, it is also this very bush that the black man shall make his exclusive territory. And he may do so with the full awareness that barren land is hardly a gift, for, in the unfolding of power inequalities, changes frequently require that rules be reappropriated so that the Master be beaten at his own game. The conceited giver likes to give with the understanding that he is in a position to take back what he gives whenever he feels like it and whenever the accepter dares or happens to trespass on his preserves. The latter, however, sees no gift (can you imagine such a thing as a gift that takes?) but only debts that once given back should remain his property, although (land-)owning is a concept that has long been foreign to him and that he refused to assimilate.

Through audiences' responses to and expectations of their works, non-white film-makers are thus often informed and reminded of the territorial boundaries in which they are to remain. An insider can speak with authority about his/her own culture, and s/he is referred to as a source of authority in this matter – not as a film-maker necessarily, but as an insider, merely. This automatic and arbitrary endowment of an insider with legitimised knowledge about his/her cultural heritage and environment only exerts its power when it is question of validating power. It is a paradoxical twist of the colonial mind: what the Outsider expects from the Insider is, in fact, a projection of an all-knowing subject that this Outsider usually attributes to himself and to his own

136

kind. In this unacknowledged self-other relation, however, the other would always remain the shadow of the self, hence *not-really-not-quite* 'all-knowing'. That a white person makes a film on the Goba of the Zambezi or on the Tasaday in the Philippine rain forest seems hardly surprising to anyone, but that a Third World member makes a film on other Third World peoples never fails to appear questionable to many. The question concerning the choice of subject matter immediately arises, sometimes out of curiosity, most often out of hostility. The marriage is not consumable, for the pair is no longer 'outside-inside' (objective versus subjective), but something between 'inside-inside' (subjective in what is already designated as subjective) and 'outside-outside' (objective in what is already claimed as objective). No real conflict.

> *Difference, yes, but difference*
> *Within the borders of your homelands, they say*
> *White rule and the policy of ethnic divisions*

Any attempts at blurring the dividing line between outsider and insider would justifiably provoke anxiety, if not anger. Territorial rights are not being respected here. Violations of boundaries have always led to displacement, for the in-between zones are the shifting grounds on which the (doubly) exiled walk. Not You/like You. The Insider's subjectivity (understood as limited affective horizon – the personal) is that very area for which the objective (understood as unbiased limitless horizon – the universal) Outsider cannot claim full authority, but thanks to which he can continue to validate his indispensable role, claiming nooow his due through 'interpretive' but still totalising scientific knowledge.

> *Anthropology is the science of culture as seen from the outside* (Claude Lévi-Strauss).[9]

> *Thus, if the natives were to study themselves, they were said to produce history or philology, not anthropology.*[10]

> *it is only a representative of our civilisation who can, in adequate detail, document the difference, and help create an idea of the primitive which would not ordinarily be constructed by primitives themselves.*[11]

Interdependency cannot be reduced to a mere question of mutual enslavement. It also consists in creating a ground that belongs to no one, not even to the 'creator'. Otherness becomes empowering critical difference when it is not given, but re-created. Defined with the Other's newly

Stills from *Naked Spaces – Living is Round* by Trinh T. Minh-ha

formed criteria. Imperfect cinema is subversive, not because science is contributing to the 'purification' of art as it 'allows us to free ourselves from so many fraudulent films, concealed behind what has been called the world of poetry';[12] not because 'the larger the grain, the better the politics'; or because a shaky, blurry, badly framed shot is truer, more sincere and authentic than a 'beautiful', technically masterful shot (shaking the camera can also be a technique); but more, I would say, because there is no such thing as an (absolute) imperfection when perfection can only construct itself through the existence of its imperfect Other. In other words, perfection is produced, not merely given. The values that keep the dominant set of criteria in power are simply ineffective in a framework where one no longer abides by them.

Non-Westerners may or may not want to make film on their own societies. Whatever the choice, the question is certainly not that of setting an opposition to dominant practices, since 'opposing' in the one-dimensional context of modern societies usually means playing into the Master's hand. For years, They have been saying with much patronising care: 'Africa to Africans'; 'We should encourage those from the Third World to make films on their own people'; 'We would like to see Asians as told by Asians'; or We want 'to *teach* people with a culture different from ours to make motion pictures depicting their culture and themselves as *they* see fit' (so that We can collect data on the indigenous ethnographic film-making process, and show Navajos through Navajo eyes to our folks in the field).[13] Again, this is akin to saying that a non-white view is desirable because it would help to fill in a hole that whites

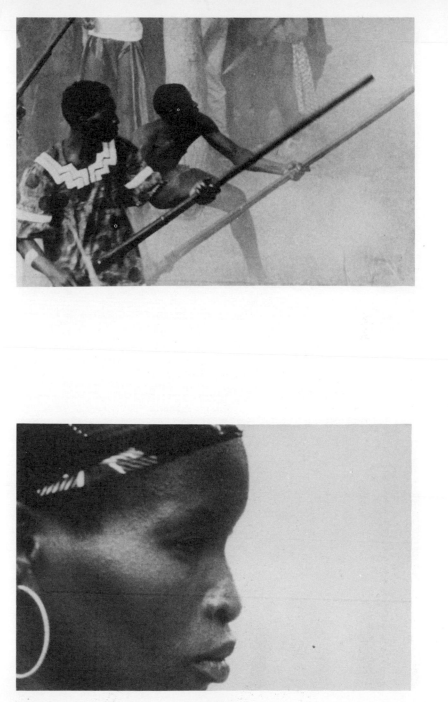

139

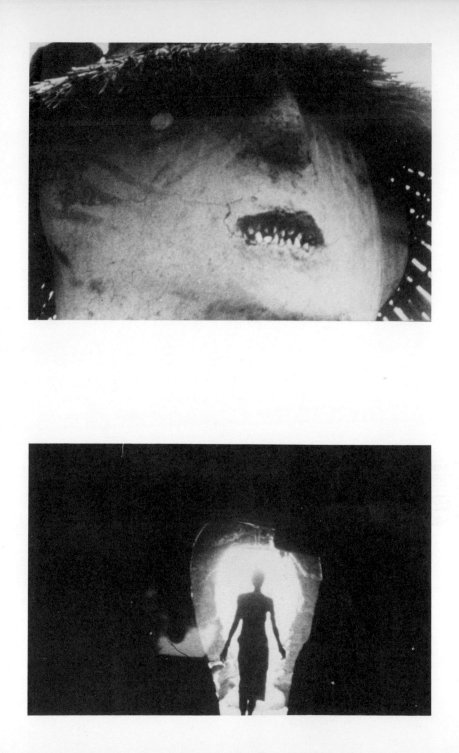

are now *willing* to leave more or less empty so as to lessen the critical pressure and to give the illusion of a certain incompleteness that needs the native's input to be more complete, but is ultimately dependent on white authority to attain any form of 'real' completion. Such a 'charity' mission is still held up with much righteousness by many; and despite the many changing appearances it has taken through the years, the image of the white colonial Saviour seems more pernicious than ever since it operates now via consent. Indigenous anthropology allows white anthropology to further anthropologise Man.

Anthropology is today the foundation of every single discourse pronounced above the native's head.

The 'portraits' of a group produced by the observer as outsider and by the observer as insider will differ, as they will be relevant in different contexts. This awareness underlies the current cry 'You have to be one to understand one'.[14]

The question is also not that of merely 'correcting' the images whites have of non-whites, nor of reacting to the colonial territorial mind by simply reversing the situation and setting up an opposition that at best will hold up a mirror to the Master's activities and preoccupations. (It has been, for example, the talk of some French anthropologists, not long ago, to train and bring in a few African anthropologists-disciples to study the cultural aspects of remote villages in France. Again, let Them – whom We taught – study Us, for this is also information, and this is how the anthropologising wheel is kept rotating.) The question rather is that of tracking down and exposing the Voice of Power and Censorship whenever and in whichever side it appears. Essential difference allows those who rely on it to rest reassuringly on its gamut of fixed notions. Any mutation in identity, in essence, in regularity, and even in physical place, poses a problem, if not a threat, in terms of classification and control. If you can't locate the other, how are you to locate your-self?

One's sense of self is always mediated by the image one has of the other. (I have asked myself at times whether a superficial know-ledge of the other, in terms of some stereotype, is not a way of preserving a superficial image of oneself.)[15]

Furthermore, where should the dividing line between outsider and insider stop? How should it be defined? By skin colour (no Blacks should make films on Yellows)? By language (only Fulani can talk about Fulani, a Bassari is a foreigner here)? By nation (only Vietnamese can

144

produce works on Vietnam)? By geography (in the North-South setting, East is East and East can't meet West)? Or by political affinity (Third World on Third World counter First and Second Worlds)? What about those with hyphenated identities and hybrid realities? (It is worth noting here a journalist's report in a recent *Time* issue, which is entitled 'A Crazy Game of Musical Chairs'. In this brief but concise report, attention is drawn to the fact that people in South Africa who are classified by race and placed into one of the nine racial categories that determine where they can live and work can have their classification changed if they can prove they were put in a wrong group. Thus, in an announcement of racial reclassifications by the Home Affairs Minister, one learns that: *'nine whites became coloured, 506 coloureds became white, two whites became Malay, 14 Malay became white ... 40 coloureds became black, 666 blacks became coloured, 87 coloureds became Indian, 67 Indians became coloured, 26 coloureds became Malay, 50 Malays became Indian, 61 Indians became Malay ...',* and the list goes on. However, says the Minister, *no blacks applied to become white, and no whites became black.*)[16]

The moment the insider steps out from the inside, she is no longer a mere insider (and vice versa). She necessarily looks in from the outside while also looking out from the inside. Like the outsider, she steps back and records what never occurs to her-the insider as being worth or in need of recording. But unlike the outsider, she also resorts to non-explicative, non-totalising strategies that suspend meaning and resist closure. (This is often viewed by the outsiders as strategies of partial concealment and disclosure aimed at preserving secrets that should only be imparted to the initiates.) She refuses to reduce herself to an Other, and her reflections to a mere outsider's objective reasoning or insider's subjective feeling. She knows, probably as Zora Neale Hurston the insider-anthropologist knew, that she is not an outsider like the foreign outsider. She knows she is different while being Him. Not quite the Same, not quite the Other, she stands in that undetermined threshold place where she constantly drifts in and out. Undercutting the inside/ outside opposition, her intervention is necessarily that of both a deceptive insider and a deceptive outsider. She is this Inappropriate Other/ Same who moves about with always at least two/four gestures: that of affirming 'I am like you' while persisting in her difference; and that of reminding herself 'I am different' while unsettling every definition of otherness arrived at.

> *It is thrilling to think – to know that for any act of mine, I shall get twice as much praise or twice as much blame. It is quite exciting to hold the centre of the national stage, with the spectators not knowing whether to laugh or to weep.* (Zora Neale Hurston)[17]

The coloured are a very emotional people, and you can't trust the Bantus. A farmer here asked his Bantu foreman once, 'Tell me, Johnny, would you shoot me?' 'No,baas, I wouldn't shoot you,' Johnny said. 'I'd go to the neighbour's place and shoot the baas there. And his man would shoot you.' (An Afrikaner)[18]

The theory behind our tactics: 'The white man is always trying to know into somebody else's business. All right, I'll set something outside the door of my mind for him to play with and handle. He can read my writing but he sho' can't read my mind. I'll put this play toy in his hand, and he will seize it and go away. Then I'll say my say and sing my song.' (Zora Neale Hurston)[19]

the only possible ethnology is the one that studies the anthropophagous behaviour of the White man. (Stanislas S. Adotevi)[20]

Whether she turns the inside out or the outside in, she is, like the two sides of a coin, the same impure, both-in-one insider/outsider. For there can hardly be such a thing as an essential inside that can be homogeneously represented by all insiders; an authentic insider in here, an absolute reality out there, or an uncorrupted representative who cannot be questioned by another uncorrupted representative.

The most powerful reason why Negroes do not do more about false 'representation' by pets is that they know from experience that the thing is too deep-rooted to be budged. The appointer has his reasons, personal or political. He can always point to the beneficiary and say, 'Look, Negroes, you have been taken care of. Didn't I give a member of your group a big job?' White officials assume that the Negro element is satisfied and they do not know what to make of it when later they find that so large a body of Negroes charge indifference and double-dealing. The white friend of the Negroes mumbles about ingratitude and decides that you simply can't understand Negroes . . . just like children.[21]

In the context of this Inappropriate Other, questions like 'How loyal a representative of his/her people is s/he?' (the film-maker as insider), or 'How authentic is his/her representation of the culture observed?' (the film-maker as outsider) are of little relevance. When the magic of essences ceases to impress and intimidate, there no longer is a position of authority from which one can definitely judge the verisimilitude value of the representation. In the first question, the questioning subject, even if s/he is an insider, is no more authentic and has no more authority on the subject matter than the subject whom the questions concern. This is not to say that the historical 'I' can be obscured or

146

ignored, and that differentiation cannot be made; but that 'I' is not unitary, culture has never been monolithic, and more or less is always more or less in relation to a judging subject. Differences do not only exist between outsider and insider – two entities – they are also at work within the outsider or the insider – a single entity. This leads us to the second question in which the film-maker is an outsider. As long as the film-maker takes up a positivistic attitude and chooses to bypass the inter-subjectivities and realities involved, factual truth remains the dominant criterion for evaluation and the question as to whether his/her work successfully represents the reality it claims would continue to exert its power. The more the representation leans on verisimilitude, the more it is subject to normative verification.

For the Inappropriate Other, however, the questions mentioned above seem inadequate; the criterion of authenticity no longer proves pertinent. It is like saying to an atheist: 'How faithful to the words of God are yours?' (with the understanding that the atheist is not opposed, but *in-different* to the believer). She who knows she cannot speak of them without speaking of herself, of history without involving her story, also knows that she cannot make a gesture without activating the to-and-fro movement of life. The subjectivity at work in the context of this Inappropriate Other can hardly be submitted to the old subjectivity/objectivity paradigm. Acute political subject-awareness cannot be reduced to a question of self-criticism toward self-improvement or of self-praise toward greater self-confidence. Such differentiation is useful, for a grasp of subjectivity as a 'science of the subject' makes the fear of ethnographic self-absorption look absurd. Awareness of the limits in which one works need not lead to any form of indulgence in personal partiality, nor to the narrow conclusion that it is impossible to understand anything about other peoples since the difference is one of 'essence'.

By refusing to naturalise the 'I', subjectivity uncovers the myth of essential core, of spontaneity, and of depth as inner vision. Subjectivity therefore does not merely consist of talking about oneself, be this talking indulgent or critical. Many who agree on the necessity of self-reflectivity and reflexivity in film-making think that it suffices to show oneself at work on the screen, or to point to one's role once in a while in the film, and to suggest some future improvement in order to convince the audience of one's 'honesty' and pay one's dues to liberal thinking. Thus there is now a growing body of films in which the spectators see the narrator narrating, the film-maker filming or directing, and quite expectedly the natives – to whom a little camera (usually a Super-8) or tape-recorder is temporarily handed out – supposedly contributing to the production process. What is put forth as self-reflexivity here is no more than a small faction – the most conveniently visible one – of the many possibilities of uncovering the work of ideology that this 'science of the subject' can open into. In short, what is at stake is a practice of subjectivity that is still unaware of its own constituted nature (hence the difficulty of exceeding the simplistic pair of subjectivity and objectivity); unaware of its continuous role in the production of meaning (as if things can 'make sense' by themselves, so that the interpreter's function consists only of *choosing* among the many existing readings); unaware of representation as representation (the cultural, sexual, political inter-realities involved in the making: that of the film-maker as subject; that of the subject filmed; and that of the cinematic apparatus); and, finally, unaware of the Inappropriate Other within every 'I'.

My certainty of being excluded by the Blacks one day is not strong enough to prevent me from fighting on their sides. (a South African writer)[22]

What does present a challenge is an organisation that consists either in close association or in alliance of black, white, Indian, Coloured. Such a body constitutes a negation of the Afrikaans' theory of separateness, their medieval clannishness. (Ezekiel Mphahlele)[23]

the stereotyped quiet, obedient, conforming modes of Japanese behaviour clashed with white expectations of being a motivated, independent, ambitious thinker. When I was with whites, I worried about talking loud enough; when I was with Japanese, I worried about talking too loud. (Joanne Harumi Sechi)[24]

Walking erect and speaking in an inaudible voice, I have tried to turn myself American-feminine. Chinese communication was loud, public. Only sick people had to whisper. (Maxine Hong Kingston)[25]

When I hear my students say 'We're not against the Iranians here who are minding their own business. We're just against those ungrateful ones who overstep our hospitality by demonstrating and badmouthing our government,' I know they speak about me. (Mitsuye Yamada)[26]

Notes

1. An article by Zora Neale Hurston. It was most likely a response to a question Hurston felt her white acquaintances were always burning to ask her. In Alice Walker (ed.), *I Love Myself* (Old Westbury, New York: The Feminist Press, 1979), pp. 152–5.
2. Clifford Geertz, *Local Knowledge* (New York: Basic Books, 1983), p. 56.
3. Ibid., p. 57.
4. Evelyn Baring, Lord Cromer, *Political and Literary Essays, 1908–1913* (1913; reprinted Freeport, New York: Books for Library Press, 1969).
5. Geertz, *Local Knowledge*, p. 58.
6. Hurston, *I Love Myself*, p. 156.
7. Ibid., p. 160.
8. Vincent Crapanzano, 'A Reporter at Large', *The New Yorker*, 18 March 1985.
9. Claude Lévi-Strauss, 'Anthropology: Its Achievements and Future', *Current Anthropology*, no. 7, 1966, p. 126.
10. Ibid.
11. Stanley Diamond, 'A Revolutionary Discipline', *Current Anthropology*, no. 5, 1964, p. 433.
12. Julio García Espinosa, 'For an Imperfect Cinema', in Michael Chanan (ed.), *Twenty-five Years of the New Latin American Cinema* (London: BFI/Channel 4 Television, 1983), pp. 28–33.
13. See Sol Worth and John Adair, *Through Navajo Eyes* (Bloomington: Indiana University Press, 1972).
14. Diane Lewis, 'Anthropology and Colonialism', *Current Anthropology*, no. 14, 1973, pp. 586–7.
15. Vincent Crapanzano, 'A Reporter at Large'.
16. *Time*, 9 March 1987, p. 54.
17. Hurston, *I Love Myself*, p. 153.
18. Dora Herzog, quoted in Vincent Crapanzano, 'A Reporter at Large: II', *The New Yorker*, 25 March 1985, p. 93.
19. Hurston, *I Love Myself*, p. 83.
20. *Négritude et négrologue* (Paris: Union Générale d'Editions, 1972), p. 182 (my translation).
21. Hurston, *I Love Myself*, p. 161.
22. Breyten Breytenbach, 'L'Aveuglement des Afrikaners', *Le Nouvel Observateur*, 20–26 June 1986, p. 48 (my translation).
23. *The African Image* (1962; reprinted New York: Praeger, 1966), p. 73.
24. 'Being Japanese-American Doesn't Mean "Made in Japan"', in Dexter Fisher (ed.), *The Third Woman* (Boston: Houghton Mifflin, 1980), p. 446.
25. *The Woman Warrior* (New York: Vintage Books, 1977).
26. 'Asian Pacific American Women and Feminism', in Cherrie Moraga and Gloria Anzaldua, *This Bridge Called My Back* (Watertown, Mass.: Persephone Press, 1981), p. 75.

Speaking of 'Ceylon', a clash of cultures[1]

Laleen Jayamanne

Anna Rodrigo:	Have you forgotten your country?
The Author:	*A Song of Ceylon* is in a way an attempt at not forgetting, among a few other things. Let's look at the other things, shall we, as the forgetting or not forgetting concerns only me and maybe you.[2]

In 1972 the island known as Ceylon was officially renamed Sri Lanka:

Herr Rutman:	Wo ist Ceylon?
Frau Lalüne:	Neither here nor there.[3]

In the absence of a relationship to the particularity of a beloved site, a land, a country, this film generates itself by parasitically appropriating the title of Basil Wright's 1935 British documentary *Song of Ceylon* and changing it into *A Song of Ceylon*. Is this appropriation simply a matter of an erudite quotation to be followed by further displays of knowledge of film history, or is the way it functions an index of some other process? If one has swallowed a lot of cinema then it is necessary to exorcise it, especially when working within the problematic of quotation from canonical texts. The question was something like how to use certain stills from classical films without simply reproducing them as quotations; and in terms of the sound, how to perform the text without embodying the mad woman.

A few teacherly asides

The conjunction of feminism and cinema in the 70s enabled forms of knowledge and ways of knowing hitherto unknown. I was not alone in feeling that knowledge, pleasure and desire, experiences which were previously painfully discrete, need no longer be so because of the radical epistemological shift in the study of the humanities marked by ambitions of interdisciplinary endeavour, which led to the constitution of the disciplinary field (disciplinary, unfortunately, in more than one sense) known as cinema studies. In this context the examination of the processes of the production of knowledge, of meaning, became central. We were methodologically equipped to enquire into the production of 'the Feminine', the notion of 'Woman' in cinema. It was not as if something called 'feminist content' lay hidden in films to be uncovered by feminists, but rather that new methods of conceptualising language and image, made possible by the conjunction of linguistics, semiotics, narrative analysis and psychoanalysis, when brought to bear on cultural artefacts like film, enabled ways of destabilising traditional meanings and interpretations which accrued to those objects. Methodologies with varying degrees of sophistication did produce new readings, ideas, values and hopes.

Anna Rodrigo:	Let's talk about the urbane drinking scene between the transvestite and the man in a suit.
The Author:	Did you like the kiss?
Anna Rodrigo:	Yes.
The Author:	What about it?
Anna Rodrigo:	The disjunction of intensity.
The Author:	What do you mean?
Anna Rodrigo:	The colours, textures and the light are sensuous, intense and produce a kind of erotic langour while the kiss itself feels like a gesture bereft of affect not unlike some of the repetitions of hand-gestures. The kiss should be intense but is not because it can't be ...
The Author:	No, not in that *mise en scène*. Have you seen Dovzhenko's *Zvenigora*?
Anna Rodrigo:	Years ago in the early 50s.
The Author:	Do you remember that marvellous drinking scene in the 'mythical' section where the woman poisons her lover. It's done a bit like silent DeMille but even more formal, more ritualistically choreographed.[4]

151

Psychoanalysis as the theory of sexual difference was appropriated by feminists in order to understand the constitution of the gendered subject *in extremis*. Through feminist work with and on psychoanalysis the possibility was opened up of a sexual economy other than the hierarchised, oppositional mode of conceptualising sexual difference. This appropriation of psychoanalysis was methodological and strategic. One of the main methodological tools was the appropriation of Lacan's theorising of the sense modality of vision in terms of the scopic drive. 'The Look', 'Spectacle' and 'Suture', the privileged cluster of concepts, were used to understand how they constructed the female form in classical cinema. 'The Look', its coding, its unconscious determinants, were used to understand how cinematic pleasure was linked to forms of gendered subjectivity. 'The Look' referring to that of the camera and the intradiegetic gaze and also to that of the observer as it constructs sexual difference, 'Spectacle' relating to the idea of *mise en scène*, and 'Suture' to a particular mode of editing as well as a certain mechanism of identification – the development of these concepts was a real advance in knowledge but it now seems unlikely that anything useful can follow from them, given the terms within which they have been theorised, which are largely those of psychoanalysis.

The blockage in the field is due to the fact that one can now only repeat the original insights through innumerable examples, through a simple model of application. The imbrication of these concepts with a form of protestant feminism has been unfortunate for feminist work in cinema.[5] Also, the way in which the elusive Lacanian discourse on the gaze has been appropriated by anglophone film theory in the 70s is in my view extremely reductive. There is enough in Lacan's oblique theorising of the distinction between the 'look' and the 'gaze' (a distinction that is not adhered to in the anglophone discourse) to generate cinematic work that can move beyond repeating ad nauseam the propositions, 'The Look is male, The Look is bad, down with The Look.'[6] I think the time is over-ripe for a practice which is not simply based on the activity of negating the classical paradigms on which much of the theorising on the cluster of concepts referred to earlier is based. It seems to me essential to maintain the difference between theoretical discourse and film work so that feminist work in film does not dutifully set out to prove the proposition of theory, even feminist theory, because the recent examples of such obedience has led, in my view, to an impoverishment of cinema, of its capacity to surprise in ways unknown and perhaps unknowable to theory.[7]

Anna Rodrigo: But you are not working within the tradition of a film like *Sigmund Freud's Dora*, are you?

The Author: The image of someone being inoculated

appeared on the leaflet soliciting articles for this publication. *Sigmund Freud's Dora* is a film in that tradition of cinema of inoculation – theoretical films which set out to illustrate a particular theory or at best take off from a theory. The least imaginative of these were crippled by servility to the idea of illustration. The best in this genre held at least a few cinematic surprises. I didn't want to make 'Obeyesekere's (the anthropologist) Somawathi' (the possessed woman), much less my own. It seems, now, that we were pursuing an idea of a more abstract body than that of an individual afflicted with hysteria, because the text was about the proliferation of bodies in the one body, many voices articulating it in a constant motion of dissolution.

Anna Rodrigo: Tell me about the supine bodies and also about the voices.

The Author: It is the most appealing posture, especially for the men, voluptuous, strange to see them thus supine.[8]

To come back to the question of reading, what has happened in this obedience to illustrating theory is that there has been a refusal to let films surprise and unsettle the feminist doxas or those of film theory. In a lot of feminist writing on cinema a limited number of theoretical propositions are plastered on to a variety of texts coming up with more of the same. The question of writing – how does one write about film? – also gets elided.

It is in the context of a thorough dissatisfaction with this state of affairs that theoretical model films have been very intensely criticised in Australia, in conversations and in journalistic rather than in scholarly writing. This subservience to theory, this unimaginative relationship to theory, is a failure of imagination and implies the return of the author as theory. This is not a criticism of theoretical work but an attempt to argue for the need for a different kind of relationship to theory vis-à-vis film so that we can overcome the poverty of reading.[9]

Under the benign shadow of the death of the author (benign because it means, as Barthes suggested, the birth of the reader) this author-turned-reader does however like to hold on to a few vestiges of intentionality, if only to understand the ways in which authorial intentions get transformed, displaced and become irrelevant to any reading of the completed word. Authors too, like you, must observe what it is that they have made and attempt to read it in the sense of inventing the text.

My favourite example of such inventiveness in reading is the answer given to the question 'Why do bodies droop, drop and swoon in *A Song of Ceylon*?' A bloke who saw the film said the bodies were falling as though unable to bear the weight, the intensity of the text. This was not the author's intention in directing bodies to fall into various extended arms, but as I said, intention pales in the face of the inventiveness of reading.

II

Beginnings

Anna Rodrigo: Have you heard or read the text in Sinhalese?
The Author: Alas, I have never read or heard it in our mother tongue. The ritual text is available to me via an anthropological reading of it from a Freudian psychoanalytic point of view. It is therefore a text already marked by a specifically Western interpretation, a particular epistemic reading of the hystericised body of woman.[10]

My main interest in this text is directly related to the work done by feminists in the domain of women and madness. The text even in translation is not simply a text about hysteria but seems to me to be a hysterical text, a text in a mode of excess. There is an investment in rewriting the text for the voices. There is no interest in it as a set of theoretical propositions but rather as a text to be performed and deformed by the voices with all that implies in terms of tone, timbre, rhythm, accent. The text, 'A psychocultural exegesis of a case of spirit possession in Sri Lanka', written by the Sri Lankan anthropologist Gananath Obeyesekere, is itself a hybrid one, for not only does it document the ritual of exorcism, it also includes interviews with the possessed woman, description of the ritual as well as an interpretation of it. The film uses all of these discourses according to its own purposes, which are quite different from those of the discourse of anthropology.

There were two prior uses to which I put this text, one being a chapter in my Ph.D. thesis on the 'Position of Women in the Sri Lankan cinema, 1947–1979',[11] the other a live performance in which it was heard as a sound tape for two voices.[12] The third stage was to find images for it – to make a film. It was clear that the images would not illustrate or represent the drama and trauma of the possessed woman. The problem then was to work out images in which the body was in various forms of transport but on an entirely different register from the possessed body

154

of the text, so that they could exist in parallel space/times without however being totally immune to each other. It was hoped that they would contaminate each other a little, for we did not want a voice-over effect but rather some idea of a tension where neither image nor text is slave to the other, where the relationships would be multiple, flexible. There is an attempt to explore the otherness of language to the body, to explore a bit the difficulty of that difference.

> Anna Rodrigo: In your writing on the Sri Lankan cinema there was a sentence about the 'narrative prodigality' of that cinema. Were you thinking in those terms when you were structuring your film?
>
> The Author: Though there is much that I loathe in my country's cinema, one of the things that I do love is its 'narrative prodigality'; the proliferation of sub-points and sub-sub-plots, arbitrary interruption and switching of modes. I have aspired to this mode of organisation in *A Song of Ceylon* but I am not sure if it really works as well as it does in the Sri Lankan generic film. The intention was certainly there, and maybe if it is not perceptible as such then something hasn't worked in the editing. Do you think it has a certain prodigality in its construction?[13]

If one thrust of colonisation is to homogenise, render readable all that is seen and heard as foreign, then a work that aspires to a different economy might render its object of desire plural, might have an investment in a certain opacity or unreadability. If the objects of desire, the proscenium theatre space, the voice, and the space designated as the feminine are already saturated with meaning, with history, if they seem somewhat exhausted by the burden of that history, then a film which explores all these elements simultaneously must also activate certain processes of gesture, of light; spatio-temporal processes that permit a certain hesitation, a stillness where it is possible to breathe and reconsider the pleasure of the spectacle. *A Song of Ceylon* explores the narcissistic body, the masochistic body, the hysterical body and maybe a few other bodies *in extremis*, and this is done by trying to bring together two different theatrical traditions from two different cultures through the mediation of cinematography. For a Sri Lankan audience of theatre there is nothing more familiar than the proscenium stage, so I am not opposing two systems of drama, South Asian open-air aural to Western renaissance structure. The post-colonial inheritance is one of hybridisation: there is almost nothing pristinely Sri Lankan, certainly

155

not in cinema. This film works with an idea of theatre which is not inimical to film, connected to the etymology of the word theatre deriving from *theomai*, which means to behold, to grasp with one's eyes but also to be held by the vision.

Therefore the centrality of the idea of spectacle is assumed for both theatre and film without moral valuation. *A Song of Ceylon* stages the body as spectacle for both the viewers within the film and of the film, which is why the place of the staging is the proscenium stage and its infamous wings. The major section of the film which is on the proscenium stage is framed both at the beginning and at the end by sequences which occur in domestic spaces. So the familial space frames the space of representation of the body on the stage.

The idea of contamination is signalled by the very opening shot of the film, an image grainy in texture, not immediately recognisable. What is it? Perhaps before there is enough time to decipher it and as if in answer to that classic expository question 'Who is this?', the title of the film and a proper name (initials, a Christian name and a surname) denoting a certain identity are projected on it. 'Ceylon', a proper name evoking a space erased from the map of the world; 'Bernadette', the author's third given name, never voiced so never heard but saturated with meaning: Catholicism, Hollywood memories of *The Song of Bernadette*, Jennifer Jones, the Virgin, visions, apparitions, seeing the invisible, etc. The body, deformed, defamiliarised by the framing, marked by a cut and a suture which runs to the breast, perhaps facilitates the deciphering of the image as being that of a woman. It is not a pristine body but one that is cut, sutured and projected on. First an image, then the image of language, sound of cicadas but no voice as yet.

When the voice is heard in the first sequence of the film it is already doubled, a male and female voice incanting 'My hands and feet grow cold . . .' slightly out of synch. Two voices without a visible body suggest a certain loss of identity, for the I's do not seem to possess the limbs which would constitute their bodily integrity. So the voices speaking of dispossessed bodies permit the autobiographical imperative to be made more oblique and, better still, set it adrift. It is through a series of formal devices (of framing, projection on the body and a particular use of voices) in the first two shots that a movement is made possible from a particular idiosyncratic body to a more generalised exploration of the body *in extremis*.

There is another segment in the film, not quite a scene, dimly lit, through which wisps of smoke rise vertically. It is over this image that the female voice says, 'Do you know who this woman is? This woman is *soma, soma, somawathi, somawathi.*' This fragmentation of the name, its rhythmic stretching and variation, is in the verbal register what this woman's body does in the register of gesture, a refusal of a unitary

156

identity, a proliferation of bodies in the one body, voices speaking in different registers, tones, rhythms and accents. The film of course does not give the particularity of 'this woman' for the viewer to see; instead it turns out that there is a *somawathi*, a possessed body/*soma* in practically every sequence, though it is not very clear who is *somawathi*, who is possessed. This contagion of possessed bodies is related to one of the structuring mechanisms of the film, which is to infuse the 'native' with the 'foreign', to never be able to see or hear the untraduced other in its pristine state.

Anna Rodrigo: The figure of the transvestite is quite central to the film. How was s/he conceptualised?

The Author: At the time I was looking at a still from *Vertigo*, where James Stewart carries Kim Novak out of San Francisco Bay. Juan Davila was suggested because he had performed as a transvestite in *Spider Woman* and also because of his work with tableaux constructions of reversed pietàs. We did not want that element of campy parody as in drag shows. We wanted some archaic echo or resonance between the textual figure of the transvestite priest and the visual figure incarnating the lineaments of classical femininity. Although I had previously worked with the spirit possession text in two other modes, it is only in the film that the possessed priest becomes quite central. A member of the crew, Gabrielle Finnane, urged me to listen to the following words of the text: 'he shakes, he shivers, he chants *gathas*'. So in a way the film has taken its cue from these words. You can see the effect of this, say in the valedictory coda, in the way the male figures come to the fore. In Sinhalese the mad woman, Somawathi, is said to be 'Aruda' or possessed, while the priest is said to be 'Akarshna' or magnetised, electrified. The point being that there is a hierarchical distinction made in their respective forms of bodily travail: one is demonic, the other divine. It is as Kali (the evil mother as opposed to the good mother Pattini) that the transvestite priest is able to tame Somawathi. In fact in the exorcist ritual there is no place for Pattini, but what we did in designing the painted backdrops was to mix motifs from

157

two quite different and incompatible rituals (i.e. the exorcist ritual where Kali is dominant and the ritual for the mother goddess Pattini, called Gammaduwa) within the one frame made of six panels. It is over the black and white image of Pattini that a pair of bodiless hands rests at the opening of the film.[14]

III

Puppets and Puppeteers, Actors and Lover

Anna Rodrigo: Is the disembodied third hand connected to the idea of the puppeteer?

The Author: If Dora's hysteria manifested itself in her throat, then here the zone of investment and terror, pleasure and pain is the hand: 'My hands and feet grow cold ... etc.' But the image does not simply mirror the text. I think it does a number of different things. Yes, the third hand is also the hand of the puppeteer-lover who holds, moulds, pulls, stretches bodies from beyond the limits of the visible frame. That is part of the desire that animated the film.[15]

Your painted teardrop does not draw tears from my eyes the way glycerine-induced tears do sometimes in the cinema. But I prefer the sign, the shape of sorrow to the obscenity of its stimulation, for it leaves me room for my own. The human body, in the agitation of performance or love, may aspire to the poised stillness of the puppet's body and face of papier-mâché or wood. If such aspirations are sustained through a variety of tribulations both mundane and ecstatic, endemic to film and love, flesh and bone may then be moulded, held, stretched and surrendered to the pull of gravity without relinquishing grace.[16]

Rex Butler:[17] You say in an interview that 'the visual ideas for A Song of Ceylon began with looking at a few film stills, which is why the segments most indebted to certain film stills have taken the form of tableaux; the arrangement of bodies in static poses held for so long as to render the body ecstatic, to empty it.' One of these tableaux is from Alfred Hitchcock's Vertigo, a moment that doesn't last more than a few seconds on screen, when James Stewart pulls Kim Novak from the water after she has attempted to drown herself. Literally here, you have held this still itself so long that it too becomes ecstatic, begins to blur, to move; it becomes *filmic* in the sense Roland Barthes uses that word in his essay 'The Third Meaning' – the filmic as precisely *the movement within the still*. Certainly, it seems you want to take us via the still, the tableau, *inside* the fragment, according to Eisenstein's final conception of montage that Barthes cites: '. . . the basic centre of gravity . . . is transferred to *inside* the fragment, into the elements included in the image itself. And the centre of gravity is no longer the elements "between shots" – the shock – but the element "inside the shot" – *the accentuation within the fragment*.' And it's this gravity, that of the Earth and the other, to which the bodies in your film are subject. You yourself say in the interview with Anna Rodrigo: 'I wanted a gesture that was aware of the body as mass, aware of its specific gravity and weight. I wanted a gesture in which the body surrenders to gravity and to another, simultaneously.' Could we generalise at this point and say that it was precisely this *motion already within the body* you wanted to discover in *A Song of Ceylon*, the fact that the body, like the still, is *already filmic*; that the 'basic centre of gravity' and the montage are not outside the body but are within it, traversing it *from the beginning*? And that the task for you, as film-maker, was precisely to *accentuate this fragment*.

That is why it is so strange to see your film described in the Sydney Film Festival notes (1985) as 'framed as a kind of self-contained, poetic response to Britisher Basil Wright's 1935 documentary classic *Song of Ceylon*, the film counterpoints Eastern and Western cultures in a challenging and mesmerising mix of sounds and imagery', when it would be the very status of such 'framing' and 'self-containment' you would be questioning in your film. To what extent, Somawathi, would it be possible to frame your own response when your own body is not even 'properly' yours, when there is already a gravity at work which is taking it beyond itself, rendering it ecstatic? In short, can there be a frame drawn around the body, the still, the text? You seem to raise all these issues yourself in that interview when you draw a distinction between the theatrical and the filmic: 'My greatest investment, in this film, lies in figuring the body. In live performance the possibilities are obviously different from those available in film. In film, lighting, editing, camera distance and movement are equally potent "performers", so that one could talk of filmic performance as including all these technical elements. These

159

elements can transform the phenomenal body to such an extent that one could say that the body that cinema materialises did not exist prior to the invention of film.' And could we talk here, following Eisenstein, of the filmic body as precisely *the space between* the various elements that make up a film – lighting, editing, camera distance, movement, etc. – precisely as a kind of *obtuseness* or resistance to them? Everything we would summarise by the separation of the body from the voice (something that existed even in silent films) – 'the absence of the voice propels the body into registers of excess that draw from a variety of performance traditions,' you say. A difference perhaps itself made possible only by film. You write: 'The separation of the voice from the body is a venerable convention in puppet theatre both eastern and western, a source of its energy and formal sophistication. A voice unfettered by a too intimate proximity to the body may speak, sing, be silent … in a manner not unlike what the puppeteer makes the puppet do. This elegant and at times grotesque distance between the body and the voice, between parts even of the same body as well as between one body and another, is all possible thanks to cinematography, the etymology of which – "writing with movement" – is good to remember even as one trembles at the prospect of directing disembodied hands to trace gestural vectors over bodies rendered still.'

I ask all these questions in the context of *Vertigo* because there too, it seems to me, the body itself is affected by a kind of vertigo, which we might define, strictly speaking, as the *motion within the body* (the vertigo that affects your characters also as they 'droop, drop and swoon' . . .). For me that film is not so much about the psychological themes of fetishism and necrophilia – which are there precisely as *tableaux*, subject themselves to a kind of vertigo that displaces and abolishes them – but rather about a certain repetition or montage *that makes the still impossible*. That is, there can be no single image of Madeline (such as the locket or 'still' of Carlotta): she is simultaneously all women (all women in their way resemble her: Judy, Carlotta, the women James Stewart mistakes her for on the street, even Madeline herself who is only acting out a part – she only *resembles* the *true* Madeline as all the others), and absolutely unique, unable to be repeated. In fact, she exists only as *an effect of those repetitions* (that is to say, Scotty only realises what was unique to her, what it was about her that could not be duplicated, when he is confronted with her exact double, Judy). As you say in your own writing on *A Song of Ceylon*, it is never a question of 'mirror-gazing at identical doubles held in the rapture of narcissistic identification'. It is rather,

160

'an ancient passion that the performer activates by gazing at her double the puppet' – the gaze between Scotty and Judy in *Vertigo*, between Ted Colless and Juan Davila, the woman and her image in the TV screen, between you and your performers (including yourself) in your film, the gesture of opening the eye we see throughout the film. There is only the puppet and the puppeteer, without knowing for a moment which is which. The fact that we cannot move without being moved ourselves. You said, 'What animated her as director of bodies was the possibility of holding, moving, pulling, stretching and moulding bodies; the actor as puppet surrendering his neck, back, arms … to the puppeteer. It seems rather difficult to move, hold, pull, stretch and mould without being moved …'

But could we say, to complete our questioning here, that your film tries to capture the still *and* the moving, the inseparability of both – the stillness of theatre, of two-dimensionality, and the movement of film, of three-dimensionality. As you write: 'When two travellers meet in transient spaces, certain ephemeral exchanges occur that are (alas) impossible in more durational spaces. So, by staging the *mise en scène* of this film (in part) in that space marked by a sense of the passing of time, of the intensity of moments, of a sense of before and after – the theatre, that denigrated space of the proscenium theatre and its infamous wings where so much happens before bodies move into the space of light and sound – by trying to traverse that space filmically, one also wants to transform the more durational places; in so doing one hopes to work in film without having to surrender the pleasures learnt (standing in the wings, waiting with other bodies) in the theatre.' You link cinema etymologically with 'writing with movement' and this seems to sum up very well all that I would like to ask you here: a certain stillness indispensable for writing (that of the desk, the letters on the page, etc.) and the movement without which writing could not be read. And thus for film: the stillness of the individual frame, the passing away of the film itself, its seductive body that is an elusive body (Raymond Bellour), that can neither be readily quoted or grasped.

Laleen Jayamanne: *A Song of Ceylon*, it seems to me, displays a fetishistic delight in the act of framing, cutting the object to fit to the measure of a certain desire, the classical lineaments of which have been described by Barthes thus:

> The tableau (pictorial, theatrical, literary) is a pure cut-out segment with clearly defined edges, irreversible and incorrupt-

161

ible; everything that surrounds it is banished into nothingness, remains unnamed, while everything it admits within its field is promoted into essence, into light, into view.[18]

As distinct from this, *A Song of Ceylon*'s economy is post-colonial in the sense that it is enamoured of corruption, processes of contamination, hybridisation. The fetishistic over-valuation of framing is, however, undermined in several ways, not the least of which is the duration of shots, a propensity to long takes. This might make one feel that the weight of time makes the 'still' image blur and move.

It seems to me that Barthes' observations on the film-still are not entirely sufficient to think through what is happening in this film. Barthes, in concentrating on what is *within* the fragment, forgets what might lie neither inside the shot (*mise en scène*), nor between shots (montage), but what the shot excludes: off-screen space, as well as the tensions and more transient movements that can be generated between on- and off-screen space.

This brings me to one of the main devices of activating the dead zones of off-screen space in this film; the third and fourth hands of the puppeteer-lover. In speaking about these bodiless limbs I will also discuss your notion that the centre of gravity lies within the still. With the appearance of these disembodied hands the integrity of the tableaux, the cut-out, is contaminated with intimations of something, some element, some movement outside the scene. These hands seem to do several things.

The disembodied hands of the puppeteer-lover first appear at the beginning of the film over the painting of the mother goddess Pattini. The gestures of these two hands indicate a structural principle of the use of gesture in the film as a whole. The right hand with its palm open and fingers slightly curved is a more or less naturalist gesture, while the left hand has the thumb extended away from the rest of the fingers, an altogether more formalised gesture relative to the other hand.

Also, these hands emerge from the 'nothingness' of off-screen space, thus activating these 'dead zones' banished from light and visibility. They are not god-like authorial hands, because they are not one, are of different shapes, sizes and energy. The vectors of energy they produce are at times articulatory and at times move to disarticulate the body of its canonical forms of the ecstatic.

So, in answer to your question 'Can there be a frame drawn around the body, the still, the text?', *A Song of Ceylon*, it seems to me, generates at least a dual movement held in a certain state of tension:

162

1) a movement of relentless cutting into beloved fragments: bodies, objects, space;
2) movements (of light, camera, spaces, voices) which work away from the pressure and delimitation of the still, cut-out fragment.

Anna Rodrigo: The two hands seem out of synch, just like some of the voices that sing classical songs.

The Author: The right hand does not know what the left hand does. This idea, which is to me conceptually quite interesting, perhaps does not work very well all the time, which may be a weakness in the film.[19]

All ritual drama re-enacts a murder, a sacrifice, not an existential death but the death of the drives, or a certain channelling of the drives which is the same thing. The exorcist ritual is a graphic demonstration of this.

Though the film draws from anthropology, it is not an ethnographic film of the body because the body it figures is not the pre-existing naturalist body but a body made possible and desirable by film itself, a body that did not and could not have preceded the invention of film. This film may be thought of as a dance film if one included the work on and with gesture and posture as being a concern of dance. The film is enamoured of the possibility of the non-standardised body, and inflects it gesturally.

Very small movements imperceptible in the theatre are here foregrounded not for their unequivocally significatory function, but because they render the body more contingent, more surprising, more tender, voluptuous. The clarity of iconic gesture is blurred by obsessive repetition rendered banal by non-obsessive performing. The almost mannerist inflection of gesture in group scenes may also be read as a certain dispersal of the unitary focus endemic to the notion of the Scene.

The urbane drinking scene between the man in the suit and the transvestite is a transformation of a histrionic scene from the Kim Novak vehicle *Jeanne Eagels* via a minimalist *mise en scène* – the abstract indeterminate space created by lighting, the solidity of the couple in that space, the static long take with the feel of a sequence shot, and the repetition of Purcell's duet for tenor and counter-tenor from the *Indian Queen*. A recognition of the Hollywood origin, though not necessary, would raise formal questions about *mise en scène* and performance, especially the gestural body.

Anna Rodrigo: There is quite a marked formal shift in the coda with the close-ups. The shift into the genre of portraiture brings the family to the fore, at the end, and connects with the ritual of swearing in the text.

The Author: The ending was a real problem. For months after the official shoot the film still had no ending, it wasn't conceptually worked out. And then someone came up with this idea and it seemed fitting to invoke 'the family' in its most canonical form of representation, portraiture. Slight movement was introduced to permutate the fixity necessary to portraiture. The smallest articulation of neck, eyes and fingers then developed into vectors of motion that passed from one still shot to another.

Anna Rodrigo: The camera is static, the only movement being of bodies within the frame and the relay of movement and looks that pass from one shot to another.

The Author: From one figure to another.

Anna Rodrigo: Figure?

The Author: Figure rather than character because these bodies in close-up are not there long enough to establish identities necessary for the recognition of them as characters.

Anna Rodrigo: The different postures and groupings are important, like the movement which changes the original configuration. Also they have all performed different functions in the previous scene in the room.

The Author: They are given oscillating functions, viewers of a spectacle but also figuring in it.

Anna Rodrigo: How did you choose the actors?

The Author: I chose some for the way they looked, some because they just happened to be there and some for personal reasons that would not necessarily enter the realm of signification. Also there are several families involved in the film but never a complete family, at least one member is missing.

Anna Rodrigo: I understand that your husband gives voice to the priest, while you voice Somawathi. What are the implications of this?

The Author: They are purely personal. The non-personal elements have to do with the different tones,

164

timbres, accents and rhythms of the voices, in fact everything you can hear.[20]

'Why do I faint into his arms after singing the Schubert *Litany*?' She could have said, 'Because I want you to, because I want you to calmly surrender your body into the arms of your son, my husband.' Would that have been simpler than saying that it was not a question of rejecting Stanislavsky for Brecht because the gesture of surrender was no simple quotation of a reversed Pietà, nor a reversal of the climactic scene in any number of Hindi and Sri Lankan films where the adult son, bespattered with blood, finally manages to work his way into an erotic maternal embrace before he dies? The passions and exigencies of the puppet/actor can never coincide with those of the puppeteer/lover, the mover of bodies, but thankfully in cinema there are other elements which move alongside those of contingent individual passion.[21]

Anna Rodrigo: It is a commonplace in cinematic history (Western) for the male director to direct his actress wife. Méliès/D'arcy, Bergman/Ullmann, Godard/Karina/Wiazemsky, Roeg/Russell come to mind. But I can't think of an example of the reverse. Is this for the first time?

The Author: You know how we Sri Lankans love the idea of 'It's the first time ...' What is more resonant culturally, however (in the context of South Asian cinema), is that a woman has directed another to surrender her body into the arms of her son, her husband, and that she did it with such grace. I am referring to that potent triangle in South Asian cinema, of mother, son, and daughter-in-law. Let's talk about the white spaces.

Anna Rodrigo: They seem to work in the way old-fashioned wipes used to wipe the screen because they are mostly moving shots.

The Author: Like a space to rest in?

Anna Rodrigo: Were you thinking of silent cinema when you were making the film?

The Author: Why do you ask?

Anna Rodrigo: Well, the static frames for one thing and then within that, gestural inflections, which is very different from the great gestural flurry and commotion say in early Chaplin. But the principle is

165

	similar. The mannerist posture reminds me of fashion photography.
The Author:	Is that good or bad?
Anna Rodrigo:	I was not making a normative statement. I would also have liked the editing to be a bit more ... prodigal. A better word would be ...
The Author:	Aberrant?[22]

Drawing highly coded gestures and sounds from different traditions, the film needed to find ways of also disembodying the bodies and spaces which are saturated with meaning and affect. Whether the film has been successful in realising this ambition is of course another matter.

By staging the classical lineaments of the feminine (narcissism, masochism, hysteria) as spectacle the film is aware of the binary schemas within which these pathological, pleasurable, traumatic states have been theorised, imaged and lived. If *A Song of Ceylon* offers an intimation of certain movements through and around these bodily states by dissolving the gendered binary oppositions within which they have been conceptualised, then the film is a spectacle not only of but also for the body *in extremis*.

Anna Rodrigo:	One last question, the hand scratching the belly of the woman in the black and white segment, it is quite arcane, no?
The Author:	I don't at all know what that gesture means, it is the only specifically Australian gesture, a tribute to a dead Australian lover.[23]

By the way, the Portuguese Catholic name of the fictional interviewer, Anna Rodrigo, is also that of my late mother.

Notes

1. The title of my paper is a composite of two comments made by two Australians in relation to *A Song of Ceylon*. To Rex Butler I owe the first part ('Speaking of "Ceylon"', *Frogger* no. 19, November 1985, Sydney); and a speaker at a Sydney Film Festival Forum in 1985 referred to the film as being about 'a clash of cultures'. This appropriation is an attempt to realise my aim of working out a structure for this paper which to some extent is isomorphic with that of the film. This paper is in three parts:

   i) some problems in the field of feminist film theory;

166

ii) aspects of the work of conceptualising the film;

iii) modes of performing and readings of the film.

The final part consists of extensive quotations from Rex Butler's interview with me for *Frogger*. As you will see, this interview, which is more like a reading, in turn uses bits from a fictional interview I wrote between a woman named Anna Rodrigo and myself as author, for another Sydney publication, *Fade to Black* (Sydney College of the Arts, November 1985). The present paper is structured by quotations from this fictional interview which you will read at irregular intervals. The interviews will usually be signalled by the names of those speaking; at times, however, it is not possible to do so because of the structure of interviews within interviews, but I hope that the inverted commas and the personal pronouns will indicate who is speaking to whom.

This work comes out of, among other things, an engagement with a specific history of feminism and film and is an attempt to work through one or two major problems in the field.

2. 'To Render the Body Ecstatic – Anna Rodrigo interviews Laleen Jayamanne', *Fade to Black*, Sydney College of the Arts Film Group, November 1985.

3. 'Puppet and puppeteers, actors and lovers', L. Jayamanne, *Cantrills Film Notes*, nos. 47 and 48, 1985.

4. Jayamanne, *Fade to Black*.

5. For a diagnosis of this problem see Aimee Rankin's review of the exhibition, 'Difference: On Representation and Sexuality', Art Network no. 16, Winter 1985. Republished in *Screen*, Winter 1987.

6. Though psychoanalysis does gender the gaze by linking the (wounded) gaze with the cock and its imagined dismemberment (castration), it does also provide a way of imagining the gaze differently in so far as it makes a distinction between the Eye and the Gaze. It is in the uneasy disjunction between the biological function and the social that drive and desire, the lure and the sense of loss, suspension and vacillation of the subject, come into being.

See Paul Foss' essay 'Eyes, Fetishism, and the Gaze', *Art and Text*, no. 20, 1986 – which is in part a comment on Rosalind Krauss' *Corpus Delicti*, *October*, no. 33, 1985 – for the relationship of psychoanalysis to Surrealism and the function of the female body in that scenario.

7. I would like to thank Homi Bhabha for one of the most interesting questions asked of me at this conference in relation to the film. He asked (I paraphrase from memory): 'What was it that resisted, at the time of conceptualising the film, at the time of making it, the very theories that you were using?' I said then that the film had taken a cue from the verbal text which said: 'He shakes, he shivers, he chants *garthas*', and had tried to develop the implications of this description in terms of the images. In so far as this is a description of the male priest *in extremis*, it shifts the burden of the hysterical body to the male figure of authority. If psychoanalysis as a discourse and profession owes a debt to the hystericised body of woman, this film attempts to spread that contagion beyond strict gender divisions in

167

order to generate itself, as well as to give the male body some voluptuous tenderness.

In a film I am currently working on, called *Rehearsing*, which functions as a sequel to *A Song of Ceylon*, we have attempted to spread this contagion of possession a bit farther afield by staging a combat of sorts between two men and a series of eight photographs, five of which are production stills from *A Song of Ceylon* showing Juan Davila being transformed into Kim Novak. It is also a sequel in the sense that the later film attempts to work through some of the formal problems in the earlier work, such as its lack of a volumetric space because of the weakness in editing.

Mandy Merck and Vivan Sundaram also asked me related questions about why I spoke more of the image than of the voice and sound in the film ('Are you hung up on the scopic drive?'), when the voices in the film seem to have a charge of their own, an ability to conjure up that which is not given by the image. The possibilities of film – sound/image disjunction, disjunctions in the register of sounds, the varieties of movements which constitute the cinematic body – can all be used to stretch, twist and also disengage from the propositions of theoretical discourse even as one works with them.

Voices were chosen for the different accents in which English was spoken, for the traces of Tamil, Spanish and Sinhalese that could be heard within English. Also the female voice started with a preference for 'Bressonian' uninflected delivery of lines, but the more I rehearsed the voice the more I realised the need for a more flamboyant theatrical gesture in the use of the voice. There was also the wish to avoid, like the plague, the feminist 'voice of sincerity'. The dialogue between the priest and the mad woman could not be read à la Bresson. But the instructions to the actors were read by me in a monotone but using a register of voice which is an attempt to tap what I think of as my 'Sri Lankan' voice, i.e. the voice that I imagine I had before I left my country some 14 years ago, so a voice that knows Sinhalese as its mother tongue and English as its second language but a voice as yet unaware of American and Australian English. The dramatic voice is a voice that tries to use vocal registers made possible by the knowledge of different theatrical traditions, and to make audible the traces of migrations on the voice.

8. Jayamanne, *Fade to Black*.
9. Feminist analysis of cinema has not done much work with, say, screwball comedy, where women display a verbal mastery and felicity unparalleled in most other genres, not to mention a certain crazy physical dexterity as well. Predictably, more attention has been paid to genres that confirm feminist ideas – i.e. domestic melodrama, film noir – than to those that may unsettle them a little vis-à-vis Hollywood. For a further analysis of this problem, see the interview with L. Jayamanne, Geeta Kapur and Yvonne Rainer, 'Discussing "Modernity", "third world" and "The Man who envied women"', *Art and Text*, Autumn 1987.
10. Jayamanne, *Fade to Black*.
11. Unpublished Ph.D. thesis, University of New South Wales, Australia 1981.
12. *Relations, a duet in black and white*, at Artspace, Sydney, July 1983. Each

use of this anthropological text of spirit possession and cure produced a
different text with different conclusions.

13. Jayamanne, *Fade to Black*.
14. Ibid.
15. Ibid.
16. *Ana Tom i – Lamentations*, L. Jayamanne, 1983. 16mm. 10 mins.
17. Rex Butler, *Frogger*, no. 19, November 1985.
18. Roland Barthes, 'Diderot, Brecht, Eisenstein', *Image-Music-Text* (London: Fontana, 1977).
19. Jayamanne, *Fade to Black*.
20. Ibid.
21. Jayamanne, *Cantrills Film Notes*.
22. Jayamanne, *Fade to Black*.
23. Ibid.

Credits

A Song of Ceylon (51 mins, 8mm and 16mm)

Director: Laleen Jayamanne.
Producer: Adrienne Parr.
Screenplay: Laleen Jayamanne (adapted from anthropological text).
Cinematography: Gabrielle Finnane, Anne Rutherford, Andrew Plain.
Editing: Geoff Weary, Laleen Jayamanne.
Art Director: Sheona White.
Sound Mix: Geoff Stitt, Adrienne Parr, Andrew Plain.

This film was funded by the Creative Development Branch of the
Australian Film Commission, 1985.

Debating the Third Cinema

Ashish Rajadhyaksha

We present Ritwik Ghatak's *Jukti Takko Ar Gappo* (*Reason, Debate and a Tale*), made in 1974, as our contribution to the debate on the Third Cinema.[1]

The film speaks of its time, of events that occurred when it was being made. It reflects the forms in which politics is discoursed as it reflects the events themselves, not only in its 'subject matter' but in the very manner of its making – these are Third Cinema characteristics.

But the film marks a clear *disalignment* with several conventions of the radical gesture, which prevailed at that time in the area of political action as in the cinema. (This was the time of the Naxalite movement, an ultra-left movement that started with the Bengali peasantry and expanded to student groups in Calcutta. It was also when Mrinal Sen was making his Latin American cinema-inspired 'street' films *Interview* and *Calcutta '71*). Ghatak himself had been close to the Indian political left since the 1940s; his first film *Nagarik* (1951) had been made in the wake of the Telengana peasant revolts, and had argued the need for direct political action. Now, however, in the vastly changed situation of contemporary India, where the Indian ruling class had totally appropriated the socialist rhetoric of the 1930s and 40s movements,[2] Ghatak was more concerned to reveal the enormous dangers inherent in such action. Sandwiched amid the juvenile activism of Naxalite youth and the cynicism of his own generation, he wanted to emphasise that every political struggle has its own *forms*. He pointed to the terrible price vital political movements had paid in contemporary India for not acknowledging the necessary *cultural* foundations for popular militancy, in unquestioningly channelling all political understanding of and opposition to what we see around us into the singular political gesture.

The political act

We must understand the consequences of this for the cinema. The 'identification' of the enemy, across all historical differences, as something static in space and time, has often been seen as one of the purposes of the Third Cinema, the first step towards liberation.[3] By 1972 Charu Mazumdar, leader of the Naxalites, had taken this to its pinnacle – demanding the 'annihilating of all class enemies and their agents' and predicting the success of the revolution by 1975 – and had thus also sealed the doom of the movement. The almost complete failure of this, and most other political struggles then,[4] led Ghatak into contemplating a position where to 'identify' with a situation in the terms prevalent was *in itself* either to face complete annihilation or cathartically to drain one's ability to fight. For the other side of political movements unable to articulate a struggle even in the immediate conditions that gave rise to them was the cynical, equally real, counterpart to the optimism of the Naxalites.

For Ghatak the crisis lay in identification. The 'piece of masking that shows only a portion of reality', in Bazin's words, opening out through the protagonist into the universe of the film, initiates a series of slippages that can take on bizarre dimensions: the masking of the frame, privileging the one thing we see out of the universe to which it belongs, is the formal parallel of our seeing into the political act, of our visual grasping of political immediacy. The resemblance to the world provided by the cinema is fixated, framed and proffered so as to induce the illusion of comprehension, rather like the affixing of a price to the commodity. Instead of the shown entering into complex relations with what isn't shown – that is, instead of the political act entering into complex relations with political understanding – the shown comes to *substitute* for the not-shown. The political act *replaces* political understanding. What is shown is all there is to be seen. There is no alternative to acting *thus*.

The moral and the ethical

A Third Cinema made under pre-revolutionary political conditions almost inevitably sets the film-maker/viewer in an antagonistic relationship with the reality sought to be portrayed. The way certain aspects of that reality are privileged over others – usually the conventionally 'radical' ones – all too often presents a discursive hierarchy that unconsciously duplicates what it is apparently opposing. The question of revolutionary identity – as distinct from 'identifying with the revolution' – is necessarily a question of political choice. But it is *not* a choice of this or that alternative within a 'given' framework: the more 'given' the political framework, indeed, the more it accepts the basic premises of the system it is supposed to oppose, the system that we by proxy are therefore also supposed to oppose. It is a question of challenging the very terms in which reality is conventionally portrayed (including all the radical gestures the conventions usually include); the choice is of the *extent* to which we wish to open the debate, the extent to which we demand change. In the absence of such an effort which would interrogate the viewer/film-maker, the terms of mediation, as much as the reality itself, what usually happens is that the artists/activists take upon themselves the entire *moral* burden of articulating exploitation and of doing something about it. This burden, which in film-seeing includes the entire edifice of distribution and exhibition, is usually imposed by the supposed 'urgency' of the contemporary situation: and it does not allow for alternative forms of articulation. It is inevitably so trapped within the economic realities shaping it that every act it performs becomes self-annihilating, guilt-ridden ...

Jukti Takko Ar Gappo is a chronicle of the contemporary, but it also refuses to endow the contemporary with a privileged position in history. Instead, the film presents what is seen to be a process, alongside the processes that shape our seeing. Here reality, along with the struggles to live in it, is seen to be a particular configuration of history in which a crucial component is the way we see it. As this history is presented, it is isolated, commented upon, with other forms of art, social organisation, even of memory. The family is rent apart, but its emotional trauma is matched alongside the historical consequences of a social division of labour. The motley quartet seek in each other a reaffirmation of the group; but the mother has been raped, the cosmology of past learning (the Sanskrit scholar) unable to account for its redundancy, and there are no 'prospects'. The unity itself is recalled through tribal forms[5] that were once the vitality of the Bengali countryside: the grandeur of the Chhou is reduced to masks for sale, the terrible dance of death now the destructive carnage mounted by the police upon the young radicals. Thus it was, says Ghatak, but he also questions if it *had* to be thus.

The isolation and questioning occurs through the most remarkable aspects of the film: Ghatak's self-interrogation. Neelkantha[6] takes upon himself the burden of guilt: he is, along with his erstwhile radical colleagues, the moral consequence of impotence. He is the identifying recipient of reality, and it is in the way that he isolates himself – isolating his inheritance, the burden that first exhausts our energies and strangulates us into silence and cynicism as we no longer have 'words to express' our reality and accept his incompetence – that he isolates the forms of history which he wishes us to view afresh. *Jukti* repeatedly defines itself against the acts of definition that surround it, and in doing so evokes within the contemporary several traditions of resistance. He evokes what Jakobson said about Mayakovsky: 'Opposed to this creative urge towards a transformed future is the stabilising force of an immutable present, overlaid, as this present is, by a stagnating slime which stifles life in its tight, hard mould ... *The revolt of the individual*

172

against the fixed forms of social convention presupposes the existence of such a force.[7] Or in Julia Kristeva's formulation: 'Murder, death and unchanging society represent precisely the inability to hear and understand the signifier as such – as ciphering, as rhythm, as a presence that precedes the signification of object or emotion. The poet is put to death because he wants to turn rhythm into a dominant element; because he wants to make language perceive what it doesn't want to say, provide it with its matter independent of its sign and free it from denotation. For it is this *eminently parodic* gesture that changes the system.'[8]

As recipient of our identification, Neelkantha swallows its history of cynicism and despair, its fragmentation – its poison. Such a breaking down is inevitable if we are to see things whole. 'It is as if the logic of systems constructed by us leave us all the time in partial realisations that militate against each other. Each art and each tradition of the art, linking itself to history and to nature, tries in despair to break itself down to re-integrate the whole of existence' (Kumar Shahani).[9] It is when the moral burden takes its toll, including its stagnant languages of an 'immutable present' and the heroic acts that sacrifice themselves to this stagnation, that a revolutionary ethics will re-place us once again in the world.

Popular/realistic: the social circulation of meaning

I know of no place in the world today where anyone can claim a 'direct', unmediated relationship with 'the people'. The enthusiastic lines that Godard made Glauber Rocha speak at the crossroads in *Wind from the East* must now give way to a discussion of the difficulties we encounter: the discourses we employ in our separate areas of practice, the traditions we invoke. Most of us live in circumstances rather different from the time when Brecht advanced his 'fighting conception of the popular'.[10] Today we find an unenlightened bourgeoisie on the rampage – nobody can remain unaffected by the megalomania of the present US administration, and that is just one, albeit crucial, example – and we have to fight just to hold our own in the face of a mass-cultural onslaught that respects nothing, weighing everything from soap to revolution as merely items of marketable merchandise.[11] We face the twin crises of a popular (read: mass) culture increasingly sealed off, by the very relations of its production and technology dependence, from any progressive potential and the almost utopian nature of any attempt to 'stand outside', to find alternatives, to look for productive cultural forms elsewhere.

In one of the only instances that actually discuss the *discursive* crises we all face in film, Paul Willemen – drawing a distinction between the avant-garde and its political antagonist, modernism – wrote about 'a growing trend, emerging in widely different areas of signifying and cultural practice, which is capable of displacing and renovating questions of the social circulation of meaning, displacing them by shifting the focus away from the determining effects of textual procedures or subjectivity to the question of the social anchorage of meaning production'.[12] Elsewhere in the same essay he argues in favour of 'an insistence on problems of reference (inherent in the refusal to bracket the signified and to be bound by the notions of media-specificity) as necessary pre-conditions for the elaboration of an artistic practice capable of representing the complexity of historical processes'.

The relevance of such formulations to Ghatak's work, as to various cinemas in the so-called Third World, as well as to aspects of the independent cinemas of Europe, is evident. But now a lot of this film practice – *Jukti* itself – demands that they be taken further.

What do we understand by 'social anchorage of meaning production' and 'reference'? All around us, we are constantly being seduced by formulations that seek to justify themselves precisely through an illusion of 'social relevance'. The advertising film-maker will simply associate the production of meaning in his film with the production of the commodity; the meaning actually attempts to receive social anchorage in the apparent 'fact' of its indispensability. At the other extreme, the 'radical' would cohere the languages that his reality 'makes available' by privileging that layer which would apparently make concrete what is often necessarily an abstraction, stultifying historical processes by congealing them into an idealist object, i.e. his 'work' and all that it is supposed to imply. In both cases, the problem lies in the discourse itself, in the very linearity of an insight being elaborated, becoming discourse, acquiring its social anchorage.

It becomes endlessly difficult for a film to refer, not to other discourses, but to *itself* through them. For the Third Cinema has to do this, 'to show the play's (film's) underlying sense by making the *surface meaning* as clear as possible' (Brecht, emphasis mine).[13] The problem, which Willemen does not emphasise enough, is that most discourses possess layers of meaning, that they inevitably bring with them their own references: that it is in the *way* discourse and reference come together – creating discursive layers which are in extreme formal, therefore historical, inequality – that the annihilation usually lies. How, here, is one to overcome 'media specificity'? How is one to 'displace' the determining effects of textual procedures?

Is the reference to the 'outside', to class struggle/imperialism/that which is documented, an underlining of the discourse? Is it in the nature of a caption to what we see (as in Godard's deconstruction of a news photograph in *Letter to Jane*)? I shall argue, as a basic issue of the Third Cinema, that almost always the reference is used to *shore up* the discourse, and that the problem begins here – in the way the reference is submerged into the discourse, and then the discourse is submerged into the political act, and the act itself into the 'choices' set before it.

I shall suggest that we must recognise that all discourses in film are a dynamic configuration of references, including those that we bring to bear when we see/participate, and each of these is 'produced' by certain traditions. These traditions are usually *qualitatively* different – popular, realistic, mythological, 'historical' – and the political issue is how they realise each other in film, as practice. It is in the way the reference signifies itself through the cinema that it illuminates the other references which go to produce the cinematic superstructure. The viewer becomes the producer; the producer the viewer. To see is to *speak*. History produces the historically transient – the commodity, and its extreme obverse, the radical 'gesture' – and neither permits understanding outside of the closed, ritualistic 'participation'. The commodity may only be understood as an act of consumption; real*ism* provides illusions of the concrete, the conventions by which we see (and for the most part accept) the contemporary and our place in it. It is perfectly possible in the cinema to duplicate this transience. But it is also possible to render the concrete as all that goes into producing it, to open out its momentness over space and time. In *Jukti* various types of historical languages are interwoven – refugees, job-seekers, trade union activists, the commerce of the street, the radical Naxalites, the Sanskrit scholar, the bootlegger, the folk, the popular as music and dance, the family – but this is not to fuse them into a neat dramatic or political whole, but in order to create the space where we can disentangle ourselves from our antagonistic/consumer-ritualistic relation with our environment. Even as the film liberates us from the drift into an instantly 'enfolding' moralist identification, Ghatak liberates 'reality' from its reductive captivations (e.g. 'miserabilism', 'Third Worldism', etc.) and restores to it the confusions, knowledges and experience of the one who encounters it.

As Kumar Shahani has written: 'To apply a reductionist approach to myths, and to saturate their meanings, as is done more often in analysis than in practice, is again to find in them a concreteness that can only become exploitative. It is thus imperative both to maintain the ambivalence of their terms, their poetry, and to place them alongside history, fact and facts, their relationship, the epic. Not the concrete. But its immanence'.[14]

Insufficiencies
In India, as in most 'Third World' areas, the problem of language takes on extra dimensions, due to what I can only call 'insufficiencies' in modern mass communications. While institutional or state-backed

media are often charged with the task of transforming languages in order to shore up and sustain the economic system the state is trying to set up, media practitioners all too often fail in, or even abdicate, their responsibility in rendering the (capitalist) transformation. In these cases the 'message' *is* the economic backing that holds them up. The deceptions fall short, the veneer does not hold. The mythic interfaces that emerge, in the transfer from earlier to newer types of social formation, collapse under the burden placed upon them. Our bourgeoisie has not, or has not been able to, set up a cultural basis for its economic system. Their economic strength, in the forms it takes, *is* their culture. Although in their specific cultural expression they depend entirely on the 'West' – either imitate it, or play up their exotic differences – here it is all too rare to see this expression successfully intervening in economic power relations. Indeed bourgeois/state cultural expression betrays its economic backing (often to the embarassment of those in power). It is as though, in every act it performs, the dominant system lays itself bare before us.

I want to suggest, somewhere in this area, a commonness of experience and purpose with colleagues in other underdeveloped regions. On the one hand, this of course leads to a very real problem of how the film-maker may work at all, for the cultural insufficiencies are usually covered up by a further strengthening of economic and political control. But on the other, it also leads to a setting up of a number of reference-points for the artist who seeks to intervene into his/her reality, to reflect the complexity of historical processes. The Indian anthropologist D. D. Kosambi writes:

> We have to go much deeper than [conventional archaeology] for the grasp of the Indian tradition. It is not the primitive tribes of other countries that are of primary interest here, nor primitive Indian survivals in marginal territory ... The social clusters that survive even in the heart of fully developed areas, say in and around cities, with others which mark all strata of a caste society as having developed at some older date from the absorption of tribal groups, constitute priceless evidence of archaeological record; their survival as backward groups also furnishes the real problem for explanation in the light of historical development. India is a country of long survivals. People of the atomic age rub elbows with those of the chalcolithic. The vast majority of countryside gods are still daubed with a red pigment that is a palpable substitute for long-vanished blood sacrifices – which also survive in a few cases, although the very idea of blood sacrifices would now come as a shock to many devotees. One finds rites practised which clearly go back to the stone age, though the votaries – often people with a modern education – are not conscious of the incredibly long continuity. Such practices may have

no foundation in Brahmin scriptures, but other portions of Sanskrit ritual works show equally primitive sacraments adopted at almost all periods down to the last century. Formulae from the Rigveda are still recited, after three millenia, at orthodox Hindu marriage and funeral ceremonies, for the higher castes; but the same rites often show features that have no Vedic justification whatever, practised with the same earnestness as the documented Vedic portion, without incongruity or contradiction felt by the participant.[15]

For us the act of signification can still be one that resonates through several centuries of our history, even as that history lives contemporaneously with the present. While this may also apply, in varying degrees, to all societies, in India the realism/modernism question, for example, that vexing opposition that is so involved with the forms of institutionalised capitalism, would not apply in the same form. Modernism here would have to be seen against the fact of large numbers of Indians living culturally outside the forms of the economic contemporary. And while, consequently, they also live in abject poverty, they have been sustained by a cultural materialism that has traditionally taken change into its stride. It is possible for us to isolate the economic contemporary, rather than submerge ourselves into it, to realise its experience in ways of seeing, and organising, that are not burdened by what we oppose *today*: the forms of and for the future.

Notes

1. For a reading of this film, see Geeta Kapur's essay in this volume.
2. Signified most particularly by the issues on which the 1972 General Elections were fought. Following the Bangladesh War in 1971, Indira Gandhi had evolved a populist socialist rhetoric that was designed simultaneously to destroy the right-wing 'old guard' and to contain a rising agrarian and industrial unrest. The slogan that characterises this populism was *garibi hatao* (down with poverty).
3. At the Edinburgh seminar, several speakers repeatedly asserted this claim of a Third Cinema: e.g. Clyde Taylor, who posited that the central function of such cinema was to present two alternatives.
4. Naxalite activity had spread to Bihar, Andhra Pradesh, Punjab and even Tamil Nadu. In addition, separate student agitations – e.g. the Chhatra Yuva Sangharsh Vahini, led by Jayprakash Narayan in Bihar – and massive industrial strikes, crucially the railway strike in 1974, were in many ways the direct stimuli for the declaration of the Emergency in 1975. See Meghnad Desai's 'India; Emerging Contradictions of Slow Capitalist Development', in Robin Blackburn (ed.), *Explosion in a Subcontinent*

(Penguin/New Left Review, 1975), for the best analysis of this period among those easily accessible to Western readers.

5. Ghatak clearly evokes Marx's own formulation on the family and the tribe: 'Division of labour in a society, and the corresponding tying down of individuals to a particular calling, develops itself, just as does the division of labour in manufacture, from opposite starting points. Within a family, and after further development within the tribe, there springs up naturally a division of labour, a division that is based on purely physiological foundations, which division enlarges its materials by the expansion of the community, by the increase of population, and more especially by the conflicts between different tribes, and the subjugation of one tribe by another. On the other hand ... the exchange of products springs up at the point where different families, tribes, communities, come into contact.... It is this spontaneously developed difference which, when different communities come into contact, calls forth the mutual exchange of products, and the consequent gradual conversion of these products into commodities' (*Capital*, vol. 1, p. 332).

6. Neelkantha: an aspect of the Lord Krishna, referring to the legend of how he swallowed the spreading poison of evil to save the people. The name literally translates as 'The Blue-throated', after the belief that the poison turned his throat blue.

7. Roman Jakobson, *On a Generation That Swallowed Its Poets*.

8. Julia Kristeva, 'The Ethics of Linguistics', in *Desire in Language* (Basil Blackwell), p. 31.

9. Kumar Shahani, 'Narrativity', Rita Ray Memorial Lecture no. 3.

10. Bertolt Brecht, 'The Popular and the Realistic', in *Brecht on Theatre*, p. 108.

11. Indian television, for example, has expanded over the last five years to a point where it is expected to reach 70 per cent of the population in the immediate future. It earned Rs 100 crore (£60 million) in advertising in 1987, 60 per cent of which came from just five multinational corporations. The cultural damage being done through the mass entertainment of 'serials' is incalculable.

12. Paul Willemen, 'An Avant Garde for the 80s', *Framework*, no. 24.

13. Bertolt Brecht, *Collected Plays*, vol. 2.

14. Kumar Shahani, 'Film as a Contemporary Art', Damodaran Lecture.

15. D. D. Kosambi, *An Introduction to the Study of Indian History* (Popular Prakashan), pp. 7–8.

Articulating the Self into History: Ritwik Ghatak's *Jukti takko ar gappo*

Geeta Kapur

Alternative cinema, with some of its major practitioners representing the Third World, has battled to represent imperialism, hunger and the preconditions of praxis. The Indian experience of cultural politics suggests that the Third Cinema, as it has come to be called, is equally about self-representation. It is about the articulation of the colonised individual, *the absent subject*, into history.

Ritwik Ghatak's last film, *Jukti Takko ar Gappo* (made in 1974), provides an appropriate text for my purpose: the film is about a failed life and an argument that goes beyond it, beyond Ghatak himself who acts out the chronicle of the life and death of this contemporary middle-class intellectual and communist. The text reclaims through its severally replayed discourse not only the absent subject but an interrogative mode of praxis that makes subject and history properly partisan within a larger utopian project.

I

The actor-author-character nexus

1. Taking himself as primary material, Ghatak puts himself on the screen as principal actor demonstrating how a person is formed by his emphatic presence. And the sensuous mobility, the plasticity of his body-presence, is rich material for the purpose. This presence is however composed into a triangular motif by its two flanking aspects: the author/director on the one hand, and the narrativised character on the other. Both aspects function in a historical dimension, so that while a sheer presence is foregrounded in the film it is also a means for testing, in full irony, models of self-representation. Thus in the sense that *Jukti* narrativises the self it is a mock-autobiography. However, as it calls into play evidence from the symmetrically composed but actual, alternative

179

histories that have been condensed into the over-determined subjectivity of Ghatak himself, the precise effect is to turn the confessional, nearly nihilist strain of the narrative back on itself by bringing ideological testimony to the subjectivity at stake.

There is the testimony of Ghatak as author with a means, through his art, of interrogating his lived history; and of Ghatak as the protagonist of a contemporary story who recounts in a third-person narrative a tragic destiny. The projective ego of Ghatak which seems to trouble everyone is undone in the full equation. It becomes a signifier in the orbit of an over-arching historicity held up by the two intentionalities of author and character. Both belong to the first young adult generation after the Indian Independence. Both examine, narratively, the choices of the Indian Left.

2. This is not the place to recount Ritwik Ghatak's biography,[1] except to emphasise his life-long relationship with the communist movement and with its cultural front organisation to which until around 1956 a large number of intellectuals and artists owed allegiance. Simply to signpost the context, we should note his reckoning from the Left position of the national struggle culminating in the simultaneous declaration of Indian Independence and the tragic Partition of the nation on communal grounds; his deeply sceptical evaluation of the gains of Indian Independence in the hands of what he would call a bourgeois-landlord ruling party; and finally his anguish at the disarray and the sectarianism of the Communist Party from the 1960s. When he made *Jukti* in 1974 he was at the end of his tether, his health and sanity disintegrating. But he was astute enough to realise that the nation polarised between, among other things, agents of political expediency and ultra-radicalism was on the brink; and if it was the last thing he did he would intervene – as an artist. To this purpose he became for the last time madly energetic, proving the degree to which he had remained engaged with contemporary politics, but more importantly the degree to which his intellect and indeed his imagination had internalised the dialectic, so that his desperate testimony was also ultimately a project for the future. *Jukti*, along with trying to pose the correct political choices, works out the problematic of praxis. This is, as we shall see, the explicit note on which the film ends.

In connection with *Jukti*, Ghatak is quoted as follows:

Which is the correct way? Society is a complex phenomenon and it should be tackled with great judiciousness. Multiple trends and tendencies cross each other continuously. The problem is which one to choose, and how to go about it.

I have emphasised that the genesis of all our present-day problems

180

is that great betrayal, the so-called Independence. But I did not specify the current phase as strictly neo-colonial. . . .

I can visualise only two alternatives: either straight Fascism or some way out of it along Leninist ideology. If you are aware of German youth during 1929–33, you will understand the tensions in our present-day youngsters, fast turning into lumpens. . . . The entire structure is crumbling down and I believe that some drastic turn is bound to come soon.[2]

In 1975, when Indira Gandhi declared an Emergency, the liberal phase of Indian democracy seemed to be over. Ghatak's prophecy about the lumpenisation, indeed the continued brutalisation, of Indian political life was correct.

3. In *Jukti* Ghatak makes the invisible, therefore manipulative, voice of the author expressly visible by acting in the film and moreover acting the role of a historical twin called Neelkanth. In this sense the authorial voice comes to us in double register, but for that very reason its hold is loosened. Once provided with a body, the author is available for anatomical operation; not only that, the various pitches, the strains and stresses of the voice, can be didactically laid out. So that if there was ever an ideal author-subject that asked like a metaphysical voice-over, 'Who is it who thus lives and dies?', it is now returned to an ontologically incomplete status, a subject in process within the narrative. But for that very reason it is also invested with a more concrete immanence within the historical realm. Ghatak's play along the actor-author-character nexus is thus a kind of hermeneutic exercise: he is interpreting for his own generation metaphysical questions that have a historical function.

4. Appropriately, the prime character in *Jukti* is first set up grandly with the very name Neelkanth, a name acquired by Siva in his moment of awesome generosity when he swallows the terrible poison that comes with the ambrosia in the great churning of the ocean by the gods and demons. (This establishes Siva's omnipotence; he is nevertheless *marked* by the event: his throat is stained blue, hence the name Neelkanth.) But having set up the protagonist in this mythical framework,[3] *Jukti*'s narrative proceeds to devolve his inconicity. Mockingly, affectionately, a transcendent figure is turned inside out into a man filled with the grand illusion but also marked: by the fallibility that always marks the martyr.

To this end an explication of the figure of Neelkanth is necessary. Neelkanth is a schoolteacher and writer; he has been a communist; now he is an alcoholic. He is the 'representative of an irresponsible middle-class intelligentsia, wasted and degenerated'.[4] The man drinks liquor with a self-destructive voraciousness, and when he says at the end 'I am burning, the universe is burning', you know that this is the martyr of all religions reduced in our own time from a blazing icon to a mere effigy yet aspiring to die on behalf of the good; to become a sign of the betrayal of the good.

And when he says, less like the omnipotent Siva and more like the earthbound saviours of humankind, that he is tired, that he is not easily tired but he *is* now tired, adding that he will not rest but qualifying later even this remnant of heroism with a stern reckoning, 'Life's imperatives are invincible', the devolution is complete. The man who speaks is addressing himself simultaneously to two sets of life-affirming youth – the nihilism of the Naxalite boys is a romantic complement to the innocence of the new-found lovers in Neelkanth's care. This man who sits and waits with the flock in the forest is speaking like a sage in history, and although this is a lower status in the iconographic hierarchy that has been sketched out by allusion to gods and saviours, it is a status at least contiguous with that of the historically incomplete viewer and stationed temporally in the *present*.

Ghatak's achievement is precisely that the positioning of the protagonist is emblematic but that he is not valorised; neither the protagonist nor the present he encloses within his life-chronicle is valorised. Life's imperatives, as the protagonist calls them, are momentarily compressed to form the present; as also they momentarily dislodge the present from the hold of causality – of both myth and history.

5. What Ghatak does in *Jukti* he does in one sense in all his films: he plays with the infinite plasticity of mythic material, then provides one figure with an iconic fixity, and another, or the 'other' of the first figure, with extreme vulnerability, and then in a game of ironic proxy between the two he exorcises the false consciousness within the very schema. But what he does in *Jukti* goes further. He works out the problem involved in the representation of the contemporary: how to construct a figure that is truly in the process of becoming, in the process of making choices while baiting death; how to figure the archetypal into the contemporary so that it burns with the mortality of the historical subject.

In *Jukti* he demonstrates – and indeed the film is a kind of pedagogical exercise – the immense condensation (in symbolic and linguistic terms) that must take place in such a figural construction. And then the series of displacements that must proceed, so that in the narrative as such the destinal figure detaches itself sufficiently from given forms of subjectivity through the game of masks. Having already distanced itself from the given forms of realism (the standard representational correlate to the historical), the figure stands somewhat tendentiously in the narrative as the 'free' signifier. But it is precisely as free as Ghatak himself,

182

and as we have seen, it is part of Ghatak's iconoclastic strategy that the covert mythology of the author is deconstructed along with that of the martyred hero in that both are contained in the person of Ghatak who shows himself falling apart.

II

Ghatak's person as subject and image

1. I began with the assertion that *Jukti*'s meaning derives from Ghatak's presence in it; I now backtrack to ask again, what is the special quality of this presence?

The first thing to note is that Ghatak was a theatre activist before he became a film-maker. During 1948–54 he participated constantly as both actor and director in the Indian People's Theatre Association (IPTA), a cultural front of the Indian Communist Party active in several regions in India, especially in Bengal.[5] And in the way Ghatak plays the protagonist, in the way he uses his body, his voice, his gesture, theatrical experience is more than evident.

IPTA activists used several models, ranging from the realist to the Brechtian to Bengal's living folk and popular forms. In *Jukti*, Ghatak provided himself with a repertoire of acting devices to make a compelling theatrical personality which is even more than Ghatak the legendary mock-iconic figure that he had by then become.

He uses the trick of dismantling the gestures, the head and limbs working separately, puppet-like, with the slightly caricatural but endearing postures of a mime. This could be a reference to the Chhau dance-dramas.[6] He loved the form no doubt because of the way it combined the heroic aspect of the Puranic gods with the comic aspect of all heroism; the way the virtuosity of the dancers topped with majestically decked-out masks may be lit up by the mischief of an accompanying band of masked monkeys leaping between the trees and the audience, the ensemble of legendary men, gods and beasts making game of the mythological battles and the status of the victor by the typical cartwheel of the *playfully absurd* on which such performances turn. So that you scarce know whether the performers are appropriating the Hindu gods humbly or subverting the pantheon in the process of adapting them to their own iconographic and ritual ends. Ghatak for his part would opt for the 'primitive' to gain a deliberately ambiguous identity for himself, inserting that into the contemporary political stage.

He also takes on the mannerism of a singularly sublime identity, that of the Baul singer, conveying the reverie, the abandonment and the grace of the crazy mendicants. (This is particularly the case in the sequence where he himself sings passionately, tenderly, the song about

183

the mother, consoling the bereft girl Bangabala who is at once the little daughter and mother of the worse bereft man.) On other occasions, especially didactic occasions, which he usually puts forth as a drunken harangue (as when he tells off his corrupt colleague who has flourished over the years writing cheap drivel, saying 'Practice thinking', but only after he has wheedled ten rupees for a drink, turning the joke on himself as a wasted ideologue), he mimics the large gestures of a Jatra actor. Placing himself in a too dramatically lit frame, he mimics as well a sort of ventriloquist's trick of throwing the voice into space, the dark space where the awestruck village audiences sit gaping at the imposing effigy-like authority of the Jatra actor, thus once again turning the joke on himself as a melodramatic actor.

However, Ghatak knows full well what happens to a body-presence in cinema, in the cinematic image. That in the cinema the encounter between the actor and spectator is incorporeal and abstract but that the person, by becoming a hallucinated figure, as in a dream, totally possesses the spectator. Ghatak projects himself on screen as both sensuous and spectral, becoming *an image of himself* by manipulating both his performance and the medium, its interpellating techniques of lighting, lensing and camera angles.

He does this at the very start of the film in one of the opening sequences. Ghatak is sprawled on the floor of a room stripped of everything but a slowly cranking fan. The simple room is carefully, artificially lit with shadows that diffuse and redefine the interior space, steeply angled by the camera positions and the wide-angle lens. In this distorted space Ghatak's figure is awry but also invisibly riveted: he commands the spatial dimensions. Even when the camera further intervenes by cutting close up to him and then to middle distance, around and above him (as he talks with his wife and son, and with Nachiketa and Bangabala), it is as if the figure turns and tilts on its own axis. This is the *mise en scène* for a self-determining presence that is at the same time remote in its final state of vagabondage. At the moment when the sensuous figure of Bangabala enters the room, the light through the window has dematerialised Ghatak's lean body, making him visually, imagistically, a far advanced liminal figure so that the narrative sequence may be taken to give us in full the equation between spiritual intransigency and the irreducible expressivity of human presence.

To restate the interposition of theatrical and filmic presentations in *Jukti*, we see how sheer presence may be turned into a virtuoso performance; and by implication we know how, by the histrionic powers of an elect soul (as in ritual and primitive drama), a person is offered to the spectator for identification and catharsis. This is a presupposition on which expressionist drama, and especially Artaud's drama, functions, including also the exhibitionist/masochistic elements of such a performance. But in *Jukti* we see further how the insubstantial image on the screen may be used to advantage in turning this offered presence, which is in a sense 'sacrificed', into an absence, the actor leaving us with the compulsion to introject this talking shadow which has survived the catharsis and become discourse.

And how often Ghatak appears on the screen with his head floating in space, the frame cutting his head from the torso at the level of the neck in what is a conspicuously unconventional framing device (memorably when he is sitting on a street bench under a starry sky quoting Yeats like a poet of all ages to the village girl; and in the scene in the forest when he quotes Lenin to the young Naxalite, his head sculpted against the dark luminosity of the long night ahead).[7] He has the audacity to project the guillotined head of an inveterate actor, nodding, laughing, teasing, and deriding itself with an inexhaustible resource for gesture and speech.

2. Now Ghatak, and this film in particular, have been attacked for being self-indulgent and exhibitionist. The charge can be conceded at the first level as a personality trait, but it must be pointed out how he makes this a self-parodying act and how this very act becomes, as part of the larger design of the film, a significant practice.

Take the aspect of himself in the form of this *actor's head* drawing attention to itself for its inimitable expressivity. The mechanism by which this seduction takes place is the camera, and behind the camera is presumably Ghatak as director, the focusing eye and ideal spectator. Ghatak, in other words, is face to face with himself, and this encounter, where the subject confirms its existence, has obvious psychoanalytic and archetypal antecedents (i.e., the mirror according to Lacan and Narcissus). I bring this up to emphasise the powerful impact of the mirror encounter: the encounter between the ideal ego with the promise of mastery and control over life's performance, and the ego experienced as still awkward, *insufficient*. Although in his last film, at the end of his life, Ghatak is accused of regression, quite the contrary is true; he actually tackles the narcissistic element in the processes of self-identification. He examines the narcissistic *relationship*, measuring the gap between self and mirrored self, transferring the weak sense of history that it implies into a paradoxical form which initiates an explicit discourse on it. In that sense the narcissistic relation forms precisely the pre-text for a discourse about the social, raising questions of identity on both symbolic and imaginary levels, levels at which a subject simultaneously articulates itself while being articulated into history. The hybrid, perhaps even self-contradictory figure that emerges in that process is the figure of the fool.

3. The figure of the holy fool, the wise buffoon, belongs to all mystic traditions and all ancient literatures, especially all dramatic literature.

Complementing the figures of the Zen monk and the Sufi poet, the mendicant minstrel of medieval India becomes the prime figure of spiritual discourse with its counterpart in the cunning figure of the *vidushaka*, the clown and didact in classical Indian drama. In Europe it gains a historical position of another order with Cervantes; and with Shakespeare, fascinated by the inquiry into the secret terrain of melancholy and madness, you get the existentially developed figure of the fool reading and rebutting destiny's signals on behalf of his companion the hero, with but the talent of speech.

This is the age of mannerism. It brings with it the slow and incipient process of individuation evolving in consonance with the material history of the Renaissance and the development of early capitalism. But this soon reaches the psychic condition of alienation such that the individual now sees himself both in charge of his destiny and unable to fulfil it within the terms of society, the economy and polity that has simultaneously evolved.[8] In painting you see subjectivity being formed (Bronzino), the subject stretching itself in a spirit of doubt and self-aggrandisement (Tintoretto). But while first this functions in favour of the subject in the world (Bruegel), alienation is imminent, where the very relationship between subject and object will snap and the bereft subject will see itself mirrored in a fantastically distorted if surreally elegant world which mocks even as it mirrors the figures and forms of an unattained selfhood (El Greco).

Mannerist art forms generate and contain excess – as emotional resource and linguistic over-supply of signifiers – and out of this excess the tragic-comic character is construed, as a pervasive discourse taking unexpected twists and turns in the unconscious. *This is the prefiguration of the romantic, which in turn prefigures the modern in its expressionist form.*

Ghatak is often called an expressionist, which is correct and which he accepts with full responsibility. What I should like to emphasise is that with Ghatak expressionist art in its full dimension does include the romantic and mannerist prerequisites. It includes working out such contradictions as mannerism threw up between the uncharted aspiration of the individual and an investigation of social anomie. It includes the dilemma of Romanticism: a glorification of the folk, of their mythic fantasy and so-called authenticity, with an understanding of the development of capitalism and the rise of an advanced working-class consciousness. And it includes, finally, an examination of middle-class conscience (the problem of bad faith) and revolutionist utopias as in the literature of the modern period. But Ghatak's expressionism finds its further reflexivity in Marxism: appropriately, he is an admirer of Brecht, and like Brecht he works on historical contradictions as such, formally and ideologically, for all to see.

186

4. To pick out some mannerist-expressionist components in Ghatak's work, let us look at his style of figuration. We have already spoken about the odd close-ups where the head floats and wobbles and of the tilted compositions. Consider again how the extremely angled shots – top angles or very low angles – distort not only the interior space (for example, the lines of the walls, the bars in a window, an open door) but also the figures so that they are tilted forward or back. See how he combines this with the use of lighting, with well worked out artificial shadows and a wide-angle lens which emphasises the depth-of-field, and you have an almost perfect description of a *mannerist image*.

I want to emphasise here that it is usually his own figure that the camera distorts, most remarkably when you see him at the end as the police bullet hits him in the stomach. You see a distorted figure and the implications are various: a) if in mannerist art such attenuation signifies alienation, a quotation from the convention can become in the Brechtian sense an alienating *device*; b) the distorted figure is seen to be at variance with our sense of gravity, whether we are positioned with the camera or in defiance of it; however we are positioned in our seats, such a figure displaces our contractual stability of space; c) and this leads to an interesting conclusion, a double conclusion: the tilted figure seems to be about to fall back or forward not to reinforce the depth of field, *not for a greater reality effect*, but for the purpose of pulling the viewer into the frame, forcibly. The viewer clutches at a figure that seems to be falling out beyond, even as Ghatak actually falls forward upon us when he dies, splashing liquor over the very lens.

Now one might say that to make the shadow on the screen and the spectator clutch each other is objectionable in that it makes identification physical, visceral. What I am arguing, however, is that Ghatak does the opposite – he breaks the pact by going too far, by defying the spectator's optical expectations of figures in space, expectations as of the Renaissance which cinema has basically internalised. If I feel dizzy or awestruck sharing the inhospitable space the character inhabits, then for all the exhibitionism he is breaking the voyeuristic spell, making me conscious of the relationship induced in cinematic viewing.

III

Narrative space

1. The relationship of the spatial with the narrative situation in *Jukti* has to be looked at further. At one level the narrative of *Jukti* is quite conventional: it is a third-person narrative whose prime character possesses the determining awareness. But there is a deviation in that the character is not guided by the psychological motivations of, say, the

realist hero, nor for that matter by those of the anti-hero, his familiar, subversive companion in whom indeed the great part of modern tragedy (in literature as well as in film) is enacted.

Correspondingly, the odd positioning of the camera in *Jukti* does not serve, as in similar uses of the convention, to encourage identification (for example, making the figure larger than life), nor to suggest alienation (for example, foreshortening and thus disfiguring the character). Nor is it quite used to mark out the psychological states of the character, his psychic stresses.

I have indicated before that in almost every film Ghatak seeks to construct a subjectivity that stands midway between an *archetypal* and a *class formation*; or rather, a subjectivity that stands apart, in a state of temporary and dynamic autonomy, from the congealed embodiment of mythic consciousness, the icon, and the cipher of history prone to be sucked into its processes. He seeks to construct what in one sense may be called a liminal figure; and the *liminal figure implies by definition a spatial disjunction*. Consistent with that, Ghatak's cinematic devices – including camera angles, lighting, lensing and depth-of-field – give the figure in space this uneasy location, on the join, as it were, between reality and irreality.

To put it another way, by interposing diagrammatic and dimensional models of spatial projection, Ghatak succeeds in making the narrative space and the figural trajectory through it a kind of manifest maze. The space is a critical area of operation, an area of doubt, of speculation, and of planned volition.

Thus a pictorial mode of positioning a figure in space becomes also a way of mapping the subject in history. (To continue the art-historical analogy, consider what happens when you move from the mannerist use of space to the Baroque, as for example in Velazquez's *Las Meninas*.) And thus Ghatak, over and beyond providing this uneasy ground to the filmic narrative, plays with meanings through a set of spatial paradigms in which we as spectators are variously positioned, every time a little askance.

2. Having concentrated too exclusively on the way Ghatak achieves this symbolic clutching together of the figural motif, I must now introduce the ways in which he *counterposes* the spatial structures in *Jukti*. For the fact is that he continually dismantles the over-determined images, suggesting not only how the principle of montage (and Ghatak regarded Eisenstein as the ulimate master of cinema) works precisely through a rhythm of closed and open forms, but further, that tight metaphoric configurations merit quite different, even converse narrative procedures.

Thus for all his expressionist tendencies Ghatak releases the image into what one might call an unmarked horizontality, a literal flatness as of many a landscape in India. Bleached and undifferentiated, such frames are in conscious contrast with the evocative, tonally rich and symbolically moulded landscapes of his other films such as *Ajantrik*, *Komal Gandhar* and *Titash Ekti Nadir Naam*. And I would like to suggest that this is a deliberate formal device which corresponds to the anecdotal mode in which *Jukti* is made.

Fully conscious of the epic form of narration (just as he is of melodrama), Ghatak knows how the epic proper comes to be inducted into the picaresque and the dramatic forms of narration (Cervantes and Shakespeare), and thence into the romantic-realism of, say, Balzac, and not least into Brecht, who then virtually draws the tail-end of realism back to its source in the epic. Ghatak speaks frequently of the epic form[9] and of Brecht. But if we want to deal with the anecdotal aspect of *Jukti* and the narrative space in which it functions, then we have to understand his interest in the documentary form of cinema,[10] and not surprisingly his affinity to aspects of Godard.[11]

Ghatak uses what could be called Godardian techniques in *Jukti*, for example the inter-spacing of neutral images whether of the city or the landscape, the insertion of documentary footage, or the abruptness of frontal address over against the fictional narrative so as to privilege the present. Indeed Ghatak adopts the logic of the cinematic present in *Jukti*, and he does this as much by the narrative style, the seemingly spontaneous performative aspect of the actors, as by the way the series of scenes are laid out, the perfunctory, nearly amateurish set-ups through which his self-exiled, anachronistic quartet wanders in and out: through the Calcutta streets punctuated by derelict tea-stalls and liquor-shops; at the river front and on park benches; trudging across the outskirts of the city and beyond into the countryside through parched fields and peasant-land; and then at the symbolic crossroads where the group meet a drunken cart-driver who directs them to their destination by saying go right, then left, then right, then left ...

Indeed the most politically motivated sequences function in a narrative space that is conspicuously unoriginal, even indifferent. For example the caricatural, very Eisensteinian montage sequence where the incoherent trade unionist is shown barking out his harangue in unison with a pariah dog; in the scene of peasant insurgency where Ghatak presents its anarchic nature in some very sketchy high-contrast, long-shot takes, with little figures running helter-skelter threatened by the landlord's gun-toting henchman, who is shown in distorted close-ups. The grand finale of prolonged cross-fire between the Naxalites and the police is, for all its inter-cut suspense, a mock-up battle, so much as to say that the meaning of the event lies not in the *mise en scène* or in the dramatisation but in the sheer *encounter*, as it is always called in police

189

reporting. That it is merely an abbreviated, notational record of the mortal struggle in lieu of which the peremptory death of the hero is pushed up, enlarged, and in a sense flattened into a rhetorical question: how do you terminate the inexorable present except by a parodic death?

Ghatak dies after delivering the coda of the film; then the corpse is picked up by the police and carried through a barren boulder landscape with the captive party in single file walking briskly – to a marching tune. This style of drumming the tragic hero across an empty stage has all of Brecht and Godard in it, but there is all of Ghatak in it too: his own black humour gained from the position of an exile to which by the end of life he was relegated.

3. That *Jukti* treats of an exile is obvious enough; that its narrative space is finally derived from a chosen indigenous tradition of exile needs to be emphasised. I have frequently referred to the hypothetical figure of the holy fool who stands in the space of exile. But then there is the Indian epic tradition of the hero's exile in the forest; there is the tradition of the peripatetic prophet and preacher, as for example the Buddha and Sankara; there are the vivid, variegated lives of the itinerant medieval saint-poets, for example Namdeva, Eknath, Kabir and many others; there are mendicants and minstrels moving across vast geographical areas, the idea of movement as such, of moving on, being quite central to their life and message: 'What is *made* will crumble, what is standing will fall; but what *is*, the living moving *jangama*, is immortal.'[12]

Therefore, though conceptually the fool stands erect, commanding the equations of the metaphysical scheme to which he belongs, the saint-poets whom we actually encounter in the Indian tradition just as systematically shed their privileges – in their itinerant life, in the grace and accessibility of their discourse, in their deliberate sociality, in the very playfulness of their presence and absence in history. And Ghatak, while formulating the narrative structure and space appropriate to the figure in exile, recalls this very *movement* of the saint-poets.

Moreover, this provides him with a way both to *humble his overriding subjectivity and to give it the power of the collective*. For we know that the saint-poets even as wanderers were embedded in the true collective of peasant and artisanal communities and that they rose beyond it, into vanguard positions of reformists and revolutionaries within the larger, hierarchically structured society. Thus it is that Ghatak, by sanction of his own tradition, has also the privilege of access to a collective and communitarian identity. Rejecting the metaphysically privileged subjectivity as also the behaviourist reading of socialised man, he can query the meaning of *action* (and non-action) from the odd position of these heretical poets.

Indeed we might say that just as subjectivity is posited in and through the spatial dimension in *Jukti*, it is posited in and through the temporal dimension also, signified as praxis. Ghatak is fully conscious that it is only when the figure is placed in such a space-time conjunction that the historical moment can be formulated, and he is fully conscious that the cinematic means are eminently capable of producing this space-time conjunction and thus redefining the ontology of the subject, as a subject in history. This brings me to a more detailed consideration of the problematic of praxis.

IV

Time, action and death: praxis problematised

1. Through a cleverly arranged narrative Ghatak himself becomes an agent in *Jukti* of the process of acting out, of enactment, and of action, in its political motivation. There is quite certainly a psychological *acting out* process in the film; Ghatak is acting out his own unresolved romanticism and he is using a well-known marker for the cause which is alcoholism. It is also true that this acting out process involves a degree of infantilism along with adult idealism. But precisely because he is also conscious of the inner core of romanticism, he is able to contain its excess: as master of the melodramatic form, he can handle the dysfunctions both of infantilism and of idealism so as to arrive, narratively, at a political resolution.

While this alcoholism is to be put down as a means of acting out, his childish play with his stoical wife, his vagabond companions, his renegade colleagues, and finally with the militant youth and the police he encounters at the end of the film – all this should be seen in terms of a conscious enactment of the many aspects of the fool. If he is the eternal child in the film, making up to its mother after every act of irresponsibility, turning her admonishments into more lavish appeals, it is in an especially Indian context where, for example, the pranks of the child-Krishna and man's childlike supplication to the goddess Kali provide a kind of cyclical energy pattern for the male consciousness. The motif of the mother, so central in the Bengali consciousness, is always present in Ghatak's films; here we have the wife-mother literally called Durga, and there is the destitute girl who is a substitute-mother equally significantly called Bangabala. Ghatak places this cruel and compassionate mother figure in her iconic form within an even larger matrix of mankind's myths (after Jung), thus converting what may be myth as mystification, a specifically construed super-structural value in Bengali culture, into the perennial source of the human unconscious. This conversion can be seen as an ideological operation with which one may be out of

191

sympathy. But so far as the playfulness of the man-child in this film is concerned, he enacts it with sufficient irony to refute any charges of false consciousness. He enacts the child in order both to appease the mother and to subsume her powers within a more existentially complex figure of the fool. This is the subject, archetypal and historical at the same time, who possesses by sanction of all tradition the prerogative of speech, and since speech is volatile it turns him into an *agent provocateur* within the social.

2. If his own alcoholism is presented in the film as an empty marker of an impossible desire for plenitude, or rather for the lost object of plenitude, which is the mother, then the relationship between two forms of infantilism is established to the advantage of the adult subject who is able to counterpose himself vis-à-vis the mother in the figure of the fool. If, however, even this figure must suffer a dissolution in death – and the death is greatly played up in the film – then there is a transferring of a sensuous object of desire to a more abstract one which is *utopia*. What is important is that it is not a transference at a psychological level alone; the supreme dissolution enacted in dying is immediately preceded by a hardheaded evaluation of his own failed life in terms of contemporary history (as envisaged in the major revolutionary figures from Marx to Che) and this self-evaluation is addressed to a young radical, in turn evaluated by him as suffering from an *infantile disorder*. The concept of utopia is thus presented in discourse as a historical project.

In this penultimate discourse Ghatak is at one level absolving himself, transferring his own kind of infantile disorder into Lenin's historical category where it is truly to be critiqued. He is transferring and also perhaps transacting between an old man and a boy the pain of alienation, the alienation of the political exile. He is attempting to split off this alienation into what could be called its defensive and reflexive parts so that the tragedy of the young Naxalite becomes disembodied idealism, while his own tragedy becomes, in exchange, a historical suicide, a full-bodied *intervention*.

3. Ghatak dies this exaggerated death standing up in the middle of the crossfire between the Naxalite and the police. As he is hit in the gut he lurches forward; he is foreshortened because the camera is set at a low angle and he appears almost horribly comic; and as if to confirm his own absurdity he reaches out one arm and spills the liquor in his bottle, pouring it out over the lens. If emptying the bottle is an ironic comment on the futile dream of plenitude, the splashed and dirtied lens, the interface between our reality and his, appears to be a comment on the impossibility of positive viewing on our part as well. The veil drawn over the lens is an anti-didactic gesture so much as to say even as the

truth slips between the Naxalite and the old man, it slips between the image and the viewer; that there is no definitive access to the out-reaching utopianism.

There is a good deal of demagogy in *Jukti*, also a good deal of vanity and caprice. But what Ghatak presents in his dying moment is the *coda* which holds compacted in it both the discourse of the speaking subject and that of contemporary history.

4. For the dying speech, as brave as it is enigmatic, modulates the tragedy of a historical suicide. As he lies dying he tells his wife a little story (by the contemporary Bengali writer, Manik Bandopadhyaya) of a weaver who, when he was admonished by his comrades for running the loom while they stood on strike against the money-lender's exploitation, replied: I run an empty loom so as not to let my limbs rust, so as to keep in practice, adding of himself as he actually dies, *one must do something*.

One must do something, one must act. This is the injunction in the *Gita*: Krishna tells Arjuna to engage in action which is his *svadharma*, which in fact constitutes him as a specific subject in a specific space and moment of history. To act irrespective of gain, irrespective even of the result. Conversely, more pessimistically, today this may also be an injunction to act even though it may result in nothing.

Praxis is here problematised, wrenched from a futurist rhetoric both of the dreamer and of the militant – or shall we say, praxis is prevented from being metaphysicalised even as death. The prime figure of metaphysics is prevented from fulfilling its function of *closure*. Where death is thus emptied of its conventional existential meaning and given an indeterminate status, where it is made to stand proxy for action, it becomes a retroactive sign, weaving a dialectical notion of time into the narrative. In a sense this is a special cinematic privilege, to enact and replay the tragedy and farce axiom of blocked history.

Notes

1. For biographical material in English see Ashish Rajadhyaksha, *Return to the Epic*, Screen Unit, Bombay, 1982; and Haimanti Banerjee, *Ritwik Kumar Ghatak*, NFAI, Pune, 1985.
2. *Chitrabikshan*, January-April 1976, pp. 75–6; English translation by Haimanti Banerjee in her *Ritwik Kumar Ghatak*, pp. 76–7.
3. This occurs not only with the main character of the film but also between characters, each with a symbolic name and a persona: a typical and an individual identity. To recount the names alone, the wife is called Durga

(mother goddess); the son Satya (truth); the young graduate Nachiketa (the young sceptic in *Kathopanishad*, burning with the desire for truth); the destitute girl Bangabala (the daughter of Bengal), and so on.

4. Ghatak, quoted in H. Banerjee, op. cit., p. 79.

5. See Ritwik Ghatak, *Cinema and I*, Ritwik Memorial Trust, Calcutta, 1987, pp. 105–11.

6. He found occasion to include a long dance sequence in *Jukti*; he had already made a documentary, *Puruliar Chhau Nritya*, in 1970.

7. We know of course that the man portrayed will be dead at the end of the film; so will the author identified in body and mind with the character; and so, tragically, was Ghatak himself a year after the film's release.

8. See Arnold Hauser, *Mannerism: The Crisis of the Renaissance and the Origins of Modern Art*, Cambridge, Mass./London, The Belknap Press of Harvard University Press, 1986.

9. See Ritwik Ghatak, 'Music in Indian Cinema and the Epic Approach', *Cinema and I*, pp. 41–3.

10. See Ritwik Ghatak, 'Documentary: The Most Exciting Form of Cinema', *Cinema and I*, pp. 46–59.

11. Ghatak had seen some Godard films; he occasionally speaks about this in his writings: 'You see I agree with Jean-Luc Godard that anything which seems to an artist to be able of [sic] conveying his message is entirely valid – be it song or dance or newspaper headlines or commentaries or just about anything ...', *Cinema and I*, p. 72.

12. See A. K. Ramanujan's 'Introduction' (to his translations of Virsaiva *vacanas*, Kannade free verse) in *Speaking of Siva*, Penguin, 1973, pp. 20–1, where he speaks about the opposition between the standing and the moving in Virsaiva religion; where 'a Jangama is a religious man who has renounced world and home, moving from village to village representing god to the devoted, a god incarnate.'

African Cinema:
Solidarity and Difference

Paulin Soumanou Vieyra

First we must define what we mean by cinema and then what we mean by African Cinema. Cinema is a generic term encompassing both the industry and the art of cinema, the latter being the cultural product represented by the film as object. The African film exists, so much is plainly evident. We have seen it, it has been the object of criticism, of studies, of doctoral theses.

The components of cinema are particularised in different stages. First there is the research which allowed the initial setting up of an industry to produce the technical materials. We know the path that has led to the discovery of the cinematograph by the Lumière Brothers in Lyon. These materials then served to produce and to direct films. These were then put on the market created for them in order to be distributed to and shown in places called cinemas.

This first and primary component of cinema does not exist in Africa. In Africa there are no film industries in this sense. The materials required to make African films are imported from all over the world. At the other end of the chain, as regards the development of film, Africa is only beginning to have its own embryonic industries with the setting up here and there of laboratories, editing studios, auditoria. This aspect of the industry can be found in Egypt and now in Tunisia, Morocco, Zimbabwe and South Africa.

While there is virtually no industrial base for African cinema, its commercial organisation is in its first and hesitant stages. It is enormously difficult to put a production apparatus in place because of the lack of an infrastructure, of resources, of capital and above all because of the lack of a positive political will. The same applies to the distribution sector, which comes up against Western hegemonies with imperial preferences and maintaining the north-south axis as the privileged route of exchange while impeding any attempts by Africans to organise this market. Finally, African exhibition, the retailing outlet, does not dispose of enough sites for it to prosper. The number of cinemas is very small: about 2,500 for the whole of Africa. This is not much compared to the 140,000 cinemas in the Soviet Union for a population which is about the same as that of the African continent. Consequently, the number of times Africans frequent the cinema is fairly low. It isn't even 2 per cent, which is the minimum number UNESCO estimated as compatible with a harmonious development of a country. I think Africa stands at about 0.5 per cent, i.e. half a seat per 100 people.

The national cinema also implies the existence of training facilities such as Film Schools and various institutions, cinémathèques, archives, libraries, etc. In the last instance a national cinema relies on an enlightened public, kept informed by its critics and historians. If we admit that cinema is all that we have just mentioned, can we say that African cinema exists?

Of course, African films do exist because film-makers exist, emerging like spontaneous developments, surviving against all expectations because films still do get made even if only on a shoestring and not very often. The Senegalese cineaste Ousmane Sembene hasn't made a film since *Ceddo* which dates back to 1976. [Sembene finished another film in 1988.] And he is considered to be one of Africa's greatest film-makers. Relief is slow in coming. It took about 8 to 11 years for members of the older generation such as the Mauritanian Med Hondo or Desiré Ecaré from the Ivory Coast to be able to make a new film. The difficulties experienced by the Malian Souleymane Cissé for his new film *Yeelen* are well known. As for the younger generation, if they do succeed in getting a production off the ground, there are few, at least in Black Africa, who could be regarded as guaranteed top value. I do not mean to question their competence, their artistic merit. Since the cultural revolution of 1968 in Europe, young African cineastes who are often university graduates have probably received better training than their elders. But how are they to acquire the necessary experience if they do not have the means or the opportunity to make films regularly?

Solidarity

Nevertheless, solidarity does exist among African cineastes, a fact attested to concretely in the form of coproductions, for example between Tunisian and Algerian film-makers, between Egyptians and Algerians, Nigerians and Malians, Nigerians and Brazilians.

We can find that solidarity in the support given to the Carthage Festival created in 1966, to the Panafrican Festival in Ouagadougou, to the Mogadishu Symposium. That will to cooperation also gave birth to the Panafrican Film-makers Federation during the first congress in Tunis in 1970 under the auspices of the Carthage Festival. This has made it possible to set up a national association of film-makers in thirty-three African countries. The FEPACI at its 2nd Congress in Algiers (1975) studied the film-makers' charter known as the Algiers Charter, which was modified and extended at the 3rd Congress in Ouagadougou in 1985. Through FEPACI, cineastes have organised a number of meetings on African cinema in its diverse aspects in order to propose solutions to the problem of organising national cinemas in the different African states. Consequently, fourteen African states created, in Ouagadougou, the Interafrican Cinema Consortium (CIDC) and the Interafrican Film Production Centre (CIPROFILM) which would take charge of distribution and production in the fourteen states. At present, these organisations are not in the healthiest of condition, again because of the lack of resources and because the states do not really show a political will to organise an African cinema in the West African area. The slow-motion functioning of these two organisations has prompted film-makers to set up a private organisation to promote their films, the Committee of African Cineastes (CAC), with offices in different African countries, using the French language and working to the benefit of any African film-maker who agrees to give them their films so that they can try to find a distributor.

The same spirit of cooperation and solidarity presided over the formation of the West African Film Corporation (WAFCO), a non-profit-making and cultural organisation aiming to help members as well as non-members to find the financial means to mount productions. This is a regional structure with the advantage of covering both French- and English-speaking areas such as Ghana, the Ivory Coast, Senegal, Guinea, Mauritania, Nigeria, Niger, Mali. Now a certain realism presides over the formation of new structures put in place privately, especially those organised by the film-makers. It remains to extend this sense of solidarity to African businessmen by stressing the possible profitability of cultural products provided there is good commercial organisation with opportunities for banks to intervene, and showing, of course, that it would be in their interest.

Differences

Since we remain on the level of African films rather than African cinema, for the reasons mentioned earlier, the differences between African films are to be welcomed if only for the range of subjects and the quality of their approaches to the various topics. This all depends on the specific characteristics of each director, their formation, their ideological choices, working methods and artistic sensibility.

Within one given country, films by different directors do not resemble each other. Their talent necessarily differentiates them even if they deal with the same subject. No doubt it is possible to find within a country's production, as in families, certain family resemblances due to biological

197

factors, similarities in the environment, the landscapes, in a particular cultural identity. In this respect, diversity makes for a country's wealth. The American cinema is rich precisely because of the diversity of its population, the multiple contributions of which open out onto the whole world and encompass all races. The African continent presents the same kind of riches as far as its population is concerned because one cannot speak of a unitary African culture with its multiplicity of ethnic groups. Its cinema reflects that diversity and will soon lead us, I hope, to speak no longer about African films but about Senegalese, Nigerian, Ivorian, Madagascan, Kenyan, Cameroonian, etc. cinemas as each of the African countries develops its specific cinema.

Then, in the light of the political organisation peculiar to the various states, there will be doctrinal choices that will determine the organisation of these different cinemas: the cinemas of the socialist states, of the capitalist states or of states with a regulated economy within a liberal framework, as for example in France where a structure such as the Centre National du Cinéma is a regulatory body allowing young film-makers to make their first film and permitting the realisation of difficult subjects through the mechanism of the advance on receipts.

Conclusion
I believe that when we speak of cinema, we now have to include the medium of TV, which is beginning to become very important in Africa as the continent develops economically and culturally. The difference necessary for our expressive wealth resides in the path of solidarity opened up and in the dialogue between cultures. With the current technological progress, planet Earth is becoming so small that only the interdependence of the populations in all their activities can assure their survival. The African Cinema that will be born, inevitably through solidarity with other cinemas, in the framework of the development of audiovisual means, will, paradoxically, affirm itself only through those differences.

Oral Literature and African Film: Narratology in *Wend Kuuni*

Manthia Diawara

Gaston Kaboré, director of *Wend Kuuni* (1983), stated, in an attempt to define African cinema, that African film-makers had not yet found a style which could characterise them as members of a film movement and differentiate them from European directors. Kaboré argued that in order to find a cinematic language which could render them singular and reflect African history and civilisation, film-makers had 'to search for their authentic inner-self. It is an endless and troublesome quest that requires the artist to constantly look for him/herself and his/her culture.'[1] Historians and critics have pointed out that African film-makers have in front of them a rich body of oral and written literature from which to take lessons on narrative devices, history and culture. It is widely believed that film and literature have much in common and that African film-makers should imitate the writer, the *griot* and other traditional story-tellers. An awareness of African literature will not only provide the film-makers with a better sense of the ambiguities of representation in Africa, it will also help them to put into an African context the lessons learned from European schools. To put it in the words of the participants of the Ouagadougou Seminar on the Role of the African Film-maker in Rousing an Awareness of Black Civilisation (1974): 'Co-operation between black writers and film-makers should find its living expression in producing films directly inspired by the works in our already rich and varied literary heritage. This would prevent the cinema from divorcing itself from literary creativity and thus from shutting itself in isolation.'[2]

The importance of literature to film was also underscored by the Ninth Ouagadougou Film Festival (FESPACO, 1985) which brought together writers, such as Mongo Beti and Sembene Ousmane, film-makers, critics and historians to discuss the possibilities of adapting African classics on film. During the colloquium, issues of representation such as *vraisemblance*, faithfulness and originality were debated with

199

regards to the film adaptation of *Kongi's Harvest* (1973) and *L'Aventure ambigue* (1984). Comparing the relative failure of *Kongi's Harvest* and *The Ambiguous Adventure* with the success of films adapted from the oral traditions, like *Wend Kuuni* (1983) and *Nelisita* (1984), some participants suggested that oral literature was a better source of inspiration than the African literatures written in the former colonial languages. The Ethiopian director Haile Gerima, for example, argued that in order for him to film a script which is in English, he must translate it first into Amharic, his mother tongue. During the translation process several cultural subtleties can be lost. The use of literature written in French, English or Portuguese as a source of inspiration/adaptation by African film-makers can also have a reverse effect on the film. The constraints of the borrowed language deterritorialise the content and form of the film, instead of enriching it with African cultural and discursive techniques. For all these reasons, Gerima stated that film-makers turn to oral rather than written literature.[3]

The influence of African literature on film has been discussed by individual scholars as well. Pierre Haffner, for example, believes that African film grew out of African theatre. To show the evolution of African cinema out of the theatre, Haffner mentions the songs of the *griots*, the performance of the wrestlers in Mali and Senegal and, especially, the enactment of the *Koteba* in Mali. He states that the theatre of the *Koteba* 'is the most dramatic among the traditional means of expression, because it puts on the stage characters who act and talk to each other.'[4] Clearly, therefore, Haffner is interested in the movement in space and the dialogues of the *Koteba*, which he sees as necessary elements of the new African film. Even though he discusses other narrative elements of the *Koteba* such as time and space, he alludes to them only to stress their influence on the spectator. Haffner does not show the manner in which elements of space and time could be used in film.[5]

Françoise Pfaff, too, in her book, *The Cinema of Ousmane Sembene*, looks at the oral tradition to show the *griot*'s influence on the film-maker. Pfaff finds that Sembene not only replaces the *griot* as the chronicler of his people's history, but his films can also be compared in some respects with traditional Yoruba theatre or the Ikaki masquerade. She states that the *griot* is physically present in a number of Sembene's works (*Niaye*, *Borom Sarret*, *Xala* and *Ceddo*), and that the films, 'like the *griot*'s renditions, provide the immediacy of visual and auditory action'.[6]

As I have pointed out above, the relation between literature and film and the influence of one on the other have been examined by historians and critics.[7] However, these studies are limited either to documenting the trace of oral literature in film (presence of the *griot*, and the use of heroes and customs borrowed from the oral tradition), or to discussing film as oral literature (analysis of repetitious patterns, formulas, proverbs, epic moments and songs). What has not been emphasised is the transformation that takes place in the narrative points of view when the film takes in charge the story from the oral tradition. As the extra-filmic elements of the story combine with specifically cinematic elements,[8] the presence of the film-maker as *auteur* takes precedence over the narrator of the literary text. This may lead to a subversion of certain characters at the expense of others, a new conception of order and closure from the original text to the film. In *The Ambiguous Adventure*, for example, the director, Jacques Champreux, emphasised the Senghorism or the symbiosis between cultures at the expense of a *vraisemblable* depiction of the Djalobés people with their dignified air.[9] As I will show, films use the material of oral literature to reflect the ideology of the time, not that of the oral tradition. Where an oral narrative advocates a return to law and order at the end, the film version desires a new order to replace the old and stagnating one.[10] Thus a *griot* is not viewed the same way in a Sembene film as in the oral tradition.

A return to the inner-self or to African culture does not therefore mean a subordination to tradition for the film-maker who uses oral literature. It is a questioning of tradition, a creative process which enables the director to make contemporary choices while resting on the shoulders of tradition. To illustrate my point, I will turn to *Wend Kuuni* and discuss the use of some narrative elements such as functions, order and voice.[11] Since the film, which won 'Le Caesar de la Francophonie' (1985) and several other awards, was adapted from oral tradition, I will attempt to show the manner in which it transforms events and characters from their original representation. Finally I will argue that the film achieves closure in a different ideological order than the oral tradition might have done. Orality is the *subject* of the film because it incorporates an oral rendering of the tale which it later subverts.

Before undertaking an analysis of narratology in *Wend Kuuni*, however, it is important to give an overview of the main narrative events in the film. It opens with a woman sitting in a hut, holding her son in her arms and crying. Her husband, who is a hunter, has been missing for thirteen months. A man comes to her door, tells her that it is useless to keep on crying, that her husband must have died or he would have returned home. She should stop being stubborn and marry another man who would become a father for her son. She refuses and states to her son her intention to run away. The sequence is followed by the credits, after which the boy is found unconscious in the forest by a trader who carries him on the back of his donkey to the nearest village. The boy is mute and cannot explain where he came from. The trader leaves him with a family until his own village and parents can be identified. After attempts to find the boy's home fail, the chief of the village decides to leave him with the family. The boy is given a name, Wend Kuuni (the gift of God), by his new parents (Tinga and Lale), who already have a little girl near the boy's age called Pongneré. Then there are several scenes showing people at their daily activities in the home, the field, and the market-place. Wend Kuuni and Pongneré, too, are shown learning social roles that fit boys and girls. Pongneré helps her mother and Wend Kuuni tends the goats. One day, Wend Kuuni sees in the forest a man hanged from a tree. The horrible sight shocks him and, as a result, he is able to speak again. He tells Pongneré his story, which is shown in a flashback. We see Wend Kuuni and his mother as they are chased out of the village. The mother is accused of being a witch and she is stoned by the villagers, who also burn her hut. Lost in the middle of the forest, tired and sick, Wend Kuuni's mother finally gives up running and sits by a big tree. Then, before she dies, we see shots of her husband hunting. Shocked by his mother's death, Wend Kuuni screams and runs away. The flashback ends and we go back to Wend Kuuni as he finishes telling Pongneré his story.

The story is presented mostly in long shots until towards the end, where there are close-up shot/reverse shots of Wend Kuuni and Pongneré.[12] Dialogue is also rare except for the daily greetings, the exchanges in the market-place and the questions and answers. Pongneré, whenever she can, breaks the general silence of the movie and talks to Wend Kuuni. There is also a voice-over narration coming in from time to time to inform the spectator of the situation. It is easy to assume on the surface that the film is an adaptation from oral tradition because of the off-screen narrator, who is comparable to the storyteller. The reduced dialogues and the long-shots also imply that there is only one narrator, the omniscient storyteller, who sees everything with objectivity.

It is also easy on the surface to see only a simple oral telling in the seemingly linear structure of the narrative. But a look at the functions reveals that we are dealing with the combination of at least three important stories in one. For example, the first function at the opening of the film, a husband missing, calls for a set of functions which constitute the deep structure of an autonomous story. The original sequence of events in this type of story is: 1) husband missing; 2) departure in search of the husband, or non-departure in which case the wife has to wait for him or remarry; 3) process of finding the husband; 4) success and return.

The representation of these functions in the film is interesting. The events of the first function are not shown; the spectator learns in the opening shots that the husband has been missing for thirteen months. The second function is narrated in flashback at the end of the film from

Wend Kuuni's point of view. The spectator also learns in the flashback that Wend Kuuni's mother dies before finding his father. Function three, which is introduced in the film before function two, had therefore to be temporarily suspended until a new agent resumed the task of finding the missing object. Function three is further complicated by Wend Kuuni's inability to speak. Thus the different attempts to restore him to his village and to his parents coincide with the search for the missing father. The fourth function is even further displaced because Wend Kuuni, who replaces his mother as the agent of the quest, finds himself instead of the missing father. A new order is established as Wend Kuuni accepts the death of his mother and father through the flashback narration at the end.

The other autonomous story from the oral tradition in the film is that of the 'wanted son', the invariant functions of which are: 1) the desire for a son;[13] 2) the attempts to get a son; 3) the arrival of the son; and 4) his coronation. Although only the third function is represented, the 'wanted son' myth is important in the film. The title of the film, *Wend Kuuni*, which means Gift of God and which is also the name of the main character, has a familiar semantic value in this type of story. Usually, when after several aborted attempts the son arrives, he is given the name Gift of God. The structure of the family in which Wend Kuuni lands shows another manner in which the 'wanted son' myth is emphasised by the use of just one function in the film. It is a family consisting of a father, Tinga, a mother, Lale, a daughter, Pongneré, and no son. Wend Kuuni is therefore needed to fill the void created by the lack of a son. The fact that a lot of film time is devoted to depicting Wend Kuuni helping the father or doing other manly duties substantiates the claim that he is the 'wanted son' or the Gift of God.

Finally, the third myth in the film concerns the 'emancipation of the daughter'. Unlike the preceding myths, which are prevalent in oral tradition, this is a new story which is contemporaneous with the advent of the emergence of written literature and film in Africa. The myth may be traced to Frantz Fanon in his studies on the Algerian woman during the revolutionary war.[14] In literature, Sembene Ousmane and Ngugi Wa Thiong'o use the myth as a metaphor of the liberation struggle of the oppressed majority in Africa.[15] But it is in film that the modes of existence and the functions of this type of story are clearly delineated. Several films by Sembene readily come to mind: *Xala*, with the story of Rama and the beggars; Princess Dior in *Ceddo*; and the women of *Emitai*. Sembene's example is followed and well executed by other directors: Haile Gerima poses the case of Beletech in *Harvest 3000 Years*; Souleymane Cissé's *Den Muso* and Ben Diogaye Beye's *Sey Seyeti*, to name only these films, are also structured around the myth of the 'emancipated girl'.

The invariant functions of the myth are: 1) oppressive order; 2) desire to break out; 3) success and creation of a new order. Function one in the film is manifest in Pongneré's situation as a girl in a patriarchal society. She has no right to the outdoor adventures into which Wend Kuuni is initiated. She is confined indoors and to the outskirts of the village activities which are safe for women. The constraints on women's freedom in the patriarchal system are earlier challenged in the film by Wend Kuuni's mother, who refuses to remarry and faces the consequences of being labelled a witch. At another point in the film, another woman, Timboko, denounces the oppressive system when she states in public that the man she is being forced to marry is old and impotent. Timboko, too, is called a witch and a snake by the social system she is putting on trial.

The events of the second function include Pongneré's friendship with Wend Kuuni, which indicates her desire to escape her condition as a girl. She goes against her mother's warnings to join Wend Kuuni in the forest and plays with him. It may be argued from the perspective of the myth of the 'wanted son' that Wend Kuuni has simply become Pongneré's brother. But it is clear that the relationship between them, as Pongneré sees it, transcends the patriarchal order constituted between brothers and sisters in the oedipal phase. Pongneré is androgynous in her relation with Wend Kuuni[15] when she says that she wishes she were a boy so she could play with him. The economisation of female and male genders in Pongneré is not without an echo of a sequence in *Harvest 3000 Years*, where Beletech too realised that she was excluded from the boys' games because of her sex.

The third function leads to events which are mostly seen from Pongneré's point of view. The frequency of long-shots diminishes to give way to subjective shots inscribed with love. It seems like a lovers' rendezvous every time Pongneré joins Wend Kuuni in the fields. The shot/reverse shots of Pongneré smiling with Wend Kuuni and the bigger than life high-angle shots of the boy isolate the youth from the day-to-day purposeful activities of rural life. Pongneré substitutes her playful world for the rigidly constructed order and, in her subversive intervention, she changes her role in the narrative from an *adjuvant* or a facilitator to a central actor or a redeemer.[16]

After this brief discussion of the use of functions in *Wend Kuuni*, it is important to show the complexity of Kaboré's transformation of the oral tradition before moving on to analyse the film representation of other narrative elements such as order and voice. Clearly the film-maker gains by turning to oral tradition where he/she learns that the chronological juxtaposition of certain functions gives birth to certain types of story. Thus the oral tradition provides not only invaluable devices of linearisation, but also montage techniques and information on how to open and close an action. In so far as the events of each function imitate actions in traditional history and culture, the return to oral tradition also helps the film-maker to chose *vraisemblable* functions in a particular story.

Beyond the wish to return to tradition for the sake of tradition, however, the film-maker must also create contemporary forms and contents out of oral literature. Kaboré's strategy in *Wend Kuuni* consists in combining the functions of three independent stories in such a manner that a new story emerges. The semantic register of the archetypal stories – 'the missing husband', 'the wanted son', and 'the emancipated daughter' – would not have been affected had Kaboré represented the stories successively in the film. But the didactic message in each of these stories is subverted either because they are not narrated in full, or the events of certain functions appear simultaneously in more than one archetypal story. For example, in the case of 'the wanted son' where only one function, the arrival of the son, is clearly represented in the film, the story is displaced and the function registers additional meanings from its new environment. In this sense, Wend Kuuni's arrival in the village is as important to the emancipation of Pongneré and to the quest for his father as it is to the family desiring a son.

The montage of the events caused by the functions in the film also silences the message of some archetypal stories. The film opens, for example, with the 'missing husband' story; but instead of continuing with the second function of that story, it poses another function with a sequence in which a trader finds Wend Kuuni unconscious in the forest. The chronological unwinding of the 'missing husband' story is thus suspended, as the function 'Wend Kuuni is lost' provokes a chain of functions represented by the search for the boy's village and parents, the proposal of substitute parents and village, the boy's relationship with Pongneré and his recovery of his voice. By the time the 'missing husband' story is completed at the end of the film, its message is suppressed, and what the narrative emphasises is not whether Wend Kuuni had found his father and mother but the fact that he has regained his memory and voice and that he is happy in Pongneré's world. One can argue here that the characters of Wend Kuuni and Pongneré dominate the different archetypal stories in the film because they always seem to transcend them instead of being contained in them as actants. This is evident in the 'missing husband' story where the spectator realises that the entire story is told in flashback from Wend Kuuni's point of view. Pongneré, too, goes beyond the construction of her character as sister of Wend Kuuni in the 'wanted son' story to become an emancipated girl at the end.

Clearly, therefore, the film works on the archetypal stories of the oral tradition by subverting the signs of their functions. As shown above, the functions from the oral narrative are used less to achieve a traditional/ nostalgic closure, and more to enunciate a new narrative posing the conditions of resistance to traditional order and the creation of a new one. The montage and the combination/confusion of the events of the archetypal stories have the effect of pushing them into the background and bringing to the foreground the story of Pongneré and Wend Kuuni. From simple and linear narratives which serve to maintain the status quo, Kaboré has created a complex plot turned against the repressive forces of tradition. Instead of limiting his characters' roles to acting in the traditional functions, Kaboré raises them above the archetypal stories and situates them in a new story with contemporary thematic overtones. The rise of Wend Kuuni and Pongneré above the tradition evokes the desire for a new order which constitutes a preoccupation for African film-makers, from Sembene to Kaboré. In *Ceddo*, for example, Sembene questions the religious order and identifies the Ceddos as the only hope for revolution; in *Finye*, Souleymane Cissé constructs a liaison between the youth, symbol of hope, and tradition, against the dictatorship of the military regime; in *Djeli*, Lancine Fadika-Kramo exposes the negative aspect of the caste system and imagines a world which is better off without it.

African film-makers distinguish themselves from traditional raconteurs by being futurists. Where the *griot*'s narrative is concerned with disorder and the restoration of traditional order, the film-maker wants to transcend the established order and create a new one. The heroes of the films are usually women, children and beggars; such concepts as neo-colonialism, techno-paternalism, polygamy and sexism are associated with the villains. The traditional functions more commonly used by the film-makers are those that work to create revolution in the state, not those that restore the status quo. Thus, in *Wend Kuuni*, the first function, 'husband missing', is not followed by wife remarrying and order being restored. It is followed instead by the wife leaving the village which accuses her of being a witch. In another sequence, when a woman defies a husband, order is not established by the woman's submission to the patriarchal system. Rather the man hangs himself, thus indicating the impotence of the system. The defiance of order is clearer with the character of Pongneré, who wishes that she were a boy because her gender limits her options.

After this discussion of the functions of real narratives and their transformation in *Wend Kuuni*, it is important now to turn to other narrative elements and analyse their use in the film. The subversive deployment of orality will once again become evident. I have already mentioned certain roles of narrative order in regard to the organisation of the functions. I will now emphasise the ordered representation of events in the film so as to compare it to the sequence of events in the story. Such a comparison will not only lead to the discovery of the manner in which the film transforms the story, it will also uncover certain elements in the film that are not in the story. First let us look at the chronology of the main events in the story: 1) Once upon a time a trader found a boy unconscious in the forest. When the boy came to, he could remember neither who he was nor where he had come from. He was mute. 2) The trader took him to the nearest village where he left him with a family. The boy was given the name Wend Kuuni. 3) There was a little girl, named Pongneré, in the family, who became a good friend of Wend Kuuni. 4) One day, Wend Kuuni found a man hanged from a tree. He was so shocked that he recovered his memory and his speech. He was then able to talk about his past. His father had disappeared during the course of a hunt; his mother was forced to leave the village because she had rejected an offer to remarry. Tired and sick, she died in the middle of the forest, leaving the boy by himself.[17]

Comparing this summary of the sequence of events in the oral tradition to the way they are edited in the film (see page 201), one notices that the first sequence of the film includes parts of the last one in the oral narrative. It is also interesting that the same sequence is repeated at the end of the film as a flashback from Wend Kuuni's point of view. There are several ways the positioning of the sequence, of Wend Kuuni's mother crying about her missing husband, at the opening of the film transforms the oral narrative, which opens with the trader finding Wend Kuuni unconscious.

On stylistic grounds, the two mediums emphasise different problems in the beginning. For the oral text, the first enigma presented is the situation in which Wend Kuuni is found. It affects the spectator by leading him/her to expect events dealing with the restoration of the boy to order. In the film, however, the first puzzle of the story concerns the character of Wend Kuuni's mother. The spectator expects her either to remarry and be reincorporated in the safety provided by the patriarchal system, or to challenge it. The narrator in the oral tradition, by begin-ning *in medias res* with the sequence of the trader and the unconscious boy, poses in the mind of the spectator questions concerning the boy's past. The opening sequence of the film coincides with the chronological beginning of the story; thus the questions raised deal more with the boy's future than with his past. Clearly, therefore, the repetition of the beginning of the story at the end of the film serves more to clarify the interpretation of events that the spectator has already been exposed to than to reveal an event of which he/she had no prior knowledge. The oral text conceals the beginning of the story until the end, thus making it the most important event that the spectator waits for.

The different temporal ordering of events in the film as a whole also affects the meaning of the story from the oral tradition. The film's opening sequence presents an individual at odds with the system; a woman, placing her desires above tradition, chooses to run away. In the oral text the opposite ideology occurs: the story begins with a lost boy in need of a home. While the film starts indoors and points toward the wilderness, the oral tradition goes from the wilderness to the village. The narrator of the oral story is interested in restoring the status quo where there is chaos, while the film-maker rejects the existing order and proposes an alternative system. This binary opposition between indoors and outdoors, tradition and change respectively, is used by other African directors. In *Harvest 3000 Years*, Beletech participates in the games of the boys while they are far away from the village. At the end of the film Berehun searches for freedom and education away from the village. In Oumarou Ganda's *L'exilé* (1982), the hero learns how to rule outside of his own kingdom. In *Ceddo*, revolution is carried from outside by the Ceddos. *Wend Kuuni*, too, ends in the fields where the two heroes have insulated themselves from the oppressive forces of tradition. This sequence is represented neither as an event of the story nor as a narrative element in the oral tradition. The film emphasises this and other outdoor sequences because they constitute liberated spaces. Indoor sequences, on the other hand, dominate in the oral text because they represent safety and conservation.

To turn now to the construction of voice in the film, I will concentrate on the way narrative point of view is constituted, and show how it too makes the oral form its subject.[18] Long shots dominate the narrative of *Wend Kuuni*; it is only after Pongneré and Wend Kuuni meet that close-ups and medium shots become important in the narration of their interaction. As pointed out earlier, along with the long shots there are extended silent moments which are regularly interrupted by formulaic greetings and rarely by conversation. From time to time an off-screen narrator summarises the course of the story, as if to remind the specta-tor of his narrative authority. Long shots and a silent soundtrack seem to be more appropriate as narrative tools than close-ups and extended conversations/arguments which stand out because of the routine provided by people always doing their work and never stepping outside their traditional roles. The point I am trying to make is that the focalisation in the film is for the most part external. The characters are seen first from the point of view of an implied narrator (off-screen narrator); they are seen from a distance, they are objects to be looked at and, until Pongneré meets Wend Kuuni, they are not allowed the off-screen glance which forms a narrative point of view. The long shots and the prolonged silence of the characters imply an objective style, a documentary of rural African life without the distortion of close-ups and individual self-imagining. The reality effect of the style brings to mind the narration in the oral tradition. The *griot*, as the keeper of traditional history, is the only narrator of the story. Each version that he tells is seen by the audience as the reality of the way things used to be. Unlike the implied narrators of modern novels and films whose skills can be measured by the way they efface themselves and let the characters carry out the narration, the *griot*'s power and mastery of the craft depends on the degree to which his audience feels his presence as he tells the story. In *Wend Kuuni*, the off-screen narrator is like the *griot* in the sense that he always manifests his redundancy by summarising the story.

However, another narrative voice is constructed in the film as soon as Pongneré meets Wend Kuuni. The external point of view which had been dominating the narrative alternates with an internal focalisation to represent Pongneré's world view. From being depicted as an object to be looked at, Pongneré becomes a subject from whose point of view the spectator sees the world of the film. The development of subjective narration, or the use of characters as narrators, as an alternative to the objective representation described above, begins with Pongneré telling Wend Kuuni about her dream. The scene is filmed with close-ups and shot/reverse shots with Pongneré kneeling down and looking up at Wend Kuuni. It is interesting that the characters are here looking up and at each other whereas before they had always looked down. The spectator sees Wend Kuuni from Pongneré's point of view as she tells him that she had a dream in which he could talk. The reaction shot of Wend Kuuni smiling and looking at her shows that she has given him hope and confidence in himself.

At another point in the film, Pongneré defies her mother's orders and joins the boys in the fields. In the scene she asks Wend Kuuni to play a tune for her; when he gestures to her to go back home lest her mother get worried, she tells him that she wishes she were a boy so that she could always be with him. There are some unusual shots in the first part of this scene: first the spectator sees a close-up of Pongneré looking off-screen and calling Wend Kuuni. After a close-up of the boy who looks towards her, a long shot reveals that Pongneré is still at some distance from the boy and not as close as the earlier close-ups implied. These types of shot, which would have been impossible in the objective mode of narration, are now valorised because they represent Pongneré's subjectivity. As a girl she is confined to certain specific spaces; she must therefore distort space or break it into pieces to find her freedom. Pongneré's voice becomes an important narrative voice through these subjective shots, for through her eyes the spectator sees the things that are either missing or not emphasised by the objective narration of the off-screen narrator. For example, after Pongneré denounces the condition of girls in the patriarchal system, it becomes easier to sympathise with the two women who refused to marry men they did not like.

209

Even though the off-screen narrator states that Wend Kuuni is troubled by things on his mind, the spectator learns his story only after Pongneré asks him to tell it to her. With her, one begins to appreciate the boy not because he is an orphan, but because he is an individual and a handsome boy. He is often shot smiling or standing tall in a high-angle shot from her point of view. The subjective narration in the film is also emphasised by the flashback narrative from Wend Kuuni's point of view. It is arguable that in the oral tradition a woman who defies the elders' advice to remarry would be considered a witch and a danger to society. But in the film, the villagers' accusation that Wend Kuuni's mother is a witch is not convincing because the woman is depicted as a harmless soul with a sick son and a husband who has been missing for thirteen months. Wend Kuuni's narrative creates a situation of sorrow with which the spectator identifies. On the other hand, the villagers who call the woman a witch, stone her and burn her house are seen as villains. It is interesting that Wend Kuuni's story was deleted from the objective narrative because, as Pongneré told the boy, only the elders were supposed to hear it. Retelling it to the girl in the fields which are outside of the traditional space is tantamount to emancipating her. The deterritorialising of the story[19] also transforms its semantic value in favour of the subversive activities at work in the film. There is no doubt that the African film-maker rests on the shoulders of the traditional storytellers such as the *griot*, but the films are already pointing toward a new order and implicating the *griot* with the old and stagnating content.

Notes

1. *Neuvième FESPACO: Cinéma et Libération des Peuples*, Ouagadougou: Secrétariat Général des Festivals Cinématographiques, 1985, p. 52.
2. *Présence Africaine*, no. 90, 1974. Special issue: 'The Role of the African Film-maker in Rousing an Awareness of Black Civilisation', pp. 14–15.
3. See my article 'African Cinema: FESPACO, an evaluation' in *Third World Affairs*, 1986, p. 408.
4. Pierre Haffner, *Essai sur les fondements du cinéma africain*, Abidjan: Les Nouvelles Editions Africaines, 1978, p. 61.
5. Ibid., pp. 88–109. More serious, however, is the generalisation Haffner makes concerning the oral tradition. He argues for example that 'African stories are rarely linear' (p. 89) and goes on to construct a theory of African cinema built on 'non-linear events' (p. 90). It seems that Haffner confuses the long digressions often seen in the stories with the non-linear or discontinuous forms that one sees in the modern novel or film. Haffner believes, therefore, that African cinema should consist of long films which contain several short stories, fewer actors and a lot of action (p. 103).

6. Françoise Pfaff, *The Cinema of Ousmane Sembene*, Westport, Conn.: Greenwood Press, 1984, p. 32.
7. See also Alain Ricard, 'Du théâtre au cinéma yoruba: le cas nigérien', in *CinémAction*, no. 26, 1983, special issue: 'Cinémas noirs d'Afrique', pp. 160–7.
8. For a definition of cinematic and extra-cinematic elements see Christian Metz, *Langage et cinéma*, Paris: Editions Larousse, 1971.
9. 'African Cinema: FESPACO, an evaluation', p. 408.
10. I am indebted to Greimas, who argued that there are two main types of narrative: 1) stories with present order accepted, and 2) stories in which the existing order is deemed unacceptable and a new order is proposed. See *Sémantique structurale*, Paris: Editions Larousse, 1966, p. 213.
11. For a discussion of narrative elements such as order and voice see Gérard Genette, 'Frontières du récit', in *Figures II* (Paris: Editions du Seuil, 1969), and 'Discours du récit', in *Figures III* (Paris: Editions du Seuil, 1972). The notion of functions is popularised by Vladimir Propp in *Morphologie du conte russe* (Paris: Editions du Seuil, 1970). See also Roland Barthes, 'Introduction à l'analyse structurale du récit', and Claude Bremond, 'La logique des possibles narratifs', in *Communications*, no. 8, 1966.
12. I am indebted to Teshome Gabriel at the University of California, Los Angeles, for our discussion on the use of long shots in *Wend Kuuni*.
13. I believe that this is an important unexplored area in West African folklore. The myth of the 'wanted son' is abundant in the folk tales, and it is the most common structure storytellers use whenever the existing order is unacceptable and a hero has to come to change it. See Djibril T. Niane, *Sundita: An Epic of Old Mali*, London: Longman, 1965.
14. In *L'an V de la révolution algérienne* (Paris: François Maspéro, 1964) Fanon argues that the Algerian woman must re-assume her body in a revolutionary manner once she enters the modern city. For him, this new dialectic of the body and the world is crucial for modern women (pp. 42–3). Fanon's discussion of the revolutionary use of the veil is also interesting in this context.
15. Ngugi Wa Thiong'o, *Petals of Blood*, New York: E. P. Dutton, 1978.
16. Greimas proposes to call 'actant' characters who only fill one action and 'actor' or 'soteriste' those who fill several functions in the story. The 'adjuvant' helps the actor to fill a function. See *Sémantique structurale*.
17. *Wend Kuuni (Le don de dieu)*, Paris: Les films du Sémaphore, 1983. The oral text is used as a synopsis for the film.
18. For definitions of point of view see Edward Branigan, 'Formal Permutations of the Point of View Shot', in *Screen*, vol. 16, no. 3; and Jacques Aumont, 'Point de vue', in *Communications*, no. 38, 1983, special issue: 'Enonciation et cinéma'.
19. Gilles Deleuze and Félix Guattari, in *Kafka: pour une littérature mineure* (Paris: Editions de Minuit, 1975), apply the binary concepts of 'déterritorialiser/reterritorialiser' to discuss the minority uses of language.

211

Black Independents and Third Cinema: The British Context

Reece Auguiste/Black Audio Film Collective

> We are coming from too much, we are moving towards too little.
> Elias Canetti

I will proceed by posing a set of questions that I believe have emanated from the historical context of black independent film production in Britain. They are questions that should concern all audio-visual practitioners who are serious about the direction of black independents.

In the general context of Third Cinema practices it is of vital importance that there is some clarification of the terrain from which we speak, that film-makers are aware of the social conditions in which they are expected to produce a politics and cinema aesthetics of relevance. The threat posed to the possibility of sustaining black independence implies that an examination of our situation is necessary. The questions which Black Audio Film Collective wish to ask are:

1. What is the precise state of black independence vis-à-vis the British cultural industries?
2. Do the history and contemporary engagements of black film-makers constitute Third Cinema practice in Britain?

These are complex questions and any resolution has to emanate from concrete analysis of the political economy of cinema in Britain. For independents the question of production has always been an issue of priority. However, the desire to produce film as commodity has a location in the market and is determined by conjunctural factors – economic, political and cultural. The sector's further development is therefore literally hemmed in by these social relations. It is important, then, that film practitioners analyse their location in relation to wider developments in the industry.

Our point of departure is propelled by the idea that each generation necessarily engages in a process of rewriting/reconstituting the past. Film-makers have to paint their own landscapes, they must breathe new life into each moment in cinema. That can only be achieved when practitioners have mapped out the field of visual representations and the film techniques they may wish to deploy. Historicity aside, the presence of British black independents is essentially a post-war phenomenon, of which the black workshops are the most recent development. Historically, the workshops have always been structured and determined by three interconnecting factors: 1) political; 2) financial; and 3) cultural. Those three interlocking categories have always determined, and will continue to do so, what is possible or not possible in an already severely racialised terrain. The space that we occupy as film-makers is increasingly becoming crisis-ridden, and thus the political economy of our independence is threatened. Undoubtedly Thatcherism, which is of course the most distinctive form of Conservative politics of the post-war years, has had multiple effects on the British cultural industries. Again, and paradoxically, the crisis is not Thatcherism itself, but of the broad Left and its inability to produce an alternative vision of Britain in the 80s. A general paralysis seems to govern the Left's political imagination in the 80s, and that is particularly pronounced in the area of cultural production.

Having said that, we must also acknowledge that the crisis of the British film industry predates the advent of Thatcherism. It appears that Thatcherite politics is merely hammering home the last few nails into the coffin. Those vital considerations aside, we still do not have a film policy on a national level that is capable of creating a vibrant and viable film and media industry; of promoting a film culture which has at its centre new and challenging visual productions, together with the necessary finances to ensure its continuation. A reformulated and viable film policy with central and local government providing capital investment would ensure full employment for film and video artists whose immense talent for the art of cinema often dies a horrendous death. Any national film policy, however, cannot afford to erase from its agenda the issues of race and representation; thus black independents have, with relentless persistence, to deliberate and ensure the inscription of race on any film policy agenda in Britain. In this cataclysmic field of multiple contradictions, of political and cultural uncertainties, which is partly determined by economic monetarism, where precisely are black independents located and how can we best arrest the tide?

From our critical evaluation and assessment of this conjunctural crisis, vis-à-vis cinema, Black Audio Film Collective believes that independent producers in this sector occupy a social space that is structured and governed by determinance of a state of emergency. If I can for a moment quote Homi Bhaba as a means of punctuating and extending this analysis: 'In every state of emergency there is emergence.' Here Bhaba's political insight opens up a space in which we can both recast and stretch the possibilities of independents. The demands and social responsibilities are quite direct: black film-makers have to rethink the political/cultural agenda, together with the possible strategic engagements for ensuring the continuation of independent film practice. It appears highly problematic to converge a politics of cultural resistance, as is practised by our diverse communities, without the prioritising of the real specificity of film production. In other words there is a danger that cultural resistance can be romanticised and thus reduced to an essentialist discourse of political practice.

If the concept 'cultural resistance' is to retain any analytical status, it will have to be substantially reworked in order effectively to address the structural crisis of the 80s. In our view multiple contestations and concrete relations, in combination with the institutional shifts within the media industries, may just constitute the albatross round the neck of romantic and essentialist readings of cultural resistance.

The conceptual binary of power/knowledge is not a given, nor does it represent static epistemological categories. As a couplet it is historically contingent because of the different power relations and knowledge productions that exist in discourse. Therefore, the debate can be most productive when it is linked to conjunctural relations of the media institutions, and the workshops' relationship to them.

Thus it is the specifity of conjunctural forces that should inform the manner in which 1) emergence takes place and 2) the political and cultural agendas can be drawn up. These are some of the strategic considerations that should contribute to film practitioners' overall understanding of the dynamic shifts occurring in the sector, and do to some extent determine the possibility of black independents. Workshops can only construct a viable challenge to the apparatus of dominant cinema when we have thoroughly and vigorously analysed the actual political economy of cultural production in this post-GLC[*] conjunctural terrain, where many are still recovering from the post-abolition blues. In fact the politics of abolition have effectively inscribed film-makers into a different amalgam of social relations where institutional, local state cultural policies, and central government, are forcing independent film producers to reassess the edifice of cultural production.

[*]In 1986, the Greater London Council and other metropolitan councils were abolished by the Conservative government. The councils, and the GLC in particular, had been a major source of support for emergent as well as established cultural practices.

Third Cinema

The conceptual apparatus called 'Third Cinema' is very broad. The manner in which the concept is loosely deployed means that it is progressively in danger of abandoning its analytical potency. In invoking the term Third Cinema practice, film artists in Britain must be politically astute to recognise that Third Cinema in its classical dimension does not exist in Britain. However, those film-makers who remain adamant about its existence should at least give recognition to its infancy.

Although there are historical reasons as to why we are in agreement with the theoretical explorations of Third Cinema practitioners from Glauba Rocha to Safi Faye, we also believe in giving privilege to historical and geographical contexts in the formation of our film sense. Independent film producers of the diaspora have a historical/cultural task which is to extend the boundaries of cinema as an apparatus capable of articulating our vision of the social world. Therefore, it is absolutely redundant to reproduce the filmic categories and organising principles of Third Cinema theory in the metropolitan centres, for this amounts to an intellectual disservice to those who for many years mentally and physically laboured to make it a viable proposition within a particular geographical context.

Debates around Third Cinema have not in my view sufficiently addressed developments in the cinema by diasporic subjects living and working in the metropolitan centres of London, Paris, New York etc. Thus it becomes immensely problematic when films from Britain are incorporated into this all-embracing conceptual framework called Third Cinema practice. Such a process does not allow adequate space for a critical evaluation of the distinctiveness of films emerging from Britain and other Western metropolitan centres. That level of analysis and critical reflection is most needed.

However, I believe that a tentative relationship does exist between Third Cinema in the Third World and that which is in the process of becoming in Britain's black communities, but the principle of reciprocity is such that it forces both a contingency and a mediacy. In our attempt to develop an alternative visual grammar it is imperative that we acknowledge influences other than that of Third Cinema. It is precisely that plurality of film form, of narrative techniques and our sense of the kind of cinema that we wish to develop, that distinguish our work from that of Latin America, Africa and India.

An intervention in visual culture that is capable of articulating the diasporic condition has to proceed from political, cultural and historical specificities, not from general filmic criteria or abstract formulations. Black film practitioners in Britain occupy a specific historical space, and it is one that has been forged by our particular experiences of

215

race, politics and cinema aesthetics in Britain. It is only through a process of experimentation that there can be new developments in film techniques, new criteria for visual representation and new voices in cinema. Only then can we make genuine claims to have made any significant contributions to that large and impressive body of work by film-makers of the 'periphery'. We should first and foremost recognise that there is a syncretic process occurring in the area of film culture, and it should be given its due celebration. Given the level of social uncertainty that presently exists in this crisis-ridden political and cultural matrix, it is important that film practitioners repoliticise the technological apparatus of visual representation. Politicisation can occur in the production process itself: that sovereign space where film-makers can radicalise the representations of gender, sexuality and the archaeologies of black subjectivity. Black workshops occupy a field of practice, theory and analysis. We are thus engaged with cinema as a technological mode of production, as a constellation of institutional conflicts, wars of shifting positions, and as a systematising of the ways in which sound, image, colour and movement signify.

Tentatively, this field constitutes an interrelated voice of multiple concerns, a voice given presences and framed by questions of technological, institutional and significatory battles, a war of meaning, a cinema of signification. The conditions of existence experienced by workshops imply that film-makers of the sector should utilise every technology of visual production that is available to them. That would of course demand an increased use of so-called marginal formats, like for example super-eight film. This also demands that an interdisciplinary approach to film-making should inform one's conception of film practice; it is a question of building a particular audio-visual style. Since its inception, Black Audio Film Collective has endeavoured to build a critical language, a grammar of precision, of movement and fluidity. It is a task that we feel will contribute to the enrichment of black independent film culture. An inter-disciplinary approach which is both constructive and engaging eradicates any conception which poses itself as a monolithic discourse of form. Indeed, our film *Handsworth Songs* is an attempt to problematise notions of narrative structure and form, questions concerning the parameters of black aesthetics and in particular the racial economy of signs.

Diasporic cinema should be a cinema of appearances, evoking and marking new inscriptions. The value of this cinema in terms of the development of independent film culture is immense. Our task should be that of developing a cinema which has a multiplicity of configurations, of identities and histories, of rewriting visual styles and evoking a dialogue between technology, class gender and language. Given that our presence in the metropolitan centres has been forged out of unequal

216

relationships between the centre and the periphery of post-colonial contradictions and presences, we passionately believe that it is apt to further inscribe meaning into those presences. A presence spoken through a system of knowledge, because there are no dark continents of meaning and there are no dark continents in cinema untouched by an aesthetics of presence. The issue is that of producing new forms of aesthetics, of visual styles and experimentation with clear-cut political and social objectives that can contribute to the development of an art form so young as the cinema.

In this manner, sound and image may assume new life and signification as one of the organising metaphors of black cinema in Britain. Diasporic film-makers can learn from the insights of the Indian film-maker Kumar Shahani: 'to open up the language, to reveal every articulation in reality by revealing every articulation in the form.' This, I believe, should be one of our many tasks and responsibilities as film-makers of the diaspora.

The Study of Third Cinema in the United States: A Reaffirmation

Scott Cooper

There are those in American universities who insist that the notion and practice of Third Cinema is outdated and obsolete. Having served a vital cultural and political function in the 1960s and 70s, they argue, such forms have now been superseded by more polished, less overtly political aesthetics, reflecting the new dynamics of cultural struggle in the 80s. Furthermore, they suggest, advances in Western critical methodologies – specifically in ideological and psychoanalytic study – have shown the theoretical underpinnings of Third Cinema to be short-sighted and inadequate. A hierarchical relationship is thus advocated, in which 'mainstream' critical methods are seen to be essential in mediating the political efforts of emerging 'marginal' Third World aesthetic forms.

What needs to be questioned in examining such arguments is the role posited for Western cultural theory, the status given to its knowledge, and the implied ends to which it is to be used. In short, such positions omit any truly self-critical consideration of how we in the West are implicated in the dynamics of cultural and cross-cultural struggle. It is in response, then, that I wish to examine our relationship as scholars of film in the United States to the practice and politics of Third Cinema, and in so doing, to reaffirm its continued importance and vitality as a tool of cultural criticism.

As has been made quite apparent at this conference, the differences among us figure quite heavily in our perspectives on the issue of Third Cinema. But rather than interpreting such differences in terms of 'marginality' and 'otherness', it would seem more appropriate and constructive to view them in terms of our varying positions within the dynamics of cultural and cross-cultural politics.

Such a perspective seems most relevant at a time in which we are witnessing an increase of Third World migration into Western nations, in which the so-called 'margins' are no longer distant and out of sight but are increasingly becoming a part of our everyday life. Prejudice and racism aside, what might be made more obvious as a result is that distinctions between First and Third World cultures are not of an 'us' vs. 'them' nature, but are rather of relations and struggles of power in which we are all positioned, by which we are all affected.

The question that we in the West must ask, then, is to what extent we shall take responsibility and transform the roles we play in this cultural dynamic. Specific to the themes of this conference are the questions of how and why Third World cultural forms are studied in the United States. In particular, we must consider how our work relates to the goals and effectiveness of politicised cultural efforts such as those of Third Cinema.

In her essay on 'Marginal Cinemas and Mainstream Critical Theory', Julianne Burton assigns to the Western critic a status which, she claims, transcends that of advocate or enthusiast, aspiring to a position of mediation as guide and interpreter.[1] What is most troubling is her insistence that it is not only for Western audiences that we are to play such roles, but for the peoples of the Third World as well.[2] As articulated by Teshome Gabriel in his response to Burton in *Screen*, the implications that our knowledge be seen as universally relevant, that our methods be seen as a universal mandate, that our considerations be couched in terms of 'marginal' and 'mainstream' cross the line into colonial discourse itself: 'To imply that mainstream critical theory should dominate and assimilate all others because of its position of power, is to speak only in economic terms and to collapse everything else, including social concerns, into it.'[3] Burton's arguments are thus undermined by the overall context of her statements. What is amiss is perspective. For who are we in the West to chart the agenda for Third World struggles? Who are we in the West to insist moreover that the people of the Third World need to understand their own situations in terms of our methodologies and theoretical positions? It is not our position to dictate; to lay claim to certain methodologies as privileged or even as 'our own' is again to fall into the trap of defining the world in terms of 'us' vs. 'them', privileged vs. deprived, enlightened vs. ignorant.

Lest we mistakenly interpret such positions as merely ethnocentric or racist, it should be added here that they are by no means inherent only in the study of Third World film and culture in the West. Rather, they are endemic to cultural and specifically to film and television studies as they now exist in the academies of the United States. What has occurred is that film and television studies, which rose twenty years ago as a rallying point for progressive, innovative and disenfranchised faculty and students in over-rigidly defined academic disciplines such as English and History, has now defined *itself* as a discipline, has now begun

219

promoting *itself* as the bearer of privileged Truth and Insight. Thus disciplinary conferences become rallying points for self-promotion. Concerns with social and public accessibility to film and television study are curtailed on the grounds of the need to maintain professionalism and the requisite development of a 'specialised discourse'.

My own most blatant observation of this occurred on a panel discussion of media journals at the annual convention of the Modern Language Association in New York in 1984. There, the issue was the increasingly inaccessible language typical in academic writing on film and television. One participant, especially irked by the notion that accessibility ought to be a priority, irately commented that no one would expect someone 'off the street' to be able to pick up a medical journal and understand it without the necessary training. Why then, he asked, should we suggest differently for film and television study?

Though it is certainly true that critical methodologies used in film and television research have proved invaluable towards illuminating subtle cultural and social phenomena, such a position raises their status to that of a Science. The discussions at this conference make clear the problematic nature of this posture: to the extent that it is meant precisely to establish and maintain a well-defined elite, it confounds the sort of broader application of methods advocated by those whose positions are politically informed and motivated. The resulting danger is that the insistence on certain methods and theoretical models will be fundamentally self-serving, concerned in fact less with the social issues they claim to address than with the desire to be uniquely qualified to address them. Of course, what then become neglected are the very issues, politics and peoples such tools might otherwise serve.

While objections to the overly jargonistic nature of such Continental methods as cine-structuralism and Lacanian psychoanalysis were, during the 1970s, lodged primarily by politically conservative and traditional faculty and critics, today's debates are taking place within the Left itself. The issue is not simply one of jargon, but rather a concern that critical methods be seen as tools, not as an ideology. Thus Gabriel's arguments concerning semiotic and psychoanalytic methods are well taken; not a rejection merely on the basis of their difficult language, but rather in so far as they have become heralded as dogma.[4]

As a student of film and television, I find it especially important to examine and compare such tools, methods and ends inherent in the forms of cultural investigation and criticism I wish to employ in my own work. Structuralist and now post-structuralist sensibilities have been and continue to be vital to my studies. However, unlike those who claim them more as ends than as means, many of us are now beginning to turn to new tools, new perspectives, to complement and broaden our inquiry to include what we feel to be the more pressing questions of the day.

A consideration of the continuing effectivity of Third Cinema requires contextualisation – an understanding of the political, cultural and economic specificity and impact of such work. But while various presentations at recent conferences in the United States have claimed to be contextualising Third World cultural products, they have done so only along formal lines, or in regard to inter-textual relationships among various cultural objects, saying little or nothing about institutional processes, social impact, reception and response.

Ours is thus a desire to broaden and re-politicise this perspective. Certainly, Western tools have proved invaluable toward such ends. The work of British Cultural Studies, for example, as exemplified by Stuart Hall and others of the Centre for Cultural Studies in Birmingham, and the writings of Raymond Williams in England and Michel Foucault in France, have been of great value in analysing and evaluating social response and political impact. But again, it must be emphasised that what is important is that we examine the relevant tools for use in a more significant project than one exclusive to the university.

Once considered in terms of specific *political* rather than merely *academic* intentions, certain methods will prove themselves to be most effective on the basis of how we might use them towards illuminating the world in which we live. It is for this reason that we insist that Third Cinema is obsolete neither as a theoretical tool nor as a cultural practice, in so far as it remains an effective means towards identifying how we are positioned within the world and in relation to its struggles, in so far as it continues to be an inspiration to efforts of politicised cultural intervention.

The call of Third Cinema is, for us, a call for social and cultural transformation. While historical contexts and aesthetic responses may change, its mandate still holds. It is obvious that, depending on where we stand, our perspectives on appropriate strategies and methods will be different. They need to be chosen on the basis of such need rather than on the basis of disciplinary or theoretical dictate. For, in spite of our intentions, to adhere to the priorities of the latter runs the risk of causing our work to be part and parcel of the problem rather than the solution, another form of cultural imperialism, another force of hegemonic containment.

The main point is that we ought to seek methods which, rather than defining borders and positions, open up the path to self-identity and recognition of one's own place in a global context, which rather than presuming to speak for others, allow all of us to speak for ourselves. Ultimately, it is such positions that will finally enable us to recognise our roles within the cultural politics of this multinational age, that will finally enable us to work not for the so-called benefit of the 'disadvantaged' or the 'underdeveloped', but towards realisation of our mutual needs and goals in eliminating capitalist and imperialist subjugation.

Perhaps most difficult is the attempt to address and resolve the more complex differences and conflicts of culture, ideology and positions of power among us. But unlike Burton, who seems to blame the Third World for the difficulty in its 'intimidating' resistance to assimilation,[5] I see this as part of the very situation we all need to appreciate and attack from our various positions and vantage points: colonialism, imperialism, and their continuing ill effects on the majority populations of the world.

This is the point of the Third Cinema advocated by Gabriel, and what might be considered a Third Criticism or Third Aesthetic being proposed at this conference to go along with it. Underlying its mandate is the conviction that only through an appreciation and celebration of the differences among us will we be able to determine and act upon our mutual needs. It is in this context that we must find and realise our most effective roles. For only then will we begin to bridge the boundaries among us, working together as colleagues towards the transformational goals which we share.

Notes

1. Julianne Burton, 'Marginal Cinemas and Mainstream Critical Theory', *Screen*, vol. 26, nos. 3–4, 1985, pp. 5, 20–1.
2. Ibid., p. 5.
3. Teshome Gabriel, 'Colonialism and "Law and Order" Criticism', *Screen*, vol. 27, nos. 3–4, 1986, p. 145.
4. Ibid., pp. 143–4.
5. Burton, 'Marginal Cinemas', p. 6.

Inner City Blues

Charles Burnett

If one has any interest in film as a means of transforming society, one can certainly sympathise with the frustrations of the main character in the novel *Bread and Wine* by Ignazio Silone. The hero, who is a revolutionary hiding from the police, disguises himself as a priest; the villagers mistake him for a real priest. He attempts to explain that their social condition could be improved, that certain things – food and shelter and the right to happiness – belong to everyone, but the villagers can't conceive those things as a part of their reality; that is something to be obtained in heaven. The question is how does one who is dissatisfied with the way things are going set about transforming society? To whom and to what should one direct the message and what will be the spark, the messianic message, to motivate people into altering their habits when reality hasn't made a stir, when the realisation of death itself has failed? However, time and again, you find in the testimony of ex-addicts and alcoholics that what made them stop and go cold turkey was that after years of destroying themselves, they looked in the mirror one day and did not recognise the person staring back at them. And having tried to change drug addicts, I was warned that no matter what logic, no matter what emotional appeal I used, it would have no effect on that person until he or she was ready to change; it is when the person has arrived at the conclusion that he or she needs help.

For a film to act as an agent for altering people's behaviour in a way that makes a neighbourhood safe, another dynamic has to have occurred and it is an ongoing process; a politicisation must be taking place. There is a polarisation and issues are clear-cut, ambiguity is at a minimum and there is a moral outrage if things don't change. Because the situation in the black community lacks leadership, it lacks direction. The inner cities are virtually infernal regions where the most inhuman behaviour manifests itself in the 'Rock House', a house where one can buy a cheap high from cocaine; it is like a black hole in space which sucks in the youth. For those of us who still have senses to offend, not to attempt to find a solution will be participating in genocide; the problem

223

of drugs, with babies being born with a drug addiction, is horrendous. When the middle class moved away and over the years a vacuum formed and an isolation, people of daring gained control and the irony is that there was a conspiracy to hide the situation.

Particularly in films that were sounding the alarm and realistically trying to dramatise concerns that were eroding the very foundation that makes a society a society, the response was, 'This makes us look bad.' To bring to light that which troubles us was being uppity, no home training, etc. The middle-class blacks wanted to emphasise the positive and the inner city wanted 'Superfly'; neither had any substance, however, both were detrimental. There is a difference between illusion and inspiration. The difference in concerns clearly marked the direction in which consciously or unconsciously the people who lived on the opposite side of the tracks were going. Surprisingly, politically speaking, there is a large reactionary and/or chauvinistic point of view in the inner city.

The commercial film is largely responsible for affecting how one views the world. It reduced the world to one dimension, rendering taboos to superstition, concentrated on the ugly, creating a passion for violence and reflecting racial stereotypes, instilling self-hate, creating confusion rather than offering clarity: to sum up, it was demoralising. It took years for commercial films to help condition society on how it should respond to reality. In the later films that strove for a reality, the element of redemption disappeared, and as a consequence the need for a moral position was no longer relevant. There was no longer a crossroads for us to face and to offer meaning to our transgressions. The bad guy didn't have to atone for his sins. He could go on enjoying life victimising innocent people. In essence this cinema is anti-life; it constantly focuses on the worst of human behaviour to provide suspense and drama, to entertain. The concerns are generally about a young white male and the rest of society and its problems are anathema. Any other art form celebrates life, the beautiful, the ideal, and has a progressive effect – except American cinema. The situation is such that one is always asked to compromise one's integrity, and if the socially oriented film is finally made, its showing will generally be limited and the very ones that it is made for and about will probably never see it. To make film-making viable you need the support of the community; you have to become a part of its agenda, an aspect of its survival.

A major concern of story-telling should be restoring values, reversing the erosion of all those things that made a better life. One has to be prepared to dig down in the trenches and wage a long battle. The problem is that we have all been given a bad name by a few adventurers. The issue is that we are a moral people, and the issue need not be resolved by a pushing and shoving match or taken in blind faith, but should be continuously presented in some aspect of a story, as for example in the negro folklore which was an important cultural necessity that not only provided humour but was a source of symbolic knowledge that allowed one to comprehend life. The issue is not necessarily to lead one to become a saint or to make the world a paradise but simply to remind us that our acts not only weigh on our souls, but also that by putting them in a narrative we make them human. A good summation on this theme would be in *Men in Dark Times* by Hannah Arendt, who in her chapter on Lessing states that 'however much we are affected by the things of the world, however deeply they may stir and stimulate us, they become human for us only when we can discuss them with our fellow ... We humanise what is going on in the world and in ourselves only by speaking of it and in the course of speaking of it, we learn to be human.' Solidarity and humanity occupy the same space. And nowhere is a common bond more necessary than in the inner city. It seems that the object of all films should be to generate a sense of fraternity, a community; however, for an independent film-maker that is the same as swimming against a raging current.

One of the features of my community is that it does not have a centre, does not have an elder statesman, and more important, does not have roots; in essence it is just a wall with graffiti written on it. Life is going to work, coming home, making sure every entrance is firmly locked to keep the thugs out, thinking on how to move up in the world or being a member of a street gang standing at neighbourhood corners, thinking about nothing and going nowhere. In both cases what is missing is not only the spiritual but mother wit. Even though there is a church on every other corner, it only holds services one day a week and it is not a dominant part of the life of the community. It is like a ship that has lost its rudder. It seems that those of us who observe tradition and have a sense of continuity can at least see the horizon. External forces more than internal forces have made the black community what it is today. There has always been the attempt to destroy our consciousness of who we were, to deny the past, and to destroy the family structure; and, since for us each day has not a yesterday or a tomorrow, to make the use of experience a lost art.

Those who live a healthy existence, meaning those who live on the other side of the tracks, gain knowledge through learning, and those who live on my side of the tracks learned about the world through conditioning based on pain and pleasure, and what has developed as a consequence is that man is wolf to man and every night is a full moon. We have always lived in a hostile environment, but not one where parent and offspring turn guns on each other. The inner city is characterised by people with irrational behaviour. The perception is that people are dangerous. Everyone is paranoid and rightfully so. It isn't the schizophrenia that is disturbing. It is that multiple personality type, people with two people inside them and more. You can witness them changing character within a breath. How do you place a chair for someone who can't sit still? In trying to find the cure, what person do you address? It is not a matter of informing someone of the truth, the facts, reality; it is only when he finds that he can't live with himself, when he has stopped deluding himself. The way back is redemption.

If film is to aid in this process of redemption, how does it work its magic? It seems that old question of why are we here, and not getting a satisfactory answer, makes man's fate intolerable. I think that it is the little personal things that begin to give a hint of the larger picture. The story has the effect of allowing us to comprehend things we cannot see, namely feelings and relationships. It may not give you answers but it will allow you to appreciate life and maybe that is the issue, the ability to find life wonderful and mysterious. If the story is such, film can be a form of experience, and what is essential is to understand that one has to work on how to be good, compassionate. One has to approach it like a job. Until there is a sharing of experiences, every man is an island and the inner city will always be a wasteland.

Mediawork's Representation of the Other: The Case of Iran

Hamid Naficy

Introduction

In recent years a number of 'image studies' have documented the stereotyped images of Third World population and ethnic and gender minorities prevalent in Western media.[1] While these studies are valuable, they limit themselves by focusing only on social portrayal, plot development and character stereotyping of minorities. Further, they place undue trust in the possibilities of realism, often ignoring that cinema and TV are themselves constructs. To understand the mechanism involved, however, we need to develop methodologies that can account for the processes that mediate between reality and its representation.

In *The Interpretation of Dreams*, Freud posited 'dreamwork' as the process which produces the manifest content of dreams from the latent dream-thoughts, which themselves reside in the unconscious and are shielded from direct observation.[2] To make manifest the latent dream-thoughts, dreamwork (to use Metz's expression) must 'get around' the censorship of secondary processes.[3] It does so by transforming the latent content by means of displacement, condensation, considerations of representability, and secondary revision. To understand these transformational processes of dreamwork itself and to unravel the mysteries of latent dream-thoughts, Freud offered his method of dream interpretation. There are other ways whereby one can gain access to, or at least get an idea of, the operations of the primary process, but these are through such privileged cases as symptoms, slips, acting out, asides and jokes.

I propose the term 'mediawork' as a theoretical framework to describe those combined operations of the 'signifying institutions'[4] or the 'consciousness-shaping industries',[5] such as mass media in Western societies, which help obtain hegemonic consensus. Mediawork, as an agency of hegemony, acts similarly to dreamwork: it manifests in its representations the latent or 'deep structures' of beliefs and ideologies.[6] But in the interests of maintaining consensus (and a sense of 'free' choice) it conceals its own operations, and reformats or disguises those deep structures and values. Thus the deep structures, the dominant ideologies, remain latent, beneath consciousness, taken for granted, and considered normal. Since they permeate everyday discourse in the form of common sense, in the words of Dick Hebdige they cannot be 'bracketed off from everyday life as a self-contained set of "political opinions" or "biased views".'[7] They are thus naturalised and depoliticised. Deep beliefs, however, do not remain absolute and constant. Indeed, as Gitlin has stated, 'Hegemonic ideology changes in order to remain hegemonic.'[8]

I submit that mediawork produces consensus through a number of processes:

1) by constantly incorporating, appropriating, and domesticating the oppositional and the subcultural Other;

2) by stereotyping (itself involving a combination of condensation and displacement);

3) by the framing of TV programmes (involving teasers, intros, bumpers, promos, and ads in newspapers and other media);

4) by the scheduling of programmes so as to establish a regular pattern of expectation and consumption (e.g., weekly series, nightly news, and stripping and chequer-boarding of re-runs);

5) by setting the agenda for national political and cultural debates (especially in the case of TV news);

6) through the use of the classical Hollywood cinema style, characterised by its economy of narrative space;[9]

7) through the replication of the panoptic regime especially by television and its allied industries (programming, ratings, advertising, surveillance).[10]

As we use psychoanalytic techniques of dream interpretation to move from the manifest to the latent level in order to decipher dream-thoughts, so too must we use methods of cultural analysis to become aware of how charged with latent ideology is an apparently impartial process, such as mediawork. Barthes has offered a method for interpreting cultural texts which is similar to that used by Freud for dream analysis. Barthes wants to move from manifest meaning (denotation) to latent content of a text (hidden dominant ideology), and for this purpose he offers connotations as a 'modest instrument'.[11] Stuart Hall, too, considers going 'from manifest meaning to the level of code' as an absolutely characteristic move in critical approach to cultural studies.[12] For both Barthes and Hall, connotations provide multi-channel, amorphous networks which inscribe mediawork within the culture to which it refers and which it also renders natural, inevitable and eternal.

Since mediawork, like dreamwork, is not monolithic, it admits a certain number of contradictions and slippages, especially in times of social upheaval. These slips, cracks and ruptures offer additional opportunities to gain access to the latent ideologies which in normal times are concealed behind a veneer of civility and normalcy.

(Mis)representing the Other

In the remainder of this essay I will focus only on one of the afore-mentioned processes of creating and maintaining consensus and I will sketch, in broad strokes, the different phases in which hegemonic mediawork in the United States produces and tames the subcultural Other – the national and ethnic minorities – in this case, Iranians since the establishment of the Islamic Republic. I have chosen this period for analysis because it is marked by two major crises in Iran-US relations: the anti-Shah revolution and the taking of American hostages. Under the pressure of these highly charged events certain cracks developed in the mediawork's consensus, which helped reveal the latent beliefs held in the US about Iranians.

Barthes contends that the petit-bourgeois is psychologically 'unable to imagine the Other'.[13] Todorov, in his analysis of the conquest of America, goes further and identifies three typologies of relations to the Other: a) axiological (involving like/dislike, superiority/inferiority); b) praxeological (involving identification with and assimilation of the Other); and c) epistemic (knowledge/lack of knowledge of the Other).[14] More to the point here, however, is the manner in which the East, the Orient and Islam, of which Iran is a part, are viewed as representing the Other. Edward Said defines Orientalism as a 'system of representations framed by a whole set of forces that brought the Orient into Western learning, Western consciousness and, later, Western empire'.[15] Interestingly, he makes a distinction between *latent* Orientalism and *manifest* Orientalism. Latent Orientalism, rediscovered around the Middle Ages, has consistently represented the Islamic Orient as 'the very epitome' of an outsider, an alien;[16] symbolising 'terror, devastation, the demonic, hordes of hated barbarians'.[17] In addition, imperialism, racism, sexism and ethnocentricism are part and parcel of this latent view of the East, which is best enunciated by classical Orientalist experts.[18]

Manifest Orientalism, on the other hand, consists of views about Oriental society, its modernisation, languages, literature, history and sociology, articulated chiefly by non-experts, such as travellers, pilgrims, statesmen and media presentations. Although certain variations and modifications have crept into this West-East model of relationship, as for example predicted by Todorov's typologies, for Said these variations have been limited to the manifest aspects, having failed to reach their latent wellsprings. Manifest Oriental experience, therefore, has not greatly influenced latent Oriental doctrine, which is dispersed throughout the deep structures of Western beliefs, appearing to be 'morally neutral and objectively valid ... [holding] an epistemological status equal to that of historical chronology and geographical location'.[19] It is, in fact, this latent view which allowed Europe to 'produce' the Orient politically, ideologically, scientifically and imaginatively during the post-Enlightenment era.[20]

Orientalism is a human production, however, not a fact of nature, and as such the East itself has also produced the West ideologically as an Other. Suffice to say that the Iranian conception of the West, for example, is no less complicated or charged with ethnocentricism and bias, especially since the establishment of the Islamic Republic. The point has been made by several theorists that there is no longer a centre but centres, no longer an other but others.

Representation of Iran

While Todorov's three typologies of relation with the Other allow some movement or variation in the relationship between centre and periphery, Us and Them, the latent-manifest model which I have borrowed from Freud and Said is fundamentally static since it rests on the stable, durable, self-preserving and self-concealing foundations of the latent, be it dream-thoughts or Orientalism. My analysis of representation of Iran by mediawork, especially since the Islamic revolution of 1978, seems to corroborate the validity of the latent-manifest model (without suggesting some sort of collusion or conspiracy), since mediawork has continued to tap into the latent Orientalist conceptions.

While such conceptions have remained largely unchanged, manifest attitudes have followed a certain trajectory correlated with political events/crises and involving three phases. The first, during the Islamic revolution itself (1978–9), was marked by denial of the revolution. The second, coinciding with the taking of fifty American hostages in Tehran (November 1979–January 1981), was marked by trivialisation and marginalisation of Iranians through their objectification as a threat and a spectacle. Finally, covering the years since the release of the American hostages, the manifest attitudes have been marked by certain attempts at domestication and assimilation of Iranians, especially those living in the US.

Phase 1: Denial. Predictably, during the first phase, the revolution was either ignored or denied by mainline media. The coverage of the 'Iran story' by the flagship newscasts of the three commercial American TV networks (ABC, CBS, NBC) increased exponentially during this period, from 9.8 minutes in 1977, a year before the revolution, to 54.7 minutes in 1978. Despite this increase, the coverage denied the revolution by largely ignoring its complex socio-cultural and politico-economical causes.

Phase 2: Threat or spectacle. The indefensible act of taking Americans hostage caused the coverage of the Iran story to peak at a high of 391.7 minutes in 1979 and 368.9 minutes in 1980. Nightly news reports of American hostages occupied the largest share of this time, so that between November 1979 (taking of hostages) until the end of 1980 ABC devoted an average of 4.1 minutes *nightly* to the hostage story, CBS 3.9, and NBC 3.1. These figures are even more remarkable when viewed in the context of a half-hour newscast, the news element of which lasts little more than 22 minutes (the rest is occupied by commercials, bumpers, and network promos).[21]

If the first phase was characterised by denial of the popular revolution against the Shah, the second phase – the hostage-taking episode – was characterised more by a perception of Iran and Islam as threats to dominant ideology: 'It seemed that "we" were at bay, and with us the normal, democratic, rational order of things. Out there, writhing in self-provoked frenzy, was "Islam" in general, whose manifestation of the hour was a disturbingly neurotic Iran.'[22] Thus a sort of 'crisis journalism' developed, which is borne out by the ever-increasing number of crisis titles on American TV, such as *Iran: The Desperate Dilemma, America Held Hostage, Crisis in Iran: The Turmoil Spreads, Raid on Iran, A Year in Captivity, Families Held Hostage, The Ordeal, Homeward Bound,* and *Home at Last.*

If the threat of the Other is perceived to be sufficiently significant, as with Iran in this phase, then mediawork seeks to capture ideologically and economically both the Other and its threat. In this case, ideological containment involved a historicising, trivialising, and caricaturing of Iran and Islam. In this regard it is worth quoting Edward Said at length:

> What seemed unfamiliar or strange to American ... reporters was branded 'Islamic' and treated with commensurate hostility and derision. ... Clichés, caricatures, ignorance, unqualified ethnocentricism, and inaccuracy were inordinately evident, as was an almost total subservience to government thesis that the only things that mattered were 'not giving in to blackmail' and whether or not the hostages were released.[23]

In the crisis atmosphere of the time, ruptures developed in the consensual manifest Orientalism produced by mediawork through which latent Orientalism itself could be gleamed. Even perceptive critics of the conservative mainline press, such as the *Wall Street Journal*, could thus note and criticise the TV coverage of Iran as 'freak show, featuring self-flagellants and fist-wavers', or as 'soap opera'.[24]

From the economic standpoint, Iran was converted to a sign system, consisting of a limited repertoire of discrete and disembodied signs often repeated *ad nauseam*: bearded and turbaned mullahs, thick frown of Khomeini, veiled women, raised fists, unruly and frantic mobs shouting 'Death to America', 'Death to Carter', and finally the image of the blindfolded American hostage which opened the ABC's *Nightline* programme throughout the so-called 'hostage crisis'.

Further, Iran as a sign system was converted into a commodity. To increase readership and audience ratings, the press and television news competed for the juiciest scoops on Iran. Khomeini had become so popular that in 1979 *Time* magazine designated him 'Man of the Year' and did a major cover story on him. Television networks vied intensely to obtain an interview with Khomeini, who had learned to play them against each other and who now was playing hard to get, causing the *Los Angeles Herald Examiner* to run the following headline: 'Ayatollah, please say yes,'[25] while *Variety* in its usual colourful manner chimed in with 'Webs Vie for Ayatollah Gabs'.[26] In fact, one such interview with Khomeini placed CBS' news magazine *60 Minutes* at the top of the ratings chart.[27] The economic benefit of high ratings is enormous and cannot be discounted. For example, *60 Minutes* generated $70 million profit for CBS, causing the programme's executive producer to call it perhaps 'the most profitable broadcast of any kind ever on the air'.[28]

The crisis had become so ensconced both in the economy of television news and in the American psyche that ABC took a fortuitous gamble and inaugurated, four days after hostages had been taken, a nightly news programme called *Crisis in Iran: America Held Hostage: Day . . . .* It was aired opposite the popular Johnny Carson's *Tonight Show* and soon drew a 30 per cent audience share, surpassing the network's previous entertainment programmes in that same time slot, and frequently beat the *Tonight Show*, causing *Los Angeles Times* columnist Howard Rosenberg to write, 'ABC *has finally* found someone who can beat Johnny Carson. Khomeini' (emphasis in the original).[29] Iran and Khomeini had reached the peak of their popularity and had so dominated the TV screens that Rosenberg satirically dubbed American television 'Ayatollah Television'.[30]

The commodification of the Iranian threat was of course not restricted to television news programmes, as other components of hegemonic mediawork such as radio, music, jokes and various artefacts (bumper stickers, buttons, dartboards, T-shirts and toilet-paper rolls) continued to sell well by employing totalisation models in caricaturing and trivialising Iranians in general and Khomeini in particular.[31] The contribution of these components of mediawork in appropriating Iran and Khomeini bears some scrutiny.

T-shirts bore slogans such as 'Don't Waste Gas/Waste Khomeini'[32] and 'Nuke Iran',[33] and demonstrators' banners declared 'Camel Jockeys, Go Home', while demonstrators themselves shouted, 'We should nuke 'em'.[34] Likewise buttons urged 'Nuke Iran' and dartboards and toilet papers carried pictures of Khomeini. Even TV ads for political candidates used the hostage issue heavily, not to mention political cartoons and strips, which had a field day with Iran and Khomeini.[35]

Soon after hostages spent their first Christmas in captivity, and especially after the departure of the Shah from the US, 'jokework' (to use Freud's term) began its operation as Iran-related jokes started cropping up regularly on *Saturday Night Live*, Mark Russell's comedy programme, Johnny Carson's monologues, at comedy clubs, improvisational theatres and Las Vegas acts, and finally on radio.[36] For example, Iranians were included in the frequently cited joke cycle 'How many ... does it take to screw in a light bulb?' (Answer: one hundred. One to screw it in and ninety-nine to hold the house hostage.)[37]

The music business propelled this commodification process even further. Barely one month after the seizure of the American embassy in Tehran, twenty anti-Iran songs had been produced, mostly by little-known artists attempting to capitalise on the crisis. Two of these, entitled 'They Can Take Their Oil and Shove It' and 'A Message to Khomeini', became national hits on the radio.[38] New songs continued to be recorded,[39] and even the popular song 'Tie a Yellow Ribbon Round the Ole Oak Tree' was re-recorded upon the release of hostages in order to take advantage of the new patriotism generated by their release.[40]

While much of this ideological caricaturing and economic commodification was criticised at the time, sometimes harshly, under such rubrics as 'Fascism Without Swastikas'[41] and 'Media Manipulating Mullah',[42] it is, I believe, a necessary part of the mediawork which seeks to tame the threat of the Other by tapping into the latent deep structures of the belief system. One consequence, to borrow from Hal Foster, is that the Other is 'socially subjected as a sign and made commercially productive as a commodity. In this way the (subcultural) other is at once controlled in its recognition and dispersed in its commodification.'[43] And this is why in capitalist societies popular culture tends to 'reproduce hegemonic ideology'.[44]

However, this is not the sole consequence of the second phase. Cultural dispersal and economic commodification can and do lead to the enlargement of the repertoire of characterisations and stereotypes, thereby allowing the Other to be recast with different, more subtle nuances. I am not suggesting that this will lead to a rapid or fundamental alteration in latent Orientalism; rather, it will make possible a gradual but significant modification of the manifest representations, reducing the negative effects of the first two phases. It is at this point, in the third phase, that mediawork will prove an effective agent of assimilation of the Other.

Phase 3: Assimilation. Significantly, the task of assimilating Iranians has been shifted from TV news and documentaries to feature films and made-for-TV movies. Some early attempts at making features about the Iranian revolution and the fate of the Shah have been reported, but none was turned into reality.[45] However, a number of feature films and television movies have come out which deal not with the Shah, but with Americans in Iran and Iranians living in the United States. Some of these, such as *Final Option* (1983), *Threads* (1984) and *Under Siege* (1986), are anti-terrorism and anti-nuclear films which do not focus on Iran specifically, but Iran figures in them as a threat and a spark of one kind or another (for example, the nuclear war in *Threads* starts over Iran). These are still phase two depictions. But there remain two theatrical films and two TV films which draw on a larger and deeper cultural repertoire of representation.

The two features, *Into the Night* (1984) and *Down and Out in Beverly Hills* (1986), both comedies, contain scenes of Iranians living in the United States. The former, directed by John Landis, is about a dope and jewellery smuggling ring in the US spearheaded by one of the Shah's sisters (never alluded to in the film) whose agents are a gang of bumbling, incompetent, cruel Iranians. *Down and Out in Beverly Hills*, directed by Paul Mazursky, does not focus on Iran much, but graphically articulates in a few short scenes another latent Orientalist stereotype, that of rich, bigamous, backward Iranians – except this time they are not living in a fantasy oasis among the sand dunes, but in Beverly Hills, California. It is true that many aspects of latent Orientalist ideology come through in these films,[46] but the mere fact that Iranians are shown living among Americans, instead of residing half a globe away in a crazy, out of control country, the fact that they are not a distant image, a threatening mob waving fists and burning the American flag, itself is a significant toning down of the phase one and two representations.

The two TV docu-dramas, the two-hour *Escape from Iran: The Canadian Caper* (1981) and the five-hour mini-series *On Wings of Eagles* (1986), take place inside Iran, the former during the hostage-taking period and the latter just prior to that event. *The Canadian Caper* deals with the story of how six Americans escaped from the captured American embassy in Tehran, were given refuge by the Canadian embassy, and ultimately spirited out of the country. This film belongs more to the second phase than the first. *On Wings of Eagles*, on the other hand, is very much a product of the third-phase operation of

234

mediawork. Intensively promoted by NBC television for two weeks before its air-date, it deals with the operation launched by Ross Perot, the head of Electronic Data Systems, to rescue two of his employees from Iranian jails during the revolution. In this film the process of assimilation is pushed further when an Iranian employee of Perot is not only shown to be resourceful and loyal but also critically important to the success of the rescue mission. In the end he is rewarded by being brought into the US without a passport but with complete acceptance by Perot and the US authorities.

This latest film about Iran demonstrates that in the third phase of mediawork's operation – assimilation – more than one phase can be present. On the one hand, *On Wings of Eagles* shows an Iranian character possessing hitherto absent heroic and laudable qualities, and on the other hand, it posits that the proper attitude towards the West for Iranians is loyalty, respect and admiration – the ultimate reward for which would be assimilation into American society. Needless to say, the sizable Iranian community and media in the US heavily criticised this film for its jingoism and for showing Iranians as American operatives and 'spies'.

The durability and strength of latent Orientalism and the success of mediawork in concealing it are perhaps a function of a) the degree to which the Self is defined by the Other, and b) of how much Western identity is interwoven with the idea of the alterity and inferiority of the Other and the Orient. But our continued coexistence will depend first on recognition of our latent Orientalism, and second on striving to achieve equality while simultaneously recognising our differences. What Todorov said still remains: 'We want *equality* without its compelling us to accept identity; but also *difference* without its degenerating into superiority/inferiority. . . . Heterology, which makes the difference of voices heard, is necessary; polygoly is insipid.'[47]

Notes

1. The following list is not exhaustive, but it provides an adequate sampling of image studies of various minorities and ethnicities. On the image of black Americans see: Daniel Leab, *From Sambo to Superspade: The Black Experience in Motion Pictures* (Boston: Houghton Mifflin, 1976), Thomas Cripps, *Slow Fade to Black: The Negro in American Film, 1900–1942* (New York: Oxford University Press, 1977), Donald Bogle, *Toms, Coons, Mulattoes, Mammies and Bucks: An Interpretive History of Blacks in*

American Films (New York: Viking, 1974), and Richard Maynard, *The Black Man on Film: Racial Stereotyping* (New Jersey: Hayden, 1974). For the image of native Americans see: Ralph Friar and Natasha Fiari, *The Only Good Indian* (Drama, 1972). For Africans see: Richard Maynard, *Africa on Film: Myth and Reality* (New Jersey: Hayden, 1974). For Latin American images see: Allen Woll, *The Latin Image in American Film* (Los Angeles: UCLA, 1980). For the image of Jews see: Lester Friedman, *Hollywood's Image of the Jew* (New York: Ungar, 1982). On North African and Arab images see: *Le Cinéma Colonial* (Paris: Seghers, 1974). On Arab images see: Edward Said, *Covering Islam: How the Media and the Experts Determine How We See the Rest of the World* (New York: Pantheon, 1981), Edmund Ghareeb (ed.), *Split Vision: The Portrayal of Arabs in the American Media* (Washington: American Arab Affairs Council, 1983), Morris International, *The Arab Image in Western Media* (London: Outline, 1980), and Jack Shaheen, *TV Arab* (Bowling Green, Ohio: Bowling Green State University Popular Press, 1984). On Palestinians see: Taylor Downing, *Palestine on Film* (London: Council for the Advancement of Arab-British Understanding, 1979). On the images of Iran and Iranians see: Hamid Naficy, *Iran Media Index* (Westport, Conn.: Greenwood Press, 1984). On the treatment of the Middle East in general see: William Adams, *Television Coverage of the Middle East* (Norwood, NJ: Ablex, 1981).

2. Sigmund Freud, *The Interpretation of Dreams*, James Strachey (trans.), (New York: Avon, 1965), p. 455.
3. Christian Metz, *The Imaginary Signifier: Psychoanalysis and Cinema*, Celia Britton, Annwyl Williams, Ben Brewster and Alfred Guzzetti (trans.), (Bloomington: Indiana University Press, 1982), p. 259.
4. Stuart Hall, 'The Rediscovery of "Ideology": Return of the Repressed in Media Studies', *Culture, Society and the Media*, Michael Gurevitch, Tony Bennett, James Curran and Janet Wollacott (eds.), (London: Methuen, 1982), p. 86.
5. Walter Benjamin, quoted by Hans Magnus Enzensberger in 'Constituents of a Theory of the Media', *Sociology of Mass Communications*, Denis McQuail (ed.), (London: Penguin, 1972), p. 99.
6. For further explanation of 'deep structures', see Noam Chomsky, *Language and Responsibility*, John Viertel (trans.), (New York: Pantheon, 1979).
7. Dick Hebdige, *Subculture: The Meaning of Style* (London: Methuen, 1979), p. 12.
8. Tod Gitlin, 'Prime Time Ideology: The Hegemonic Process in Television Entertainment', *Social Problems*, vol. 26, no. 3 (February 1979), p. 263.
9. Stephen Heath, *Questions of Cinema* (Bloomington: Indiana University Press, 1981).
10. For a discussion of the panoptic system see Michel Foucault, *Discipline and Punish: The Birth of the Prison*, Alan Sheridan (trans.), (New York: Vantage, 1979).
11. Roland Barthes, *S/Z*, Richard Miller (trans.), (New York: Hill and Wang, 1974), p. 6.
12. Hall, 'The Rediscovery of "Ideology" ', p. 71.

13. Roland Barthes, *Mythologies*, Annette Lavers (trans.), (New York: Hill and Wang, 1972), p. 151.
14. Tzvetan Todorov, *The Conquest of America: The Question of the Other*, Richard Howard (trans.), (New York: Harper & Row, 1982), p. 185.
15. Edward Said, *Orientalism* (New York: Vantage, 1979), pp. 202–3.
16. Ibid., pp. 70–1.
17. Ibid., p. 59.
18. Ibid., pp. 204–7.
19. Ibid., p. 205.
20. Ibid., p. 3.
21. These figures are compiled from William C. Adams (ed.), *Television Coverage of the Middle East*. For details and a comprehensive list of all nonfiction films and television news and documentaries about Iran, see Hamid Naficy, *Iran Media Index*.
22. Edward Said, *Covering Islam*, p. 77. This ideological threat was augmented by an additional apprehension that the rise of 'fundamentalist' Islam, exemplified by Islamic Iran, might force Middle Eastern and North African countries, which formed an 'arch of crisis' or 'crescent of crisis', to revise their economic and military relations with the United States.
23. Said, *Covering Islam*, p. 124. Of course, while these stereotypical representations are somewhat inaccurate or unfair, there are some truths undergirding them.
24. *Wall Street Journal*, 29 January 1979. It should be stated that in line with my definition of hegemony allowing certain slippages, a number of oppositional, anti-hegemonic programmes were aired by the commercial and public broadcasting networks, such as some of *Bill Moyers's Journal* (PBS) programmes, *Iran File* aired by *60 Minutes* (CBS), and *America Held Hostage: Secret Negotiations* (ABC).
25. Frank Torrez, *Los Angeles Herald Examiner*, 17 November 1979, p. 85.
26. 'Web Reporters Vie for Interview with Iran's Ayatollah K.', *Variety*, 21 December 1979.
27. *Los Angeles Times*, 21 November 1979.
28. John Weisman, 'Network News Today: Which Counts More – Journalism or Profit', *TV Guide*, vol. 33, no. 43, p. 8. See also Tom Shales, 'Networks Love TV Newsmagazines', *Los Angeles Times*, 31 May 1985, and Howard Plotskin, 'Flashy. Gutsy. Unpredictable. Incisive. Appalling', *TV Guide*, vol. 33, no. 48, p. 16.
29. Howard Rosenberg, 'Unplugged in Iran: The Network Shuffle', *Los Angeles Times*, 14 January 1980. *Crisis in Iran: America Held Hostage* soon became a regularly scheduled nightly news programme which continues with the title *Nightline*.
30. Howard Rosenberg, 'Iran: The Ayatollah Television', *Los Angeles Times*, 23 January 1980. Interestingly, in Iran itself the television network was derisively called 'mullavision'.
31. Significantly, even the *scheduling* of previously produced TV entertainment programmes seems to have been influenced by this hegemonic process: whatever is oppositional and is felt to be a national ideological threat sets the agenda not only for newscasts *but also* for the production *and* the

scheduling of entertainment programmes. My unfinished analysis shows that during one week *prior* to the hostage-taking episode (week of 20 November 1979) there were six programmes and films on TV dealing with kidnapping or hostage-taking in general. At one of the high points *during* the hostages drama in Iran (week of 13 December 1979) a total of 10 entertainment programmes featured hostages and kidnappings (unrelated to Iran), and long *after* the end of the Iranian hostage affair (week of 19 October 1985) there were only 5 such films. This analysis is based on programme descriptions in *TV Guide* and thus is limited by that fact. Interestingly enough, Russians and Arabs, prominent in current newscasts because of the anti-Soviet stance of the Reagan administration, the Chernobyl power plant accident, and the various acts of 'Arab' terrorism, have spawned a spate of anti-Soviet and anti-Arab television programmes. In the same week in 1979, there was only one film dealing with the Soviet Union, while in the week studied in 1985 there were six films about the Soviet Union and four about Arabs. While this data is not sufficient to establish a definitive link, it is suggestive of TV news influencing not only the production but also the scheduling of previously produced entertainment programmes.

32. Lynn Simross, 'Frustration Goes Public in a Climate of Crisis', *Los Angeles Times*, 23 January 1980.
33. Peter Schrag, 'Politics', *Inquiry Magazine*, 7–21 January 1980, p. 10.
34. 'The Perils of War Fever', *Inquiry Magazine*, 24 December 1979, p. 3.
35. For an example of one political TV ad for a major presidential candidate which backfired, see Dave Van Dyck, 'Iranian in Iowa Feels Sting of Baker's Jab in TV ad', *Los Angeles Times*, 18 February 1980, p. 16.
36. Peter H. Brown, ' "Take My Ayatollah, Please": Breaking the Gag Barrier', *Los Angeles Times Calendar*, 20 January 1980. See also in the same issue James Brown, 'Ayatollah as Comic Foil'.
37. According to anthropologist Alan Dundes, who has studied jokes extensively, these jokes emanate from 'our own potential lack of sexual and political power'. See Alan Dundes, 'How Many Hands Make Light Work or Caught in the Act of Screwing in Light Bulbs', *Western Folklore*, vol. XL, no. 3, July 1981, p. 266. The Iran-Contra arms scandal, too, generated its own share of jokes and humorous songs. For details see 'Songsters to Reagan: "Try to Remember" ', *Los Angeles Times*, 29 March 1987.
38. Graham Stewart, 'Songs Vent U.S. Frustration Over Iran', *Los Angeles Times*, 20 December 1979.
39. 'New Iran Disk Released', *Variety*, 2 January 1980, p. 2.
40. Robert Hilburn, *Los Angeles Times*, 29 January 1981. Caricaturing is still popular, as indicated by the enduring signs of 'Iran Sucks' which appear regularly at ringside whenever the Iranian 'bad guy' wrestler the 'Iron Sheik' has a wrestling match. Interestingly, he is usually teamed with another popular bad guy, the Russian Volkof. Of course, these two characters themselves are part of mediawork, trying to capitalise on the popularity of the bad guy image of their respective governments.
41. Fergus Bordewich, 'Fascism Without Swastikas', *Harper's*, July 1980, p. 65.

42. 'Whose Side is NBC News On?', *Aim Report*, December 1979, p. 2.
43. Hal Foster, *Recodings: Art, Spectacle, Cultural Politics* (Port Townsend, Washington: Bay Press, 1985), p. 167.
44. Douglas Kellner, 'TV, Ideology, and Emancipatory Popular Culture', *Socialist Review*, vol. 9, no. 3 (May–June 1979), p. 26.
45. For example, in 1979 one film with the working title of *Kill the Shah* (later changed to *Shah of Iran*) was to have starred Gilbert Roland as the Shah and Linda Cristal as his empress (Roderick Mann, 'The Shah's Story: Half a Truth', *Los Angeles Times*, 23 October 1979). Another film was to have been based on the bestseller book *The Crash of '79* (Roderick Mann, 'Evans Takes a Rugged Turn', *Los Angeles Times*, 22 November 1979). In 1980 yet another film, apparently to be produced by Carlo Ponti, was to have had Sophia Loren playing the part of the empress (Barbara Saltzman, 'Cagney, O'Brien to Meet Royalty', *Los Angeles Times*, 29 November 1980).
46. This did not escape a local critic who offered the following assessment: '*Into the Night* spews its own kind of nastiness. Not only does it seek laughs from the murder of women and animals, but it uses racist stereotypes as the tactic. One gets sick of watching Iranians wear stupid expressions, cop feels from their female victims, slaughter everything that moves, and have a four-man pile-up from running into closed doors.' (John Powers, 'Landis Grows Up (A Little)', *L. A. Weekly*, 29 March–4 April 1985, p. 39.)
47. Todorov, *The Conquest of America*, pp. 249–51.

Bibliography

Books

Allen, Robert C. and Gomery, Douglas: *Film History: Theory and Practice*. New York: Alfred A. Knopf, 1985.

Aprà, Adriano (ed.): *America Latina: Lo schermo conteso*. Venice: Mostra Internazionale del Nuovo Cinema, Pesaro/Marsilio Editori, 1981.

—— (ed.): *Teorie e Pratiche del Cinema Cubano*. Venice: Mostra Internazionale del Nuovo Cinema, Pesaro/Marsilio Editori, 1981.

—— (ed.): *Brasile 'Cinema Nôvo' e dopo*. Venice: Mostra Internazionale del Nuovo Cinema, Pesaro/Marsilio Editori, 1981.

Armes, Roy: *Third World Film Making and the West*. Berkeley, University of California Press, 1987.

Bachy, Victor: *Le cinéma au Mali*. Brussels: OCIC/L'Harmattan, 1983.

—— *La Haute-Volta et le cinéma*. Brussels: OCIC/L'Harmattan, 1983.

—— *Le cinéma en Cote d'Ivoire*. Brussels: OCIC/L'Harmattan, 1983.

—— *Le cinéma au Gabon*. Brussels: OCIC, 1986.

Bakhtin, Mikhail, M.: *Speech Genres and Other Late Essays*, trans. Vern W. McGhee. Austin: University of Texas Press, 1986.

Balogun, Françoise: *Le cinéma au Nigeria*. Brussels: OCIC/L'Harmattan, 1984.

Banerjee, Shampa (ed.): *Ritwik Ghatak*. New Delhi: Directorate of Film Festivals/NFDC, 1982.

Barker, Francis, et al. (eds.): *Europe and its Others*, vol. 1, Essex Sociology of Literature Conference. Colchester: University of Essex, 1985.

Bestman, Martin, T.: *Sembène Ousmane et l'esthétique du roman négro-africain*. Quebec: Eds. Naaman, 1981.

Boughedir, Ferid: *Le cinéma africain de A à Z*. Brussels: OCIC, 1987.

Brecht, Bertolt: *Brecht on Theatre*, ed. and trans. by John Willett. London: Eyre Methuen, 1964.

Buhle, Paul (ed.): *C.L.R. James: His Life and Work*. London: Allison & Busby, 1986.

Bürger, Peter: *Theory of the Avant-Garde*, trans. M. Shaw. Manchester: Manchester University Press, 1984.

Burns, E. Bradford: *Latin American Cinema: Film and History*. Los Angeles: UCLA Latin American Center, 1975.

Camera Nigra: Le discours du film africain. Brussels: OCIC/L'Harmattan, 1984.

Chanan, Michael: *The Cuban Image*. London: British Film Institute, 1985.

—— (ed.): *Twenty-five Years of the New Latin American Cinema*. London: British Film Institute/Channel 4 Television, 1983.

Cinema dei paesi arabi. Pesaro: Mostra Internazionale del Nuovo Cinema, 1976.

240

Danvers, Louis and Tatum, Charles Jr.: *Nagisa Oshima*. Paris: Editions de L'Etoile/*Cahiers du Cinéma*, 1986.

Dorfman, Ariel: *The Empire's Old Clothes*. London: Pluto Press, 1983.

Dorfman, Ariel and Mattelart, Armand: *How to Read Donald Duck: Imperialist Ideology in the Disney Comic*, trans. David Kunzle. New York: International General, 1975.

Downing, John D. H. (ed.): *Film & Politics in the Third World*. New York: Automedia Inc., 1986.

Fanon, Frantz: *Black Skin, White Masks*, trans. C. L. Markmann, foreword by Homi Bhabha. London, Pluto Press, 1986.

—— *Toward the African Revolution*, trans. Haakon Chevalier. New York: Grove Press, 1967.

Fusco, Coco (ed.): *Reviewing Histories: Selections from New Latin American Cinema*. New York: Hallwalls, 1987.

Gabriel, Teshome, H.: *Third Cinema in the Third World*. Ann Arbor, MI: UMI Research Press, 1982.

Gates, Henry Louis Jr. (ed.): *'Race', Writing and Difference*. Chicago: University of Chicago Press, 1986. Essays in this volume originally appeared in *Critical Inquiry* vol. 12, no. 1 and vol. 13, no. 1.

Gendzier, Irene L.: *Frantz Fanon: A Critical Study*. London: Wildwood House, 1973.

Ghatak, Ritwik: *Cinema and I*. Calcutta: Ritwik Memorial Trust, 1987.

Gramsci, Antonio: *Selections from Cultural Writings*, trans. W. Boelhower, eds. D. Forgacs and G. Nowell-Smith. London: Lawrence and Wishart, 1985.

Gugelberger, Georg M. (ed.): *Marxism and African Literature*. London: James Currey, 1985.

Hennebelle, Guy (ed.): *Les Cinémas africains en 1972*. Dakar: Société africaine d'édition, 1972.

Hennebelle, Guy and Gumucio-Dagron, Alfonso (eds.): *Les Cinémas de L'Amérique latine*. Paris: *CinémAction*/Lherminier, 1981.

Hong Kong Cinema Survey: 1946–1968. Hong Kong: Urban Council, 1979.

Huyssen, Andreas: *After the Great Divide*. Bloomington: Indiana University Press, 1986.

Jameson, Fredric: *The Political Unconscious: Narrative as a socially symbolic act*. London: Methuen, 1981.

Jay, Martin: *The Dialectical Imagination: A History of the Frankfurt School and the Institute of Social Research, 1923–1950*. Boston: Little, Brown and Co., 1973.

Johnson, Randall and Stam, Robert (eds.): *Brazilian Cinema*. Cranbury, NJ: Fairleigh Dickinson University Press, 1982.

Kapur, Geeta: *K. G. Subramanyan*. New Delhi: Lalit Kala Akademi, 1987.

King, John and Torrents, Nissa (eds.): *The Garden of Forking Paths*. London: British Film Institute, 1987.

Lau Shing-hon (ed.): *A Study of the Hong Kong Swordplay Film (1945–1980)*. Hong Kong: Urban Council, 1981.

Lears, T.J. Jackson: *No Place of Grace: Antimodernism and the Transformation of American Culture 1880–1920*. New York: Pantheon, 1981.

241

Li Cheuk-to (ed.): *Changes in Hong Kong Society Through Cinema*. Hong Kong: Urban Council, 1988.
—— *Cantonese Opera Film Retrospective*. Hong Kong: Urban Council, 1987.
—— *Cantonese Melodrama, 1950–1969*. Hong Kong: Urban Council, 1986.
—— *The Traditions of Hong Kong Comedy*. Hong Kong: Urban Council, 1985.
—— *A Study of Hong Kong Cinema in the Seventies*. Hong Kong: Urban Council, 1984.
Lin Nien-tung and Yeung, Paul (eds.): *Cantonese Cinema Retrospective (1950–1959)*. Hong Kong: Urban Council, 1978.
Martin, Angela (ed.): *African Films: The context of production*. BFI Dossier no. 6. London: British Film Institute, 1982.
Mattelart, Michelle and Mattelart, Armand: *Le carnaval des images: La fiction brésilienne*. Paris: La Documentation française, 1987.
Mattelart, A. and Siegelaub, S. (eds.): *Communication and Class Struggle*, 2 vols. New York/Bagnolet: International General/International Mass Media Research Center, 1979 and 1983.
Mattelart, Armand: *Mass Media, Ideologies and the Revolutionary Movement*, trans. Malcolm Coad. Brighton: Harvester Press, 1980.
Mbye, Cham and Watkins, Claire (eds.): *BlackFrames: Critical Perspectives on Black Independent Cinema*. Cambridge, Mass.: Celebration of Black Cinema/MIT Press, 1988.
Mercer, Kobena, (ed.): *Black Film/British Cinema*. London: ICA Document 7/ British Film Institute, 1988.
Michaels, Eric: *For a Cultural Future: Francis Jupurrurla Makes TV at Yuendumu*. Sydney: Artspace, 1987.
Müller, Marco and De Vincenti, Giorgio (eds.): *Cinemasia*, 2 vols. Venice: Mostra Internazionale del Nuovo Cinema, Pesaro/Marsilio Editori, 1983.
Nelson, Cary and Grossberg, L. (eds.): *Marxism and the Interpretation of Culture*. Urbana: University of Illinois Press, 1988.
Ngugi wa Thiong'o: *Decolonising the Mind: The Politics of language in African Literature*. London: James Currey, 1986.
Nuovo cinema taiwanese, Il. Pesaro: Mostra Internazionale del Nuovo Cinema, Pesaro, 1988.
Oshima, Nagisa: *Ecrits (1956–1978): Dissolution et jaillissement*. Paris: *Cahiers du Cinéma*/Gallimard, 1980.
Paranagua, Paulo Antonio: *O Cinema na América Latina*. Porto Alegre: L & PM Editores, 1984.
—— *Le cinéma brésilien*. Paris: Centre Georges Pompidou, 1987.
Passek, Jean-Loup (ed.): *Le cinéma indien*. Paris: Centre Georges Pompidou/ l'Equerre, 1983.
Passek, Jean-Loup and Quiquemelle, Marie-Claire (eds.): *Le cinéma chinois*. Paris: Centre Georges Pompidou, 1985.
Pfaff, Françoise: *The Cinema of Ousmane Sembene*. Westport, Conn.: Greenwood Press, 1984.
Pick, Zuzana M. (ed.): *Latin American Film Makers and the Third Cinema*. Ottawa: Carleton University, 1978.
Pierre, Sylvie: *Glauber Rocha*. Paris: *Cahiers du Cinéma*, 1987.

Rajadhyaksha, Ashish and Müller, Marco (eds.): *Le Avventurose storie del cinema indiano*, 2 vols. Venice: Mostra Internazionale del Nuovo Cinema, Pesaro/Marsilio Editori, 1985.

Rajadhyaksha, Ashish and Gangar, Amrit (eds.): *Ritwik Ghatak: Arguments/ Stories*. Bombay: Screen Unit/Research Centre for Cinema Studies, 1987.

Rajadhyaksha, Ashish: *Ritwik Ghatak: A Return to the Epic*. Bombay: Screen Unit, 1982.

Ramachandran, T.M. (ed.): *70 Years of Indian Cinema (1913–1983)*. Bombay: Cinema India-International, 1985.

Rocha, Glauber: *Revisión crítica del cine brasilero*. Havana: Ediciones ICAIC, 1965.

Rockett, Kevin, Gibbons, Luke and Hill, John: *Cinema and Ireland*. London: Croom Helm, 1987.

Said, Edward: *Orientalism*. London: Routledge and Kegan Paul, 1978.

—— *The World, the Text and the Critic*. London: Faber, 1984.

Salmane, Hala, Hartog, Simon and Wilson, David (eds.): *Algerian Cinema*. London, British Film Institute, 1976.

Shu Kei (ed.): *A Comparative Study of Post-war Mandarin and Cantonese Cinema*. Hong Kong: Urban Council, 1983.

—— *Cantonese Cinema Retrospective (1960–1969)*. Hong Kong: Urban Council, 1982.

Solanas, Fernando E. and Getino, Octavio: *Cine: Cultura y Descolonización*. Buenos Aires: Siglo XXI Argentino Editores, 1973.

Study of the Hong Kong Martial Arts Film, A. Hong Kong: Urban Council, 1980.

Todorov, Tzvetan: *Mikhail Bakhtin: The Dialogical Principle*, trans. W. Godzich. Manchester: Manchester University Press, 1984.

—— *The Conquest of America: the question of the Other*, trans. Richard Howard. New York: Harper & Row, 1982.

Vieyra, Paulin Soumanou: *Le cinéma au Sénégal*. Brussels: OCIC/L'Harmattan, 1983.

Willemen, Paul and Gandhy, Behroze (eds.): *Indian Cinema*. BFI Dossier no. 5. London: British Film Institute, 1982.

Williams, Raymond: *Culture*. London: Fontana, 1981.

Articles

Alea, Tomás Gutiérrez: 'The Viewer's Dialectic'. *Jump Cut*, nos. 29, 30 and 32, 1984–7.

Allen, Richard: 'The Aesthetic Experience of Modernity: Adorno, Benjamin and Contemporary Film Theory'. *New German Critique*, no. 40, Winter 1987.

Anderson, Perry: 'Modernity and Revolution'. *New Left Review*, no. 144, March/April 1984.

Bagchi, Jasodhara: 'A Statement of Bias'. *Journal of Arts and Ideas*, no. 3, April/ June 1983.

Bhabha, Homi: 'Representation and the Colonial Text: A Critical Exploration of Some Forms of Mimeticism', in Frank Gloversmith (ed.): *The Theory of Reading* (Brighton: Harvester, 1984).

—— 'The Other Question – the Stereotype and Colonial Discourse'. *Screen*, vol. 5, no. 6, November/December 1983.

Bharucha, Rustom: 'Peter Brook's Mahabharata'. *Framework*, no. 35, 1988.

—— 'Letter to an Actress'. *Framework*, no. 35, 1988.

Bhaskar, Ira: 'Myth and Ritual – Ghatak's Meghe Dhaka Tara'. *Journal of Arts and Ideas*, no. 3, April/June 1983.

Buck-Morss, Susan: 'The Flaneur, the Sandwichman and the Whore: The Politics of Loitering'. *New German Critique*, no. 39, Fall 1986.

—— 'Benjamin's Passagenwerk: Redeeming Mass Culture for the Revolution'. *New German Critique*, no. 29, Spring/Summer 1983.

—— 'Walter Benjamin – Revolutionary Writer (1)'. *New Left Review*, no. 128, July/August 1981.

Butler, Alison: 'Contextualising Rocinante'. *Framework*, no. 32/3, 1986.

Diawara, Manthia: 'The Cinema of Ousmane Sembene'. *Framework*, no. 32/3, 1986.

—— 'Technological Paternalism – Subsaharan African Film Production'. *Jump Cut*, no. 32, 1987.

Feuchtwang, Stephan: 'Fanon's politics of culture: the colonial situation and its extension'. *Economy and Society*, vol. 14, no. 4, November 1985.

Freiberg, Freda: 'The "Difference" of Japanese Film', in Barbara Creed et al. (eds.): *Papers and Forums on Independent Film and Asian Cinema* (Australian Film and Television School/Australian Screen Studies Association, 1983).

Gabriel, Teshome H.: 'Ceddo'. *Framework* nos. 15/16/17, 1981.

—— 'Colonialism and "Law and Order" Criticism'. *Screen*, vol. 27, nos. 3/4, May/August 1986.

Gibbons, Luke: 'The Politics of Silence: Anne Devlin, Women and Irish Cinema'. *Framework*, nos. 30/31, 1986.

Gilroy, Paul: 'C4 – Bridgehead or Bantustan?'. *Screen*, vol. 24, nos. 4/5, July/October 1983.

Gokhale, Shanta: 'Mani Kaul', in *The New Generation – 1960-1980* (New Delhi: The Directorate of Film Festivals, 1981).

Hansen, Miriam: 'Benjamin, Cinema and Experience: "The Blue Flower in the Land of Technology"'. *New German Critique*, no. 40, Winter 1987.

—— 'Early Silent Cinema: Whose Public Sphere?'. *New German Critique*, no. 29, Spring/Summer 1983.

Harris, Wilson: 'Adversarial Contexts and Creativity'. *New Left Review*, no. 154, November/December 1985.

Huaco-Nuzum, Carmen: 'Matilde Landeta'. *Screen*, vol. 28, no. 4, Autumn 1987.

Jameson, Fredric: 'Third World Literature in the Era of Multinational Capitalism'. *Social Text*, no. 15, Fall 1986.

—— 'The Politics of Theory: Ideological Positions in the Postmodernism Debate'. *New German Critique*, no. 33, Fall 1984.

Jayamanne, Laleen: 'Rehearsing ...'. *Cantrills Filmnotes*, nos. 55/6, May 1988.

—— 'Passive Competence'. *Screen*, vol. 28, no. 4, Autumn 1987.

Johnston, Claire: 'Maeve – Interview with Pat Murphy'. *Screen*, vol. 22, no. 4, 1981.

—— 'Popular Memory'. *Framework*, no. 19, 1982.

Khac Vien, Nguyen: 'Apocalypse Now'. *Framework*, no. 14, Spring 1981.

Kipnis, Laura: 'Aesthetics and Foreign Policy'. *Social Text*, no. 15, Fall 1986.

Lamche, Pascale: 'Interview with Merata Mita'. *Framework*, no. 25, 1984.

Lindner, Burkhardt: 'Hallucinatory Realism: Peter Weiss' Aesthetics of Resistance, Notebooks, and the Death Zones of Art'. *New German Critique*, no. 30, Fall 1983.

Malkmus, Lizbeth: 'A Desk Between Two Borders'. *Framework*, no. 29, 1985.

Martin, Angela: 'Four West African Film Makers'. *Framework*, no. 11, Autumn 1979.

Mercer, Kobena: 'Third Cinema in Edinburgh'. *Screen*, vol. 27, no. 6, November/December 1986.

Michaels, Eric: 'Bad Aboriginal Art'. *Art & Text*, no. 28, March-May 1988.

Minh-ha, Trinh T.: 'Un Art sans oeuvre: L'Anonymat dans les arts contemporains'. Troy, Mich.: International Book Pub., 1981.

Morris, Meaghan: 'Tooth and Claw: Tales of Survival and *Crocodile Dundee*', in *The Pirate's Fiancée* (London: Verso, 1988).

Naficy, Hamid: 'Iranian Documentary'. *Jump Cut*, no. 26, 1981.

Ngugi wa Thiong'o: 'The Language of African Literature'. *New Left Review*, no. 150, March-April 1985.

Nowell-Smith, Geoffrey: 'Popular Culture'. *New Formations*, no. 2, Summer 1987.

Peña, Richard: 'Nelson Pereira dos Santos: Presentation and Interview'. *Framework*, no. 29, 1985.

Pfaff, Françoise: 'The Films of Med Hondo'. *Jump Cut*, no. 31, 1986.

Pick, Zuzana M.: 'Chilean Cinema in Exile'. *Framework*, no. 34, 1987.

Pines, Jim and Gilroy, Paul: 'Handsworth Songs – Interview'. *Framework*, no. 35, 1988.

Pines, Jim: 'Territories: An interview with Isaac Julien'. *Framework*, no. 26/7, 1985.

—— 'The Passion of Remembrance'. *Framework*, no. 32/3, 1986.

Price, Derrick: 'Photographing the Poor and the Working Class'. *Framework*, no. 22/3, Autumn 1983.

—— 'So That You Can Live – A Welsh Response'. *Framework*, no. 19, 1982.

Rajadhyaksha, Ashish: 'Gandhiana and Gandhiology'. *Framework*, no. 22/3, Autumn 1983.

—— 'Neo-Traditionalism: Film as Popular Art in India'. *Framework*, no. 32/3, 1986.

—— 'Moving Beyond the Source: K.K. Mahajan'. *Framework*, no. 35, 1988.

Rentschler, Eric: 'The Use and Abuse of Memory: New German Film and the Discourse of Bitburg'. *New German Critique*, no. 36, Fall 1985.

Rocha, Glauber: 'The History of Cinema Nôvo'. *Framework*, no. 12, 1980.

Rohdie, Sam: 'Capitalism and Realism in the Italian Cinema: An examination of film in the fascist period'. *Screen*, vol. 24, no. 4/5, July-October, 1983.

Said, Edward: 'Intellectuals in the Post-Colonial World'. *Salmagundi*, no. 70/1, Spring/Summer 1986.

Schulte-Sasse, Jochen: 'Toward a "Culture" for the Masses: The Socio-Psychological Function of Popular Literature in Germany and the u.s., 1880–1920'. *New German Critique*, no. 29, Spring/Summer 1983.

Taylor, Clyde: 'One Struggle, Many Fronts'. *Jump Cut*, no. 23, 1980.

—— 'New u.s. Black Cinema'. *Jump Cut*, no. 28, 1983.

Trommler, Frank: 'Working Class Culture and Modern Mass Culture Before World War I'. *New German Critique*, no. 29, Spring/Summer 1983.

Wang, Yuejin: 'The Old Well: A Womb or a Tomb'. *Framework*, no. 35, 1988.

Willemen, Paul: 'Notes on Rocinante'. *Framework*, no. 32/3, 1986.

—— 'In Search of an Alternative Perspective'. *Framework*, no. 26/7, 1985.

—— 'An Avant-Garde for the 80s'. *Framework*, no. 24, Spring 1984.

Wollen, Peter et al.: 'Place in the Cinema'. *Framework*, no. 13, Autumn 1980.

Special issues

CinémAction 3: 'Cinéastes d'afrique noir'. Paris [1978].

CinémAction 14/*L'Afrique littéraire* no. 59–60: 'Cinémas du maghreb'. Paris, 1981.

CinémAction 17: 'Jean Rouch, un griot gaulois'. Paris, 1981.

CinémAction 26: 'Cinémas noirs d'Afrique'. Paris, 1981.

CinémAction 29–30: 'Les cinémas indiens'. Paris, 1984.

CinémAction 33: 'Youssef Chahine, l'alexandrin'. Paris, 1985.

CinémAction 34: 'Sembène Ousmane'. Paris, 1985.

CinémAction 39: 'Le cinéma sud-africain est-il tombé sur la tête?'. Paris, 1986.

CinémAction 43: 'Les cinémas arabes'. Paris, 1987.

Cultural Critique nos. 6 and 7: 'The Nature and Context of Minority Discourse', Abdul R. JanMohamed and David Lloyd (eds.). 1987.

Discourse no. 8: 'She, the Inappropriate/d Other', Trinh. T. Minh-ha (ed.). Winter 1986–7.

Framework no. 7/8: 'African Dossier'. Spring 1978.

Framework no. 10: 'Latin American Dossier'. Spring 1979.

Framework no. 11: 'Latin American Dossier'. Autumn 1979.

Framework no. 28: 'Brazil – Post-Cinema Nôvo'. 1985.

Framework no. 29: 'Dossier on Amos Gitai'. 1985.

Framework no. 30/1: 'Dossier: Kumar Shahani'. 1986.

Inscriptions no. 3/4: 'Feminism and the Critique of Colonial Discourse', Deborah Gordon (ed.). University of California at Santa Cruz, 1988.

Journal of Arts and Ideas, no. 5: Special cinema issue. October–December 1983.

Jump Cut nos. 21 and 22: 'Brazilian Renaissance', special dossiers. 1979–80.

Jump Cut no. 27: 'Third World Film' dossier. 1982.

The Oxford Literary Review vol. 9: 'Colonialism and other essays'. 1987.

Screen vol. 24, no. 2: 'Racism, Colonialism and the Cinema'. March/April 1983.

Screen vol. 26, no. 3/4: 'Other Cinemas, Other Criticisms'. May/August 1985.

Third Text nos. 1 and 2: London, Autumn 1987 and Winter 1987–8.